Teaching American History:
The Quest for Relevancy

D1073597

COVER: Photograph by Arthur Tress from *The Dream Collector*,
published by Avon Books, New York, New York
Reproduced by permission of Photo Researchers, Inc., New York, New York

Contributors

Vernon O. Adams
Ronald K. Atwood
O. L. Davis, Jr.
Cathy Lyn Domann
Geneva Gay
Marsha Hobin
Francis P. Hunkins
Allan O. Kownslar
Allen P. Lawrence
Gerald A. Ponder
Virginia M. Rogers
Mary Lee Wright

NATIONAL COUNCIL FOR THE SOCIAL STUDIES
A National Affiliate of the National Education Association

1201 Sixteenth Street, N.W., Washington, D.C. 20036

NCSS 44th Yearbook 1974

Teaching American History: The Quest for Relevancy

Allan O. Kownslar, Editor

NATIONAL COUNCIL FOR THE SOCIAL STUDIES

The National Council for the Social Studies is a National Affiliate of the National Education Association of the United States. It is the professional organization of educators at all levels—elementary, secondary, college, and university—who are interested in the teaching of social studies. Membership in the National Council for the Social Studies includes a subscription to the Council's official journal, *Social Education*, and a copy of the Yearbook. In addition, the Council publishes bulletins, curriculum studies, pamphlets, and other materials of practical use for teachers of the social studies. Membership dues are $15.00 a year. Applications for membership and orders for the purchase of publications should be sent to the Executive Secretary, 1201 Sixteenth Street, N.W., Washington, D.C. 20036.

A very special thanks for criticisms from
Marguerite L. Kownslar, Jack P. Risher,
Terry L. Smart, Donald E. Everett, and Philip F. Detweiler,
and appreciation to Donald Treadwell, whose photographs
of teachers and students using the lessons in this yearbook
appear at the introduction to each chapter.

Allan O. Kownslar

Foreword

Innovation is a very much overworked word. We have trivialized it in much of the educational literature by applying it to a wide variety of materials, curricula, and teaching procedures. Some of these may be genuinely innovative. Many fall in the category of old wine in new bottles. Thus what was previously termed a unit of work may become a module or a learning package. An audio-visual device becomes a multimedia presentation. The child-centered curriculum becomes alternative learning styles.

This yearbook rightfully merits the term "innovative." It is addressed basically to the classroom teachers, not to the curriculum designer. It is practical, not theoretical. It demonstrates how to do it rather than explicates grand designs. And if these criteria do not merit an innovative label, then let the possessor of previous volumes in the yearbook series try to place this one alongside the others on his neat 10-inch-high shelf. It won't fit evenly.

The difference in physical appearance of this yearbook is not an insignificant item. It tacitly transmits a non-standard message to the reader. "I'm different," it says. "Don't judge me by the old standards. And don't use me in the same way. If we mutually respect these differences, we might even live happily together in the classroom."

But innovation *per se* is no virtue. Allan Kownslar, the editor, and his various able chapter contributors recognize this truism by incorporating within their novel lessons the kind of cognitive content that has substance and the kind of affective learning that gets under the skin of the pupils. And if we accept change in behavior as a working definition of learning, it is apparent that the lessons contained in the book are highly calculated to achieve this goal.

A yearbook of this kind also tends to trigger off some introspective thoughts about our teaching field or at least that part of the social studies that deals with history. It affords us the opportunity to reflect on the history of the teaching of history. To Herodotus history was the telling of a story. To Ranke it was a meticulous effort to "tell it like it really was"—*wie es eigentlich gewesen*. And well into the twentieth century the prevalent mode for the teaching of history conformed to the "bucket theory"—content poured from a dispenser (teacher) into cranial containers (students). It is rather significant that not a single lesson in this yearbook is presented exclusively or even predominantly in this expository mode.

Yesterday's fads have a way of becoming today's style and tomorrow's fashion. What current learning and teaching styles will become the fashion of tomorrow? That, nobody can assuredly say. But one prediction is safe. Some new fads and styles will emerge. For example, scientists are already experimenting with ways of feeding data directly into the brain without the "learner" even being conscious of the process. Such learning could presumably take place while the learner is sleeping. This should at least give rise to some novel variations on students' oft-heard themes about dozing through such and such a course. But aside from these jocular implications, what do such new learning processes portend with respect to such persistent issues in history teaching as *what* material should be scheduled for inclusion in the curriculum, *who* should determine what content should be selected, and what *values* should the materials reflect? So the quest goes on. How these and related questions are answered in 1974 is reflected in part by the various chapters in this yearbook. How they will be answered in 1984 and beyond will be largely determined by the school children who are now entrusted to us, the history and social studies teachers of today.

Stanley P. Wronski, President
National Council for the Social Studies

The Authors

Vernon O. Adams has been a classroom social studies teacher since 1958 and was head of the department of social studies at Alamo Heights Independent School District in Texas from 1965 to 1972. Since then he has become Assistant Principal in charge of secondary curriculum for Alamo Heights High School. He holds the B.A. degree from Southwest Texas State University and the M.A. from the University of Denver.

Ronald K. Atwood received the B.S. and M.A. degrees from Murray State University, the M.S. from New Mexico Highlands University, and the Ed.D. at Florida State University. Before becoming an Associate Professor in the Department of Curriculum and Instruction at the University of Kentucky, he taught at Calvert City, Kentucky; Murray, Kentucky; and Florida A. & M. University. Dr. Atwood is also the author of numerous articles published in professional journals.

O. L. Davis, Jr., is a Professor of Curriculum and Instruction at The University of Texas at Austin. He has been a classroom social studies teacher on both secondary and elementary levels in Texas and Tennessee schools. He holds the B.A. and M.Ed. degrees from North Texas State University and the Ph.D. from George Peabody College for Teachers. Dr. Davis is general editor and co-author of *Exploring the Social Sciences*, an elementary social studies program for grades 1-6, and has contributed numerous articles to professional and research journals in both education and history. He has been a member of the Publications Board and Research Committee of the National Council for the Social Studies and a member of the Executive Council and editor of the 1976 yearbook of the Association for Supervision and Curriculum Development. He has also served as Vice-President of the American Educational Research Association.

Cathy Lyn Domann and **Mary Lee Wright** hold B.A. degrees in history from Trinity University and have just begun their careers as social studies classroom teachers. Ms. Domann teaches in the Northeast Independent School District in San Antonio, Texas and Ms. Wright teaches in Galveston, Texas.

Geneva Gay is Associate Executive Secretary, Association for Supervision and Curriculum Development. She received her B.A. degree in comprehensive social studies and M.A. degree in history at the University of Akron and her Ph.D. in Curriculum and Instruction from the University of Texas. Dr. Gay was formerly a high school social studies teacher and has participated in NDEA Institutes at Georgetown and Purdue Universities. She is a consultant and co-author of *Investigating Man's World*, an elementary social studies series, and has contributed to *Language and Cultural Diversity in American Education*, *Curricular Concerns in a Revolutionary Era* and the *43rd Yearbook* of the National Council for the Social Studies.

Marsha Hobin is an undergraduate history major at Trinity University in San Antonio.

Francis P. Hunkins, a Professor in the Department of Curriculum and Instruction in the College of Education at the University of Washington, received the B.S. from Salem State College, the M.Ed. from Boston University, and the Ph.D. from Kent State University. Before joining the staff at the University of Washington, he taught in the Gloucester, Massachusetts, schools and was a Research Assistant for the Bureau of Educational Research at Kent State. Dr. Hunkins is author of *The Influence of Analysis and Evaluation Questions in Achievement and Critical Thinking in Sixth Grade Social Studies*, *Questioning Strategies and Techniques*, *Social Studies for the Evolving Citizen*, and is a contributing author to all levels of *Exploring the Social Sciences*, an elementary social studies program for grades 1–6. He has also contributed numerous articles to professional journals.

Allan O. Kownslar is Associate Professor of History at Trinity University in San Antonio, Texas. He was formerly a Research Historian at Carnegie-Mellon University where he received his doctorate in history. Prior to that time he was a social studies teacher in San Antonio, Texas; Amherst, Massachusetts; and Pittsburgh, Pennsylvania. Five of his twelve years as a classroom teacher were spent in inner-city schools. Dr. Kownslar is managing editor and co-author of *The Americans: A History of the United States*, co-author of *Discovering American History*, co-author of *Inquiring about American History: Studies in History and Political Science*, and author of *The Texans: Their Land and History*, *The Progressive Era: Tradition in a Changing So-*

ciety, and *Manifest Destiny: American Expansionism in the 1840's*, as well as a number of articles in professional journals. In 1973 Dr. Kownslar became a member of the Curriculum Steering Committee for the Texas Council for the Social Studies.

Allen P. Lawrence has been a classroom teacher of minority group students since 1959. He has taught in the El Paso, Texas, and San Antonio Independent School Districts and holds a B.A. in history from the University of Texas at Austin and an M.A. in history from Southern Methodist University.

Gerald A. Ponder has been a history instructor in North Little Rock, Arkansas; New Orleans, Louisiana; and at Loyola University in Louisiana. From 1971 to 1973 he was supervisor of secondary social studies student teachers at the University of Texas at Austin. He received the B.A. and M.A. in history from the University of Arkansas and the Ph.D. in Curriculum and Instruction from the University of Texas at Austin. Currently he is an Instructor of Secondary Education at North Texas State University.

Virginia M. Rogers is an Associate Professor, Department of Curriculum and Instruction in the College of Education at the University of Kentucky. She holds a B.A. in Primary Education and an M.A. in Elementary Education from Northwestern State College in Natchitoches, Louisiana, and a Ph.D. in Curriculum and Instruction from the University of Texas at Austin. From 1957 to 1966 she taught in elementary schools in DeRidder, Louisiana; Shreveport, Louisiana; and Irving, Texas. Before assuming her present position, Dr. Rogers was an Assistant Instructor in the College of Education at the University of Texas. She is a co-author of the *Teacher's Guide for Asking About the U.S.A. and Its Neighbors*, a contributor of numerous articles to professional journals, and serves on the Advisory Board for *Social Education*.

Teachers Who Helped Evaluate Lessons in This Yearbook

The authors wish to express their sincere appreciation to the following teachers who helped to evaluate some or all of the lessons which appear in this Yearbook: Linda Foster, Abilene, Texas, ISD; Louie Lee Carrico, Elizabeth Fearing (student), Frances Finkbeiner, and Joni Timmins, Alamo Heights, Texas, ISD; Bettie Herrin, Anton, Texas, ISD; James O'Hara, Austin, Texas, ISD; Mary Anne Gilleland, Corpus Christi, Texas, ISD; Juanita Tankersley, Corsicana, Texas, ISD; Domingo Regaldo, Dallas, Texas, ISD; John Hurley, Deer Park, Texas, ISD; Robert Fitch and Mary Wilder, Dickinson, Texas, ISD; Rebecca Bailey and Sidney Hilton, Edgewood, Texas, ISD; L.E. Treadway, Floresville, Texas, ISD; Mary Bell, Floydada, Texas, ISD; Russell Marie Boatright and Joyce Johnson, Fort Worth, Texas, ISD; Virginia Cleave, Harlandale, Texas, ISD; Kenneth McCullough, Holland Hall School, Tulsa, Oklahoma; Don Craig and Willie Gay, Houston, Texas, ISD; Peggy Duffy and Joanne Furtek, Houston-Galveston Diocese; Patricia Muston and Elaine Tondre, La Porte, Texas, ISD; Dorothy Higgins, Lubbock, Texas, ISD; Yvonne Booker, Agnes Hudspeth, Alma Marshall, Lee Roy Shannon, and Bertha Starks, Midland, Texas, ISD; Marjorie Blaylock, Wanda Curtis, Helen Elkins, Donna Fontaine, Diana Groves, Elizabeth Hinkle, Linda Miller, Jean Morgan, Thomas Parsley, Olive Paschal, Robert Rock, Margaret Sims, Edith Speert, James Sprinkle, Janet Stanberry, Nellie B. Towles, Joseph Vasquez, Helen Watson, Nathalee White, Willie Whitehead and Cecilia Wittles, Northeast, Texas, ISD; Lyn Hicks, Wanda Moody, and Sybil Roberts, Northside, Texas, ISD; Joyce Herbert and Sandra Scott, Pasadena, Texas, ISD; James Herron, Pearsall, Texas, ISD; Milton Hausmann, Port Lavaca, Texas, ISD; Barbara Gray, Prairie View College; Lynn Franzen, Round Rock, Texas, ISD; Amy Jo Baker, Page Berler, Yolanda Campos, Etta Crutsinger, Kenneth Crutsinger, George Fraige, Bettye Gatlin, Earl Hessong, Janice Hill, B. J. Naegelin, Rose Saenger, Fannie Mae Stallings, and Richard Warren, San Antonio, Texas, ISD; Karen Wambaugh, Schertz-Cibolo-Universal City, Texas, ISD; Mary Catherine Franz, St. Martin Hall, San Antonio, Texas; Wilma LaRue, Temple, Texas, ISD; Frances Finkbeiner, Texas Military Institute, San Antonio, Texas; Curtis Ersparner, Wardine Guthrie, Robert Miller, and Charles Youngblood, graduate students at Trinity University; Doris Pheif, Ursuline Academy, San Antonio, Texas; Velma Sutherland, Uvalde, Texas, ISD; and Alma Kimball, Victoria, Texas, ISD.

Purposes and Format of This Yearbook

There is no doubt that discussions of educational theory and formulation of objectives for American history courses (or for any courses) are invaluable experiences which contribute to clarity and direction in teaching and in learning. However, during the past few years, many teachers have suggested that social studies publications should now deal more with how theory and objectives can be applied directly in the classroom. The NCSS Publications Board, sensitive to this issue, requested that the content of this yearbook, without ignoring in any way theory or desired objectives, emphasize their *practical* application. The result was formation of specific lessons, *created and class-tested especially for inclusion in this yearbook*, which focus on how a study of the American past might be made more relevant in meeting the needs of our students.

The yearbook appears in three sections. Part I is a rationale for why the teaching of American history should remain a vital part of the quest for relevancy within the school curriculum. Subsequent chapters focus on lessons which can be used to implement that rationale in the classroom.

Part II, "History in the Classroom," concentrates primarily on how students can begin to understand better the nature of the discipline of history and how the teaching of history can assist students in further developing a mode of inquiry, concepts, a sense of empathy, and ways for dealing with suspected myths and stereotypes. Chapter 2 focuses on suggested ways in which the basic processes of inquiry can be used to illustrate the incomplete and interpretative aspects of history. O.L. Davis in Chapter 3 deals specifically with how students can utilize a process of inquiry as they try to piece together what may have transpired in the past. In Chapter 4 Cathy Domann and Mary Wright use the term "liberation" as the basis for a sample lesson on concept development in an American history course. Virginia Rogers and Ronald Atwood in Chapter 5 suggest two ways in which students can empathize with problems of people with whom they are not familiar. In Chapter 6 Gerald Ponder and Geneva Gay present a case study which depicts formation of a historical myth, applications of that myth to a specific racial group, and which shows how students might establish criteria for detecting and checking the validity of any suspected myth.

Part III focuses more on how historical topics can be expressly utilized to assist students in coping with issues which may arise in the future.

Francis Hunkins in Chapter 7 has a dual purpose; first, to help students learn what questions they can ask about a historical topic and secondly, how to utilize those questions in the future when processing information, arriving at conclusions, and judging the appropriateness of those conclusions. Marsha Hobin in Chapter 8 uses objective historical data to help students analyze and clarify what opinions they may have about a question which might concern them today and which should definitely concern them in the future. In Chapter 9 Allen Lawrence raises the question of whether the students themselves are relevant to history by having them consider how their present actions might affect the future developments of our nation. Chapter 10 contains a questionnaire which has been developed and used by many teachers as a tool in helping to evaluate available history classroom materials. Vernon Adams in Chapter 11 speculates about what might result if more students approached any examination of the past by seeking out relationships between historical topics and relevant issues.

All the Chapters except 1, 10, and 11 contain sample lessons designed to illustrate how major points made in the rationale can function in practice for elementary or secondary-level American history students. These lessons are intended primarily for use in grades 5 through 12, since those are the levels at which most American history is taught in public and private schools.

Chapters 2-9 follow a format which includes:

1. A brief introduction and rationale for suggested use of the sample lesson plan and student materials
2. Title of the lesson or lessons
3. Intended student audience
4. Suggested time for classroom use of the materials
5. A description of materials included for classroom use
6. Major objectives for the lesson
   a. Objectives within the cognitive domain
      (1) Knowledge goals
      (2) Skill development
   b. Objectives within the affective domain
      (1) Value clarification
      (2) Empathizing
      (3) Social participation
7. Teaching suggestions
   a. A brief overview of the lesson
   b. How to introduce the lesson
   c. How to implement the lesson
   d. How to conclude the lesson
   e. Predicted outcomes (where appropriate)
   f. Alternate teaching suggestions (How else this lesson might be used and with what kinds of students.)
8. Annotated bibliography of additional sources (both secondary and original) suggested for teacher and/or student use on the historical and educational topic for that chapter
9. Student materials required to implement the lesson in the classroom

(Teachers are encouraged to utilize in their classrooms the sample lessons that appear in this book. However, where the material is not in the public domain and where the copyright is held by a publisher other than the National Council for the Social Studies, teachers should write directly to the individual publisher for permission to reproduce student materials for classroom use.)

This format is partially the result of suggestions made by the many teachers who helped to evaluate the lessons which appear in Chapters 2-9. We are especially grateful for the criticisms of those dedicated teachers and the time they generously gave in assisting us during preparation of this yearbook. It was the particular desire of all of us to share not only specific lessons but also ideas, some old and some new, which might be transferred directly to the history classroom, inservice sessions, and teacher-preparation courses. More than anything else, we most sincerely hope that this yearbook will be useful in helping to make the teaching of history more relevant to our students.

Allan O. Kownslar

Contents

PART THREE: Coping with Future Issues

EPILOGUE

PART ONE

Why Teach American History?

"The need for relevancy led increasing numbers of teachers to work toward making history signify more than just the story of our past—more than a 'story' neatly bound on printed pages with color photographs between the hard covers of a textbook."

Allan O. Kownslar

1
Is History Relevant?

A Beginning for Many of Us

Many of us who were teachers during the pre-*Sputnik* era all too often regarded the study of history as nothing more than an experience for students which involved memorizing and quickly forgetting dates, events, and names of people. It was a learning process which embodied little if any relevance to the present or preparation for the future.[1] In such a sterile atmosphere students failed to grasp how history can enlarge life experiences, how it can enable man and woman to know more about themselves, or how history teaches the inevitability of change. The goal, rather, was the accumulation of data strictly for knowledge's sake.[2]

Such primary emphasis on learning "the story" was in part a result of patterning our courses and teaching techniques after those scholars under whom we had studied history. This "filtering down" process resulted in history courses in the elementary and secondary schools that seemed irrelevant to most students.[3] Memorization of "everything" from the past was not one of several goals but *the* primary reason for teaching history.[4] We somehow failed to grasp a point made recently by Edgar B. Wesley that the mandate for remembering historical data "has never been established, and whatever need may once have existed has largely disappeared since the invention of printing and other handy methods of duplicating and recording."[5]

Mass introduction during the late 1950's of non-textual materials and hardware, described by some critics as "gimmicks," contributed little to relevancy. Phillip D. Ortego invented the term "technorriculum"—a "curriculum heavily invested in gadgetry like tape recorders, slide projectors, *et cetera*, in the hope that somehow technology may help overcome what has been otherwise deemed impossible." Unfortunately, as many of us have come to realize, these gadgets were only as good as the educators who used them.[6] Instructorial television, team-teaching, multi-colored chalkboards, moveable chairs or walls, supplementary textbooks, programmed instruction, movies, and transparencies seemed at first like wonderful additions to the teaching of history or social studies. We soon discovered, however, that they were wasteful and ineffective when their use in the classroom served only as proof of Parkinson's Law of Triviality.[7] It was all too easy to have students memorize, rather than analyze critically, what they saw on a transparency, on television, or in a movie or what they read in any textbook. Neither was it an approach likely to motivate a generation of blasé

3

students attuned to the multi-media of the Sixties.

Resistance appeared from students discontented with their roles as passive note-takers, passive listeners only, or passive memorizers. The cry of "What good's this gonna do me?" was heard not only from dissatisfied ghetto students or bored white, middle-class suburbanites, but even from those in rural schools, usually the last to rebel openly against what they regard as outdated pedagogies. Students began to demand tools which might enable them to cope with an unpredictable future. Gimmickry alone was no longer an acceptable alternative to relevant learning processes.

The New Social Studies and the Sixties

The need for relevancy led increasing numbers of teachers to work toward making history signify more than just the story of our past—more than a "story" neatly bound on printed pages with color photographs between the hard covers of a textbook. Emphasis was on having students relate their own experiences with some of the facts and figures spread before them in social studies texts. Efforts in that direction soon became part of a curriculum revolution now commonly referred to as the New Social Studies.

One approach led more teachers to encourage students to realize that history is what happened—that no event is more "historical" than another, although events can differ in the significance historians place on them.[8] We devised new materials and teaching strategies which enabled students to understand that in examining the contents of any secondary source, they were reading what a historian or writer had said about an event or period in history and that such writings were *interpretations*. They learned that an interpretation is the way a person pictures an event; that it is another word for the conclusions one forms from examining available *historical evidence*. As part of this process, students began to distinguish differences between *original*

sources and *secondary* sources. Very early in the grades we wanted them to become aware of the fact that an original source, whether it is historical evidence in the form of a diary, letter, journal, or folklore, represents a first-person eyewitness account on which historians base their interpretations or secondary accounts.

As a result, students had ample New Social Studies programs designed to encourage them to discover how historians assembled all the available data at their disposal and then recorded their interpretations of what happened and why it seemed to happen. Most importantly, it allowed a class the opportunity to discover *how* historical interpretations are formed and *how* written history itself takes shape.[9]

Another approach led students to discover that most of what happened in the past has never been recorded. They began to understand, as R.G. Collingwood, Henry Steele Commager, George Kitson Clark and many other historians have long argued, that knowledge of the past was a collection of fragments set down by observers who did not tell everything.[10] Those observers had recorded what they thought was significant—*their* interpretations—but sometimes they dismissed as unimportant what others may have thought meaningful. This subjective reporting, a trait of all human behavior, was now more frequently demonstrated in the classroom. Elementary students examined diaries kept by schoolmates, conducted interviews with their fellow students, or wrote separate accounts of what occurred on a class field trip. When compared, their completed work usually demonstrated their differences of opinion about what transpired and why. Multiple accounts also illustrated that no one on the field trip could remember or even keep detailed notes on *everything* that occurred—the point being that any two observers might emphasize different particulars about an event and use different "facts" to describe it. There was, therefore, no such thing as a "complete story."

While experimenting with New Social Studies techniques many teachers re-examined the use of formal written objectives as they acknowledged that the study of history might well begin with definitions of objectives one can expect students to accomplish. There resulted a renewed focus on goals within the *cognitive* domain, involving a closer look at the mental processes by which knowledge is acquired and analyzed. Soon pioneers in the New Social Studies began to classify various cognitive-type processes, with major emphasis on modes of inquiry.[11] Their findings can be summarized in a five-step process whereby the student was expected to:

(1) *Recognize a problem.* (For example: How are we able to know some things about American Indians who lived long ago?)
(2) *Arrive at a tentative conclusion or hypothesis* in answer to the problem. (We might be able to learn more about early American Indians after examining available archeological finds, observations by European explorers, and Indian folklore.)
(3) *Analyze and interpret available sources of information* about early American Indians under consideration.
(4) *Form and support a generalization* in answer to the problem. (We are able to learn much about early American Indians through an examination of a variety of available sources.)
(5) *Synthesize* or combine information, concepts or generalizations about early American Indian life with other peoples who long ago lived elsewhere and arrive at a new generalization. (We are able to discover much about early American Indians for many of the same reasons that we can learn some things about the ancient African.)

Emphasis on cognitive-type objectives in the area of inquiry-oriented skill development did not preclude the uses of factual data or more basic skill development in reading, speaking, listening, viewing or writing. Students must first examine some data and perform some of the more elementary intellectual skills in order to analyze and interpret available information. They then proceed to communicate its meaning silently to themselves and perhaps orally to others. This they continue to do while examining material and questions associated with any social studies course. Students must first read, view, or listen to something which will enable

them independently to recognize a problem or begin to ask questions about it. The need for utilizing some data and study skills becomes all the more apparent if anyone has ever attempted to inquire about *nothing*.

To proponents of the New Social Studies, development of these inquiry-oriented skills became all the more important if students were to become educated critical thinkers. Applying this five-step process in the study of history afforded pupils the opportunity to show why their *own* generalizations or syntheses were valid. Once this procedure became second nature through repeated practice, students were less likely to be fooled or misled by vague statements, myths, or stereotypes in textbooks, or those advanced by some politicians, journalists, salesmen, teachers, neighbors, or friends, and, equally important, by the students themselves. Neil Postman and Charles Weingartner have termed such training the development of an ultra-sensitive "crap detector."[12]

An integrated, disciplined, and consciously acquired mode of inquiry often became a natural approach for students as they viewed the world around them. They developed an inner discipline relevant enough to equip them with the courage and ability to question rather than always accept, to challenge what appeared to be a myth or an unsupported generalization on any matter of opinion which is treated as fact, and they learned to form their own generalizations and defend them when questioned by their peers or teacher.[13]

Closely integrated with development of inquiry skills, a renewed interest in concept-formation enabled students to distinguish clearly the meanings of terms used in recognizing problems, formulating hypotheses, testing their validity, and arriving at sound generalizations. Within the framework of the New Social Studies the term "concept" came to signify any word or phrase which evoked an appropriate image. For the student, development of any concept meant to elaborate on the many definitions which applied to it.[14]

As part of our continued quest for relevancy, concept development often began with personal concerns or experiences of the students. We searched for fresh data and new teaching strategies which would further illustrate how the study of history provided a vehicle by which concept development began naturally with the students' environment or with something with which they were familiar, building from the present to the past. Relying on experiences of students who had viewed historical material in museums, on television, through reading, or as a result of accidental "finds," we dealt with such artifacts as American Indian or Native American spearpoints which fall into the conceptual category of concrete-type triangular objects. We then could show with pictures how an examination of the Clovis, Folsom, and Plainview spearpoints could illustrate differences among them as varied as the many ways a triangle can appear. The same variety of differences likewise applied to the concept "Indian" or "Native American" especially when students examined the Iroquois, Natchez, and Mohaves—groups whose living patterns and philosophies were sometimes more different than similar. Similar results occurred when classes examined in depth people with Spanish surnames, Blacks, Jews, Italians, Asian-Americans, or Anglos, or those who called themselves Hippies, Roman Catholics, Protestants, Republicans or Democrats.

Concept development as a part of the New Social Studies likewise served as a vehicle for students to identify and analyze various forms of behavior. They might be asked to consider the term "revolt," a form of behavior many have at least contemplated against parents, teachers, or government officials. Examinations of revolt sometimes began by having students consider: What is a "revolt" and under what circumstances would they rebel? Open class discussion revealed that all students would not rebel for the same reasons or manifest the same forms of behavior when rebelling. Some students, although content with parental guidance, might have rebelled against school policies which they felt threatened a cherished right. Others inclined to revolt against a teacher whose authoritarian classroom procedures they resented. Still others, content at home and school, would rebel against governmental policies they deemed unfair or negligent. Potential revolt options ranged from passive (refusing to participate in class discussions—"the silent treatment") to violent (threatening the safety of personal life or property).

Once the concept of revolt was defined, proponents of the New Social Studies further clarified it with comparisons as to reasons people might have rebelled in the past. An analysis of the American Revolution of 1776 revealed both passive (refusal to pay taxes) and violent behavior (military force); it was both resistance to authority and also a rebellion aimed primarily at preserving political, economic, and social rights. Related questions seemed obvious. Do people (like you, your classmates, or those early American colonists) revolt for the same reasons? Does revolt always take the same form of rebellion? What, then, does "revolt" mean?

Abstract ideas likewise received special attention as part of concept development in the New Social Studies. Building on elementary students' familiarity with an abstract idea such as "discover," they were asked what it meant to them. Most would respond that to "discover" is to learn or encounter for the first time. Any group of fifth graders when asked "Who *discovered* America?" would immediately reply "Columbus." But did he? A recording from a portion of the *Journal* of his first voyage to what Europeans regarded as a New World quickly reveals that he found people there. Did Columbus then actually *discover* America? What could "discover" signify when applied to Columbus' well-publicized journey of 1492? Possible answers by ten-year-olds were seemingly unlimited: (1) That Columbus *discovered* for himself the existence of lands previously unfamiliar to him, (2) that others had *discovered* those lands before his arrival, (3) that Columbus *discovered* lands previously unknown to most people in Western Europe, or (4) that Indians already living here *discovered* Columbus in 1492. "Discover" came to mean something very different for each individual student as he encountered something new for the first time. Similar results can be expected from concept developments of any abstract idea, including such terms as "liberal" or "conservative."[15]

Emphasis during the Sixties on concept development and acquisition of a mode of inquiry therefore supported the contention that a study of history or any discipline within the social studies can be relevant to students; that, as John Dewey long ago argued, the best academic discipline for the child comes from one which taps first his actual experiences and progresses into an examination of related examples from the past. Through such a process, learning a historical "fact" or concept enabled students to use it functionally to find out other facts and meanings of a concept, or, more fundamentally, to learn something more about themselves or their society.[16]

The "New" New Social Studies and the Seventies

The "Old" Social Studies and the "New," with renewed emphasis on the uses of data, skill development, and concept formation, provided a cognitive foundation with which to make history and social studies courses more relevant to students. In so doing many teachers placed a renewed emphasis on content selection, focusing on strategies and topics *affective* in nature. As their primary purpose these processes seek to stimulate or affect some kind of response which directly involves the student. Unless involved through this sense of relevancy, some students, turned off by the past, persisted in their dependence upon peer groups, television, drugs, films, contemporary movements, or other academic disciplines which seemed to satisfy a craving in their efforts to cope with contemporary life.

This renewed emphasis on affective-type goals which build upon cognitive objectives might readily be termed the "New" New Social Studies of the Seventies. Current strategies associated with this movement utilize historical and social studies content in an endeavor to impel students to question, express interest, experience empathy, or seek to analyze objectively and clarify their own values or those held by others, past and present.

Empathizing, for example, has become a vital part of the "New" New Social Studies. Being affective in nature, empathizing deals primarily with emotions, attitudes, and values as a means of conveying an understanding so intimate that the feelings, thoughts, and motives of one person can readily be comprehended by another. Any study of American history or of any social studies course abounds with examples by which students can begin to empathize with people of the past. What history teacher at one time or another has not focused on empathizing as a classroom strategy by having students role-play in debates, act out short skits, or perform in some kind of simulation or game? Its usage as a teaching strategy in a quest for relevancy does not mean that history repeats itself, only that certain basic problems or dilemmas are continuous in man's and woman's experiences.

To illustrate the impact of empathizing as a teaching strategy in the social studies curriculum, consider the uses of *Star Power,* a simulation developed by R. Garry Shirts. *Star Power* has proven effective with elementary, secondary, and college-level students in American history courses. Through the distribution of wealth in the form of plastic chips it is a game which builds a mobile three-tiered society.[17] Students playing the game have chances to move from one level of society to another by amassing wealth as the result of trading chips with one another. Once a given society has been established, that group with the most wealth receives the right to determine the rules for the remainder of the game. This "wealthy" group usually makes rules which the other groups of students feel are unfair, dictatorial, or racist. What usually results is protest or revolt against the rules as well as the rulemakers. Once this occurs, or is about to occur, the point is made and the teacher must end the simulation!

Particularly noteworthy is the effectiveness of *Star Power* as students empathize with the "haves" or "have-nots" and raise questions which draw on historical parallels about the uses of power in democratic or totalitarian societies. Causes which drive the "have-nots" in the classroom to revolt can readily apply to other forms of rebellions—the Civil Rights movement of the 1960's, the Civil War of 1861, or the American Revolution of 1776. Questions arise almost without prompting: Did rebels during those historical periods revolt for reasons similar to those of the "have-nots" of *Star Power*? What other reasons might you have for rebelling against certain forms of authority? Could the *feelings* of the "have-nots" in the class be compared to any experience of people living in poverty-ridden nations of today?

Classroom strategies, like those employed in *Star Power*, illustrate how history courses should include pedagogies which allow students to empathize with another group of people, past or present: to afford, for example, white, middle-class, suburbanite pupils the opportunity to empathize with the unwritten rules of war, poverty, hunger, or revolt.[18] In other words, if teachers are to have students pretend, let them role play in a situation which reveals that questions in the game have something to do with *them*.[19] Only then is a class prepared to relate to similar problems or experiences in the past, realizing that their concerns, while significant, are not entirely original for this day and age.

As with empathizing, the teaching of American history within the framework of the "New" New Social Studies also lends itself readily to value clarification. By "value" is meant something cherished, represented by an attitude toward an object, an event, a type of behavior, or a particular phenomenon.

Value clarification, of course, does not mean the imposition or inculcation of a value system, but an attempt to have students carefully re-examine, explain, and justify whatever it is they cherish and why. It involves having students realize possible or logical consequences of positions they choose to take and assumes that no one has the "right" set of values, although people may agree on many absolutes.[20] Thus, students need to analyze objectively those values held by others in order to better understand their own. Any process of value clarification also requires that students "learn to identify their own value assumptions along with those of others, to project and evaluate consequences of one value stance to another."[21] In essence, students should learn to appreciate diversity rather than be told there is only one "right way."[22] If we believe this, our responsibility is not one of training students but in educating them; not in indoctrinating them, but in developing classroom strategies which produce a knowledgeable sense of values that will endure for a lifetime.

These classroom techniques call for a greater use of strategies which exploit the principles of Socratic dialogue. Socratic questioning techniques have strong motivational value as teachers build from students' contributions rather than their own. In a Socratic dialogue the teacher converses with a single student while the remainder of the class listens. The purpose is to help an individual student examine both unstated assumptions and the logical implications of her or his position, while other students share in the same learning process. Any such open classroom dialogues are recommended only with a relatively secure child. The length of time for any dialogue depends on the interests of the class. A short example of this method follows, taken from actual transcripts of a recording made in an American history class of junior-high-school slow learners and non-readers who were just beginning a study of the Battle of Lexington:

Teacher: This gets to the most important point: Would you have fought to help save Hancock and Adams?

Student: No.

Teacher: Why?

Student:	What's the sense in it? They were strangers.
Teacher:	Would you have fought if your friends were the ones in jail or threatened?
Student:	Yes.
Teacher:	You would? Why?
Student:	I'd want to save my friends.
Teacher:	Why? Why do you think it is right to help your friends?
Student:	Because I would want to help them.
Teacher:	Do you think that is more important than the chance that you might be killed?
Student:	Yes.

Here the teacher used a Socratic dialogue to make the student define the conditions under which *he* would fight. The discussion then turned to a consideration of whether or not the student always would help a friend or whether there were limits to his loyalty.[23]

At times the clarifying response can also be used to encourage students to make other kinds of choices freely. Witness this example from dialogues recorded in another class:[24]

Teacher:	Would you have joined the Revolutionary army in 1776?
Student:	Yes.
Teacher:	Why?
Student:	Because they were fighting for self-government.
Teacher:	So, you would join a revolution, if it were fighting for self-government.
Student:	Yes.
Teacher:	Why do you think self-government is so important? What ideas do you base your decision on? Let's talk about this issue during class tomorrow.

As part of the "New" New Social Studies, the need for more attempts at value clarification by history teachers becomes apparent as students seem readier to detect contradictions in beliefs of their elders past and present. Discrepancies discovered by students, one study indicates, are commonly associated with adult hypocrisy.[25] At the same time, however, many of those same students fail to notice contradictions in their own beliefs and practices. Some students, for example, are quick to condemn the alleged right of governmental officials during the Vietnam War (or the Mexican War or the War of 1812) to keep secrets from the public while these same students fail to tell members of a student body all that occurred in a high school Student Council meeting. Students clamor for more civil liberties while some polls indicate that high school students have very little knowledge about the historical origin and evolution of the basic freedoms found in the Bill of Rights. Nearly half of those students questioned in one poll stated that police should be able to use torture on *other* people suspected of committing a crime.[26]

To counteract these discrepancies more teachers now utilize a cyclical approach to value clarification by moving from a present-day emotional problem to a parallel issue in the past and finally back to a similar relevant-emotional one. This approach bridges the gap between two supposedly unrelated issues by relating a contemporary problem to one in the past. A cyclical pattern emphasizing value clarification in an American history course will avoid the danger of too much emphasis at an emotional level which, producing unwarranted student anxiety, may interfere with learning processes. A cyclical approach which moves from emotional to contextual to emotional, as in the two previous dialogues, also allows students to consider alternative value positions, inasmuch as students often do not possess rigid mind-sets or frames of references about issues in the past. Any such examination of historical issues through the cyclical method thus provides numerous opportunities for students to attempt to analyze value alternatives objectively before finally comparing them critically with what they cherish.[27]

Use of the cyclical approach is also another form of teaching history "backwards" whereby a class can: (1) begin with a contemporary issue of special concern, (2) trace causes for the emergence of that problem or examine similar instances of that problem in the past, and (3) then compare them to reasons for concern today. In so doing, students realize that neither the problem nor the proposed solutions are unique to the present.

Assume, which seems credible, for example, that the extent to which any governmental official has the right to keep policy matters a secret from the public will remain a relevant issue. Students in a secondary-level class discussing this subject might support the right of a people to live under a government free from any form of censorship. To assist those students in further clarifying the freedoms or rights and the responsibilities inherent in that expressed value, the teacher can take the class backward in time, examining recent issues first: (a) Our secret bombing of Cambodia from 1969 to 1971, (b) The "Jack Anderson Papers" concerning the India-Pakistan War of 1971, (c) The Pentagon's *Secret History of the War in Vietnam*, (d) Secret investigations by the Central Intelligence Agency during the Cold War, (e) Undercover work conducted by the Federal Bureau of Investigation on organized crime, (f) Secret plans formulated by the Allies prior to the Normandy invasion of June 1944, (g) The Army's O.S.S. activities in determining Nazi operations during World War II, (h) Closed foreign policy meetings between President Franklin D. Roosevelt and Prime Minister Winston Churchill in 1940, (i) Activities of President Woodrow Wilson's George Creel Propaganda Committee during World War I, (j) Closed cabinet meetings conducted by President James K. Polk during the Mexican War, (k) Closed door proceedings of the Constitutional Convention of 1787, and (l) Secret meetings held by Samuel Adams and the Committees of Correspondence immediately prior to the outbreak of the American Revolution.

Elementary students, starting from "the here and now," can begin a study of history backward by first asking themselves: What is my own city, community, or neighborhood like today? How did it get that way? What sources or places will I need to investigate in order to obtain possible answers? Can I ever know *all* that ever happened in my community which made it what it is today? Why or why not? What does my answer show me about the study of the history of any community or people?

Students who are led to ask questions like these feel involved. Lack of such involvement illustrates how futile it is to train students to be aggressive, independent, inquirers and then force them to focus their curiosity, for example, *only* on ways people in the past made their living. Teaching history backwards helps to avoid this pitfall by teaching them to sense what is worth learning and allowing them to play an active role in determining the process of solution.[28] Use of the cyclical approach by teaching history "backwards" stimulates students as they begin— not stop—with a contemporary issue of special interest. After objective consideration of the topic in its historical setting, the students go about clarifying their own ideas concerning the problem at hand. For whatever the area—be it grammar, auto mechanics, music, or history— unless an inquiry seems in some way relevant to students, it is unlikely that any real learning will occur.

Real learning as part of the "New" New Social Studies ultimately leads us to a point stressed by Alvin Toffler in *Future Shock*; namely, that our society is often geared to prepare people for survival in a system that will possibly be dead before they are.[29] Another writer, John Holt, likewise has emphasized how quickly knowledge changes and how much of the data a student now "learns" will someday prove false or inaccurate. His theme is that we cannot know precisely what knowledge will be needed forty, twenty, or even ten years from now.[30] Terry Borton has estimated that a student who began the first grade in 1970 will, on reaching the twelfth grade, encounter four times the amount of knowledge of those who began school twelve years earlier. Today's problems are compounded by this projected expansion of knowledge which teachers cannot utilize today because they cannot know what it will be.[31] Thus, teachers are faced with the problem of how to educate students for an increasingly uncertain future; as Charles Silberman put it more cogently, teachers must deal with students who "need to learn far more than the basic skills. For children who may still be in the labor force in the year 2030, nothing could be more wildly impractical than an education designed to prepare them for specific vocations or professions or to facilitate their adjustment to the world as it is."[32]

To assist students in their continuing adjustment to the world of tomorrow, the study of American history should arouse those questions that serve to cope with both old and new ideas, movements, and developments. Students might well consider, for example, what questions they would raise about any contemporary or historical topic before studying it. If our efforts to make the course relevant are fruitful, students would have been educated to respond by asking significant questions about those authors who have written or spoken on the topic. What are their values? How can one determine what their values are? Are the authors authorities on the subject? Why did they write or speak out? How did they make known their opinions or prejudices? Were they directly associated with the topic? How well did they support their viewpoints? What were their main sources of information and why did they use those sources? Are these the best and most accurate sources of information? How were they obtained and when? Can I really trust the "facts" in the sources? Do points made by the author conflict with arguments made by other people? Does the topic under consideration relate to anything I have read prior to this? If so, how? Will consideration of this topic be useful to me in later life? Will asking these questions be useful to me? If so, how?[33]

Whatever the responses, they can determine to some degree whether the course has served to help prevent or soften the blow of possible future shocks. One of our principal tasks must be to analyze carefully student replies and use them as possible criteria for materials, topics, and teaching strategies which could form the basis for subsequent study of history or the social studies. In so doing, we would be taking a vital cue from Margaret Mead, who observed that many of the young say "the future is now. This seems unreasonable and impetuous, and in some of the demands they make it is unrealizable in concrete detail; but here again . . . they give us the way to reshape our thinking. . . ."[34]

Perhaps students may not offer us *the* means, but they can provide some of the many ways to begin the restoration of history as a relevant academic discipline. Youth certainly can offer suggestions designed to bring what Jerome Bruner calls social relevance to personal relevance and vice versa; to bring knowledge and conviction together; to link directly a historical issue with personal conviction.[35] As argued recently by Postman and Weingartner, this means that we should educate students to a literacy which allows a "high degree of competence in analyzing . . . propositions, evaluating them and correlating them with reality. Anything less than that is letteracy, not literacy."[36] Seen this way, the teaching of history can lend itself naturally to a developmental interplay between objectives within the cognitive and affective domains. The "New" New Social Studies relates the utilization of historical data and critical thinking directly to further clarification of values and attitudes.

What Seems to Be at Fault?

Educational critics such as Edgar B. Wesley, George E. McCully, and even Harry Golden, have emphasized that political scientists, economists, anthropologists, and geographers have now made the study of their disciplines more attractive and relevant for elementary and secondary students than have historians.[37] Some critics go so far as to call for the abolition of history classes below the college level. Their criticisms, however, do not fully take into account two major considerations. First, historians have utilized and are increasingly utilizing data and insights from related social studies disciplines. Moreover, most teachers agree that many history materials of sound quality are now available for classroom and their integration of information from related disciplines is ongoing. More significant, any proposal to abolish history from the curriculum fails to consider adequately whether it is the materials available or their use which perpetuates irrelevance. Perhaps shortcomings in the presentation of materials are responsible for the cry of irrelevance—a protest repeated all too often during the past two decades by many students who believed that teaching strategies in history classes fostered a senseless examination of the past. If such criticism has validity, then the quest for relevance should not suggest the abolition of history courses but rather *alteration in the ways history classes have been taught.* Students must be led to understand how and why a study of the past does have meaning and practical application as they face a difficult present and an uncertain future.

Teachers of history or social studies have students at best 180 out of their allotted 8,760 annual hours, or only about two per cent of the time in a given year. What we do with students during those crucial class hours should easily withstand the rigors of the Five-Year Test. In other words, much of what we teach students should continue to affect or to have an impact on them five years thereafter. Having students absorb large doses of historical data will not provide us with a very satisfactory evaluation. But history taught as a quest for relevancy, incorporating the best qualities of the Old, the New, and the "New" New Social Studies, should not only improve our rating but make the teaching of history more challenging each year. For wherever it appears in the school curriculum, a study of history can readily serve as a vehicle by which students can acquire an applicable mode of inquiry, develop useful concepts, successfully empathize with the past, continue to clarify values, learn to recognize and to cope with suspected myths and stereotypes, and to ask critical questions about the past, present, and future. If our goal, then, is to effectively teach American history as a quest for relevancy, students should never need ask: "What good's all this gonna do me?" They'll already know.

FOOTNOTES

[1] The lack of obvious relevance has occurred for many reasons, the first of which can be traced to curriculum trends during the past century. During the nineteenth century, for example, the McGuffey *Eclectic Readers* were supposed to provide training necessary to help make young Americans well-informed citizens. While examining the *Readers*, students supposedly learned the three R's with hero-worship a major focus of the history materials. In the twentieth century Russell Baker recently described such a "learning" process as one in which those "among us who were cunning had learned the importance of grades. Good grades meant that you were getting ahead, and because we soon perceived that it was important to get ahead whether we were learning anything or not, we became grade pursuers of intense, Byzantine artifice." Russell Baker, "School Daze," San Antonio *Express*, September 13, 1972, p. 3E.

[2] Counteracting student boredom and the discipline problems so often associated with it has not fallen quite so hard on some experienced social studies classroom teachers who began their careers before the New Math, New Physics, or New Social Studies eras. Since the New Social Studies did not exist before 1961, none of these teachers had received the formal academic training necessary to cope with the Social Studies Revolution. Long before the advent of *Sputnik* or before the New Social Studies even had a name, those teachers, instead of pretending to represent a walking set of encyclopedias, remained the experienced leader, director, and a constant and constructive critic to student opinions. These teachers found ways to actively involve students in long-lasting learning processes. They somehow managed to find the time and energy to use their own imagination and initiative in developing new materials and teaching strategies which presented factual data in an appealing, challenging, and effective way to their pupils.

[3] Perpetuating the trend of irrelevancy was the requirement begun in Massachusetts in 1827 that American history be a required subject for pupils attending the equivalent of present-day public schools. The American Historical Association during the 1890's and the National Education Association in 1916 helped to solidify this trend by strongly recommending the teaching of European history at grade 7, geography at grade 8, and American History at grade 9. Most students in the early part of this century seldom matriculated beyond grade 9, apparently a determining factor in not requiring more history for the high school grade levels. Similar mandates for other grade levels gradually increased until the 1940's when most states required students to study American history in grades 5, 8, and 11. More often than not, their examination of the American past at those grade levels represented three surveys of the American past—each hopefully a little more sophisticated than the previous one. Until the past decade, publishing houses of textbook materials traditionally have also encouraged this curriculum trend. Publishers in particular feared to risk stockholders' money on allegedly radical new approaches which might fail on the market. Thus one American history textbook usually resembled all the rest and likewise lagged far behind the latest research and teaching techniques. See Ambrose A. Clegg, Jr., and Carl

E. Schonburg, "The Dilemma of History in the Elementary School: Product or Process?", *Social Education*, May, 1968, pp. 454-456; Frederick R. Smith and C. Benjamin Cox, *New Strategies and Curriculum in Social Studies*, Rand McNally and Company, 1969, p. 114; and Edwin Fenton, *The New Social Studies*, Holt, Rinehart and Winston, 1967, p. 2.

[4]One writer recently claimed that this filtering-down process had resulted in the presentation of data "desecrated and distorted beyond recognition." See George E. McCully, "History Begins at Home," *Saturday Review*, May 16, 1970, p. 75.

[5]See Edgar Bruce Wesley, "Let's Abolish History Courses," *Phi Delta Kappan*, September, 1967.

[6]Phillip D. Ortego, "The Education of Mexican Americans," in *The Chicanos: Mexican American Voices*, Ed. Ludwig and James Santibañez (eds.), Penguin Books, 1971, pp. 160-161.

[7]For a fuller discussion of this, see Chapters I and V in Neil Postman and Charles Weingartner, *Teaching As a Subversive Activity*, Dell Publishing Company, 1969.

[8]Put another way, "all men think about what happens; there are better and worse ways in which to go about it. With the right kind of training, a person should be able to learn how to do it better, and this should improve his competence in life. This is where school history could be useful and relevant." McCully, *op. cit.*, p. 86.

[9]The same procedure worked in reverse when a class examined the raw data or source material cited by a historian in footnotes used to support his interpretations. Once that footnoted material had been examined, and sometimes compared with any other kind of information the class found appropriate, the students next formed their own conclusions about how they would interpret the available historical information. Placed in paragraph form, the topic sentence signified the conclusion and the remainder of the paragraph included evidence and references which supported the thesis. Conclusions were then compared to those offered by the historian, with particular emphasis on possible reasons for any discrepancies in interpretations.

[10]See R. G. Collingwood, *The Idea of History*, Oxford, 1946; Henry Steele Commager, *The Nature of History*, Merrill, 1965; and George Kitson Clark, *The Critical Historian*, Heinemann, 1967.

[11]See, for example, Barry K. Beyer, *Inquiry in the Social Studies Classroom: A Strategy for Teaching*, Charles E. Merrill, 1971; Benjamin S. Bloom (ed.), *Taxonomy of Educational Objectives, Handbook I, Cognitive Domain*, Longmans, Green and Company, 1956; C. Benjamin Cox and Byron G. Massialas, *Social Studies in the United States*, Harcourt, Brace and World, 1967; Edwin Fenton, *The New Social Studies*, Holt, Rinehart and Winston, 1967; and Edwin Fenton (ed.), *The New Social Studies for the Slow Learner: A Rationale for a Junior High School American History Course*, American Heritage and Holt, Rinehart and Winston, 1969.

[12]See Chapter I in Postman and Weingartner, *Teaching as a Subversive Activity*.

[13]For a fuller discussion of this point, see Nat Hentoff, *Our Children Are Dying*, Viking Press, 1966, pp. 31-34. Jerome Bruner has described this as understanding of how generalizations are formed; that what is learned is competence in good problem-solving performances. Jerome Bruner, "The Skill of Relevance or the Relevance of Skills," *Saturday Review*, April 18, 1970, p. 67. On the subject of how the debunking of myths can be made relevant to students as they study American life, see the teaching strategies suggested for use by Barry K. Beyer, Director of Project Africa at Carnegie-Mellon University. Beyer, in particular, utilized a mode of inquiry to have students clarify values and refute myths commonly associated with Africans living south of the Sahara. Throughout the lessons, where the latest research findings about sub-Sahara African life appear in the form of written materials, slides, transparencies, and recordings, students constantly compare available data to prevalent myths or stereotypes about Africa. This includes those which portray Africa as a hot, primitive, savage, dark continent "filled with witch-doctors, drums, straw huts, and rich deposits of precious gems." Similar teaching strategies and use of available evidence are readily at hand for debunking myths about American life, past and present. One needs only to begin with Oliver La Farge's or Hazel W. Hertzberg's study about myths commonly associated with the American Indian. W. J. Cash made a classic examination of Southern white chivalry in *The Mind of the South*. Thomas F. Pettigrew set a new pace with a treatment of popular prejudices, ideas, and fallacies which concern Blacks in his *Profile of the Negro American*. Henry Nash Smith debunked the yeoman farmer and Garden of Eden images in his *Virgin Land: The American West as Symbol and Myth*. Richard Hofstadter carefully examined the agrarian myth in his *Age of Reform*. Feliciano Rivera has a discussion in *The Chicanos* of faulty assumptions about Mexican-American contributions to our way of life. And Janice Law Trecker recently made available a study about stereotypes commonly associated with women in United States history books which can limit girls' aspirations. See Barry K. Beyer, *Africa South of the Sahara: A Resource and Curriculum Guide*, Thomas Y. Crowell Company, 1969, p. V; Oliver La Farge, "Myths That Hide the American Indian," *American Heritage Magazine*, October, 1956; Hazel W. Hertzberg, "Issues in Teaching about American Indians," *Social Education*, May, 1972, pp. 481-485. Here you may also wish to examine the entire May, 1972, issue of *Social Education*, which is devoted to teaching about American Indians; W. J. Cash, *The Mind of the South*, Alfred A. Knopf, 1942; Thomas F. Pettigrew, *A Profile of the Negro American*, D. Van Nostrand, 1964; Henry Nash Smith, *Virgin Land: The American West as Symbol and Myth*, Harvard University Press, 1950; Richard Hofstadter, *The Age of Reform: From Bryan to F.D.R.*, Random House and Alfred A. Knopf, 1955; Feliciano Rivera, "The Teaching of Chicano History," in *The Chicanos: Mexican-American Voices*, Ed. Ludwig and James Santibañez (eds.), Penguin Books, 1971; and Janice Law Trecker, "Women in U.S. History High School Textbooks," *Social Education*, March, 1971, pp. 248-261, 338. A collection of scholarly articles about most myths in American history can be found in Nicholas Cords and Patrick Gerster, *Myth and the American Experience*, Volumes I and II, paperback, Glencoe Press, 1973.

[14]For a more detailed discussion of concept formation, see Barry K. Beyer and Anthony N. Penna (eds.), *Concepts in the Social Sciences*, NCSS General Bulletin No. 45, 1971, and James C. Tyson and Mary Ann Carroll, *Conceptual Tools for Teaching in Secondary Schools*, Houghton Mifflin Company, 1970.

[15]The term "destiny" was another abstract idea which received special attention as part of the New Social Studies movement. Most adolescents are vitally concerned with themselves and their possible destinies. Ask any group for a definition of "destiny," and many will maintain that it signifies the inevitable lot assigned to an individual or to a group of people. Some astute students may qualify this definition by stating that destiny can be partially determined by consideration of past experiences and pre-planning on the part of individuals or nations. A closer look at the concept in an American history course focusing on the nineteenth and twentieth centuries can reveal even more variations of the term. It can mean what John Louis O'Sullivan stated in 1845 that it was "our manifest destiny to overspread the continent allotted by providence for the free development of our yearly multiplying millions . . . ." Yet the concept of national or manifest destiny, like that of "discover," can signify different things to different people—especially when students consider how certain individuals have viewed the destiny of their people. Cecil Rhodes, a builder of the British empire in South Africa, saw English national destiny as justification for the fact that the English were "the first race in the world, and that the more of the world (they inhabited), the better it would be for the human race." Adolf Hitler in 1937 described the bonds holding the German people together not as economic interests, history, religion, or custom but "our common destiny, this compelling common destiny from which none can escape, our life's destiny in the world." And President Lyndon B. Johnson twenty-eight years later proclaimed that "For every generation, there is a destiny. For some, history decides. For this generation the choice must be our own . . . Our destiny in the midst of change will rest on the unchanged character of our people, and on their faith." After students examine these or similar interpretations of destiny, we can ask: Do these meanings of "destiny" agree? Do they compare favorably with your own definition of "destiny"? Does "destiny," then, always assume the same meaning? See John Louis O'Sullivan, "Annexation," *Democratic Review*, 1845; J. G. McDonald, *Rhodes: A Life*, Robert M. McBride and Company, 1928, p. 36; Norman H. Baynes (ed.), *The Speeches of Adolf Hitler*, Oxford University Press, 1942, pp. 939–941; and *Congressional Record*, 89th Congress, 1st Session, pp. 985–986.

[16]Richard H. Brown, "A Note to the Teacher," in *Discovering American History* by Allan O. Kownslar and Donald B. Frizzle, Holt, Rinehart and Winston, 1970, p. XVI.

[17]See R. Garry Shirts, *Star Power*, Copyright 1969 by Western Behavioral Sciences Institute.

[18]Wallace Roberts, "No Place to Grow." *Saturday Review*, March 21, 1970, pp. 62–64, 80.

[19]Postman and Weingartner, *op. cit.*, p. 49.

[20]Sidney B. Simon, "Values-Clarification vs. Indoctrination," *Social Education*, December, 1971, p. 902. For additional reading on value-clarification, see Robert D. Barr (ed.), *Values and Youth*, NCSS Crisis Series Bulletins, No. 2, 1971; Lawrence E. Metcalf (ed.), *Values Education*, NCSS Forty-first Yearbook, 1971; and Michael Scriven, "Values in the Curriculum," *Social Science Education Consortium Newsletter*, No. 2, 1966.

[21]"Social Studies Curriculum Guidelines," NCSS Task Force on Curriculum Guidelines, *Social Education*, December, 1971, p. 858.

[22]Charles A. Reich, *The Greening of America*, Random House, 1970, p. 392.

[23]Edwin Fenton (ed.), *The New Social Studies for the Slow Learner: A Rationale for a Junior High School American History Course*, American Heritage and Holt, Rinehart and Winston, 1969, pp. 47–48. Additional examples of such clarifying responses can be found in Louis E. Raths, Merrill Harmin, and Sidney B. Simon, *Values and Teaching: Working with Values in the Classroom*, Charles E. Merrill, 1966.

[24]Fenton, *The New Social Studies for the Slow Learner*, p. 49. For additional examples of the Socratic dialogue, see Donald W. Oliver and Fred W. Newmann, *Cases and Controversy*, *The Public Issues Series*, Harvard Social Studies Project, American Education Publications, 1967.

[25]Lawrence E. Metcalf and Maurice P. Hunt, "Relevance and the Curriculum," *Phi Delta Kappan*, March, 1970, p. 359.

[26]John Holt, *The Underachieving School*, Pitman Publishing Corporation, 1969, p. 134.

[27]For a more detailed discussion of the cyclical approach, see Fenton, *The New Social Studies for the Slow Learner*, pp. 46–50.

[28]Postman and Weingartner, *op. cit.*, p. 52.

[29]Alvin Tofler, *Future Shock*, Random House, 1970, p. 399.

[30]For a more detailed discussion of these points, see John Holt, *How Children Fail*, Pitman Publishing Corporation, 1964, pp. 167–181.

[31]Terry Borton, "What's Left When School's Forgotten?", *Saturday Review*, April 18, 1970, p. 69.

[32]For a more detailed discussion of these points see Charles E. Silberman, *Crisis in the Classroom*, Random House, Inc., 1970. Harold G. Shane made a point quite similar to Silberman's when he wrote of children that "we must espouse the more tangible goal of teaching them *how* to learn." See Harold G. Shane, "A Curriculum Continuum: Possible Trends in the 70's," *Phi Delta Kappan*, March, 1970, p. 391. Jerome Bruner also recently elaborated on this point by stating that any education for the Seventies and beyond should provide a situation where a student can act on his own—to be able to demonstrate and to realize a sense of results—and provide models so that students can acquire and structure them so as to be able to cope with new situations. Jerome Bruner, Talk at "Educating a Nation: The Changing American Commitment," *Symposium on Education*, The Lyndon Baines Johnson Library, January 24, 1972.

[33]Postman and Weingartner recently asked questions quite similar in nature to these. Their special plan was for all educators to reflect on them and others they might generate. Their questions included the following, all of which could be utilized by students in history courses: "What do you worry about most? What are the causes of your worries? Can any of your worries be eliminated? How? Which of them might you deal with first? How do you decide? Are there other people with the same problems? How do you know? How can you find out? If you had an important idea that you wanted to let everyone (in the world) know about, how might you go about letting them know? . . . How do you want to be similar to or different from adults you know when you become an adult? What, if anything, seems to you to be worth dying for? How

did you come to believe this? What seems worth living for? How did you come to believe this? At the present moment, what would you like to be able to do? Why? What would you have to know in order to be able to do it? What would you have to do in order to get to know it? . . . At the present moment, what would you most like to be doing? Five years from now? Ten years from now? Why? What might you have to do to realize these hopes? What might you have to give up in order to do some or all of these things? . . . What is 'change'? What are the most obvious causes of change? . . . What kinds of changes are going on right now? Which are important? How are they similar to or different from other changes that have occurred? . . . Where do new ideas come from? . . . If you wanted to stop one of the changes going on now (pick one), how would you go about it? What consequences would you have to consider? . . . What are the most important changes that have occurred in the past ten years? Twenty years? Fifty years? In the last year? In the last six months? Last month? What will be the most important changes next month? Next year? Next decade? How can you tell? . . . What's worth knowing? How do you decide? What are some ways to go about getting to know what's worth knowing?" Excerpted from *Teaching As a Subversive Activity* by Neil Postman and Charles Weingartner. Copyright © 1969 by Neil Postman and Charles Weingartner. Used with permission of Delacorte Press.

[34]Margaret Mead, "Youth Revolt: The Future Is Now," *Saturday Review*, January 10, 1970, p. 113.

[35]Jerome Bruner, "The Skill of Relevance or the Relevance of Skills," *Saturday Review*, April 18, 1970, p. 68.

[36]See Neil Postman and Charles Weingartner, *The School Book*, Delacorte Press, 1973.

[37]See discussion of Harry Golden's comments in *AHA Newsletter*, May, 1971, pp. 13–15; Edgar Bruce Wesley, "Let's Abolish History Courses," *Phi Delta Kappan*, September, 1967; and George E. McCully, "History Begins at Home," *Saturday Review*, May 16, 1970.

PART TWO

History in the Classroom

"Development of inquiry-oriented skills becomes all the more important if students are to become educated critical thinkers."

Allan O. Kownslar

2
History As an Incomplete Story

Many students assume that a history textbook is *the* history of whatever topic appears on the title page. Few realize that all history is interpretation, that we know only a small portion of everything which happened in the past. In a single lifetime no one person can examine all the evidence about an important set of events. Nor can history textbook authors possibly read all the literature produced about any major event. Instead, they must make selections at each stage of their investigative process, and selection naturally implies interpretation.

If all this is so, then perhaps as teachers we should *begin* our courses by educating students to recognize that any history or story is both incomplete and interpretative in nature. In the process we can also show students how a mode of inquiry might be applied to any study of the past.

Most students do not realize that they, as well as all of us, use the processes of inquiry every day. Without trying to oversimplify those processes, consider, for example, how on the first day of any school year your students might *identify a problem* (How much work is this teacher going to require of us?). After several days of

class the students begin to *form hypotheses* in answer to the problem (We have already had three lengthy reading assignments; it seems we will be doing a lot of work in this course.). During the year, the class will continue to *check their hypotheses* for validity (The reading assignments require much effort, but the tests are not so difficult. Maybe this course is not going to require more work than any of my other subjects.). Finally, at the end of the year, the students will *arrive at a more definite conclusion* (The teacher did require a lot of work, but most of us managed to meet satisfactorily the requirements of the course.).

And since inquiry is a part of all our everyday lives, it would seem only logical that such critical thinking processes should lend themselves readily to the teaching of history in ways which involve students. One way of actively involving the students is suggested in the lesson plan and student materials included in this chapter. Throughout the lesson, special attention is devoted to how the basic processes of inquiry can be used to illustrate both the incompleteness and the interpretative characteristics of the discipline of history.

Sample Lesson for Teaching:
Inquiring about Early American Indian Life:
The Jumanos

LESSON PLAN

Intended Student Audience   Upper elementary and secondary levels.

**Suggested Time for
Classroom Use of Materials**   2–4 class periods (100–200 minutes).

Materials for Classroom Use   Ten information cards on Jumano Indian Life. Student assignment sheet: "Relating the Materials to Your Own Life." (Pages 29–39.)

Major Objectives for the Lesson

**Objectives
Within the Cognitive Domain**   Upon completion of this lesson the students will:

Knowledge Goals

(a) Know that the Jumano Indian way of life ceased to exist by 1800 A.D.
(b) Know that although incomplete, a variety of historical evidence is available about the Jumano Indians of the Southwest.
(c) Know that any written history is interpretation.
(d) Know that the history of any people or person must be classified as incomplete.
(e) Know that although incomplete, the history of any group or individual can nevertheless tell us much about them.

Skill Development

(a) *Interpret* and *compare* information from readings, sketches, and a map.
(b) *Recognize a problem:* How are we able to know some things about a people, the Jumano Indians, who ceased to exist by 1800 A.D.?
(c) *Formulate a hypothesis* (a tentative answer or educated guess) about how we can learn something about that life.
(d) *Test the validity of the hypothesis* by examining some available evidence about the Jumanos.
(e) *Form a generalization* about how we are able to know some things about Jumano life.
(f) *Make a listing* of the sources or kinds of historical evidence available about their lives.
(g) *Write a paragraph* or a short essay consisting of a topic sentence(s) and additional sentences as supportive evidence which form the student's history of what occurred in one social studies class.

Upon completion of this lesson the students will:

(a) Be *willing* to work in groups while examining and discussing samples of available evidence about early Indian life.

Teaching Suggestions

To illustrate the incompleteness and interpretative nature of history, this lesson first focuses on the Jumano (Hoo ma no) Indians who once inhabited parts of the American Southwest. Students may view samples of what we know about Jumano life by examining some of the many forms of historical evidence available on Jumano culture.

The Jumanos are especially appropriate for illustrating how incomplete the history of any people can be. Once a contented hunting and farming population which numbered about 15,000, the Jumanos by 1800 A.D. had ceased to exist. Plagued by poor crops and droughts, epidemics, slave raids by Spanish troops, war parties from the Apache nation, and the false lure of a better life by working for pay in Mexico's silver mines, the Jumanos either died or were quietly assimilated into the Mexican or Apache cultures by the beginning of the nineteenth century. All that has remained of their culture are bits of evidence recorded by early Spanish explorers and ruins and artifacts discovered and studied in great detail only during the past forty years by archeologists and anthropologists. The history of the Jumanos, then, is much like the story of many American Indian tribes—one of plunder, intrusions, epidemics, and finally, assimilation into alien cultures. It is also a history which is quite incomplete, since firsthand accounts or any forms of recorded sources by the Jumanos either have long since vanished or never existed at all.

Typical examples of the kinds of historical evidence which are available appear on the ten cards accompanying this lesson. A brief identification of each follows:

Card 1 contains questions to be considered as the students examine the information on Cards 2–10. The questions will help focus the students' inquiry.

Card 2 has a map which identifies all locations mentioned in the lesson.

Card 3 contains a description of where the Jumano Indians lived and why they ceased to exist as a people.

Card 4 tells about how uncertain scholars are of the exact origin or correct spelling of the word "Jumano."

Card 5 is an account about early Jumano life by Cabeza de Vaca.

Card 6 is a 1583 account about early Jumano life by Perez de Luxan, another Spanish explorer.

Card 7 is a 1583 account about early Jumano life by Antonio de Espejo, a Spanish explorer.

Card 8 is a 1581 account about early Jumano life by Hernan Gallegos, another Spanish explorer.

Card 9 contains a modern-day drawing depicting one aspect of Jumano life as described in 1581 by Gallegos.

Card 10 contains an illustration showing how archeologists have been able to reconstruct a typical Jumano pueblo-type dwelling.

Introducing the Lesson

Before they examine the information about Jumano life, ask the students: What is the meaning of "historical evidence"? What kinds of historical evidence might one expect to find available about a people, all of whom had ceased to exist as much as two hundred years ago—most of whom had vanished even before the American Revolution of 1776 or before the United States was even a nation. To emphasize this point, on the chalkboard draw the following time line, later substituting "Jumanos" after you have introduced the term for "the people we will next examine."

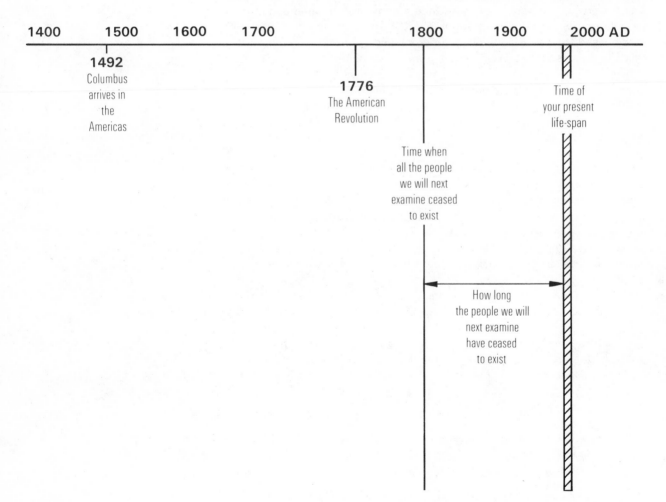

Then ask: How, for example, could we possibly begin to reconstruct a history of a people who left us no written records and who ceased to exist long before the inventions of radio, television, and movie or photograph cameras? What kinds of evidence could we begin to search for? Student suggestions could include artifacts, ruins, and possibly old written accounts by other peoples who had observed Jumano life.

Predicted Outcomes

Whatever their answers, the students will have *recognized a problem for inquiry* (How are we able to know something about a people who have long since ceased to exist?) and *offered some hypothesis* or tentative answers (Maybe we can learn something about those people by studying available evidence in the form of artifacts, ruins, or written accounts by outsiders.).

Then tell the students that they now are to imagine themselves as detectives or investigators attempting to piece together a story that in the past has remained a mystery. This they will do while examining the sample forms of available historical evidence we have on the Jumanos.

Here you may wish to write on the board "How are we able to know about the Jumano Indians?", pronouncing aloud the term *Jumano* and explaining to the class that this was a group of American Indians most of whom for many reasons ceased to exist at least two hundred years ago. Then tell the class that in order to begin to determine how we are able to begin to solve the mysteries of how the Jumanos lived, we will first begin to look at some kinds of evidence available on their life—evidence that has somehow survived long after the Jumanos vanished.

Before your students examine that evidence, you may also want to pronounce and write on the chalkboard the following locations, terms and individuals, telling the class that information about each will appear in their materials for this lesson. These words are: Rio Grande River, Rio Conchos River, Chisos Mountains, drought, Cabeza de Vaca, Alonzo del Castillo, Andres Dorantes, Estevanico, Perez de Luxan, Antonio de Espejo, pueblo, Hernan Gallegos, archeologist.

Implementing the Lesson

For this assignment have your students work in groups of fives, duplicating a set of cards for each group, and have them decide what story, although incomplete, can be pieced together about Jumano life by using evidence available on the cards. For ease of handling and care, you may wish to dry-mount and laminate each of the cards. Depending on the make-up of your class, you may also want to have each group contain certain representative proportions of what you regard as slow, average, and bright students and allow each group, once formed, to select a leader to later report its findings about Jumano tribal life.

As part of each group's organization, you may wish to assign Card 1 to the group leader and distribute Cards 2–10 to the other group members. The group leader can then ask the remainder of the group answers to those questions which appear on Card 1. After the students have received the cards, allow each group adequate time to survey them. Emphasize that while seeking answers to questions asked on Card 1, group members should feel free to express different opinions as they begin to piece together the lives many Jumanos led. While working on this group project, tell your students that they may take one or more class periods to complete the assignment.

When examining information on the cards, you may prefer to have your students, especially those who experience difficulty in communicating orally or in reading, illustrate what they have read on Cards 3, 5, 6, 7, and 8. This would allow these pupils the opportunity to obtain a sense of accomplishment by being able to successfully contribute to the lesson other than by speaking or reading.

Once the groups have completed their examination of information on the cards, each leader should then be prepared to report group findings, especially those in response to the last three questions which appear on Card 1.

Predicted Outcomes

In completing this part of the lesson the students, while interpreting, analyzing, and comparing information about Jumano life as it appears on the cards, will have *tested the validity of their hypotheses* (by determining if early accounts and archeological finds can tell us something about Jumano life), and finally, will have *formed a generalization* (by reaching a conclusion about how one can know about that life).

To facilitate group-work discussions when your students examine information on Cards 2 and 3, you may wish to tell the class that recent studies have shown that before 1000 A.D. the Jumanos were once part of the Puebloan culture which at one time was scattered over a wide area that included present-day Northern Arizona, New Mexico, Colorado, and Utah. According to many scholars this distinctive and rich Pueblo culture was based on a well-developed agricultural system where people raised beans, squash, sunflowers, cotton, tobacco, and several different kinds of corn, often by use of irrigation. Men worked the fields and did some hunting while women kept house, prepared the food, and made elaborate baskets and pottery. By 1400 A.D. this Indian culture had spread southeastward about 300 miles down the Rio Grande River past present-day El Paso and at least 40 miles into present-day northeastern Mexico. While this migration of Jumanos occurred, they probably met and assimilated into their tribes scattered bands of local Indians whose existence depended on a hunting and gathering culture. By the 1500's, the region down river from El Paso and between the lower Rio Conchos and Davis and Chisos Mountains came to be populated mainly by the Jumanos. There they generally remained until their final assimilation into other Mexican cultures.

When discussing the information on Card 10, you may wish to tell the class that according to one scholar of Indian life, the jacales (thatched-roof huts) found today in the Big Bend-El Paso region are probably survivals derived from the older Jumano pueblo-homes. The modern jacal, for example,

is usually small and normally is used only as a storehouse or shed, but otherwise it duplicates many of the features of the prehistoric houses. A shallow floor is excavated, corner posts, usually of cottonwood, are raised, and horizontal stringers are lashed to them or rest in their crotches. The walls and the roof are normally made of prickly ocotillo stalks, laid vertically and tied together, over which a liberal coating of adobe is plastered. These structures are cheap to build and are surprisingly durable in this dry climate. (W. W. Newcomb, Jr., *The Indians of Texas*, Copyright © 1961 by the University of Texas Press, pp. 242–243. Used by permission.)

To be more specific during group reports of their findings, ask the students: How many points can you now list about Jumano life? How many different kinds of sources have you examined about the Jumano Indians? What are some other questions you might ask about Jumano life? Why would you ask those questions? What other kinds of evidence might be available about the lives of the Jumanos? Why would you look for those kinds of sources? Where could one begin to look for those possible sources? Even if we found all the evidence that was available today about Jumano life, would this tell us *everything* about that life? Does this mean we cannot ever reach any conclusions or decisions about the Jumanos? Why or why not? Then conclude this part of the lesson by asking the students to consider, before the next class meeting, whether a history of any people, including *themselves*, would be an incomplete story.

When the students reassemble, remind them that they have examined some of the forms of historical evidence we now have available about the Jumano Indians. The students also reached some decisions on what we can learn about Jumano life, realizing that because of the amount of limited evidence available we cannot piece together a complete history for that group of early Indians. Yet we are nevertheless able to learn much about their life even from the evidence which is available. Now the class should be prepared to begin to consider if the history of any people or person can ever be absolutely complete.

Concluding the Lesson

Here you will need to duplicate and give each student a copy of "How Complete Is Your Life History?", which asks them to consider: (1) What sources or kinds of historical evidence are available about *your* life? (2) Once assembled and examined, could these sources be used to write a *complete* history of your life? (3) If not, does this mean that someone should never attempt to write a history of your life? (4) What is meant by the term "interpretation"? (5) Suppose two or more people used that information on the Jumanos and each wrote a history or story about those Indians. Would their *interpretations* necessarily be the same? Explain why or why not. (6) Could two different interpretations about the Jumanos be *different* and yet *valid*? Explain why or why not. (7) If someone wrote a history of *your* life, *how* would the interpretations formed about you depend on the available evidence? (8) Imagine that two or more people each wrote separate histories or stories of your life. Could they arrive at *different* interpretations about your life? Tell why or why not. (9) If you had two or more histories written about your life, could the interpretations in each be *valid* and yet *different*? Tell why or why not. And (10) Is it possible your answers to questions 5-9 could apply to the writing of any history? Explain why or why not.

While the students, possibly working in groups of fours or fives, consider these questions, you may need to ask also: What historical evidence in this room or building might be useful to historians studying our lives 5000 years from now? Would that be the same kinds of evidence those historians would seek to learn about how you lived?

Predicted Outcomes

When considering student answers to these questions, notice to what extent the students maintain that sources about themselves could include a diary, letters, report cards, school papers and tests, notes transferred in class, photographs, home movies, tape recordings, school newspaper articles, and accounts or interviews conducted with family members, peers, or teachers.

Conclude the discussion by then asking: Even if all this evidence was assembled for each of you, would it still be enough for someone to write a complete—second-by-second—account of your life? If not, what else would a writer about your life have to have in order to write its complete history? What, then, does all this tell you about piecing together the history of any people—whether it is about yourself, the Jumano Indians, or anyone else?

The class should begin to realize (1) that the written history of any people or person must be classified as "incomplete," (2) that although incomplete, the history of any group or individual can nevertheless tell us much about them, (3) that formation of any generalization greatly depends on how available evidence or information is used, (4) that often more than one conclusion on a common topic can be valid, depending on what aspect of the evidence is emphasized, and (5) that the writing and support of any generalization is essentially interpretation based on the use of available evidence.

Alternate Teaching Suggestions

Before or after your students examine and discuss the questions with "How Complete Is Your Life History?", you may wish, especially in the case of elementary-level pupils, to have them prepare in one paragraph (or a brief essay) a *history* or *story* of what transpired in class the preceding day. In essence, the students should write a paragraph(s) with a topic sentence(s) and supporting evidence in which they give *their interpretation* of what happened on the day before during which time the class completed their examination of the cards depicting Jumano life.

If you think some of your students might require a review of paragraph formation, write and discuss the following example on the chalkboard.

The Topic Sentence: Today we still strive to learn more about unknowns.

Supporting Evidence. Space exploration, for example, has taken man to the moon and unmanned space flights have been directed as far as Venus, Mars, Mercury and Jupiter. Plans are now being made to send even men to Mars someday.

If by this time you have recognized those students who require special attention in developing writing skills, you may prefer to have them work in teams of twos with more capable students. If you feel your class is not yet ready for paragraph formation, have the students write only topic sentences (generalizations) in answer to the central question.

Whatever the case, have the students begin their "history" by completing the following topic sentence:

Our social studies class yesterday was _____.

Once the students have completed their topic sentences and included supportive evidence, encourage each pupil to tell what he concluded and why. Student generalizations in answer to the question may differ, and yet each might seem valid. When this occurs, write several of the different topic sentences on the chalkboard and complete the paragraphs by including student supportive evidence for each. Those paragraphs which appear on the board can then be used as the basis for comparing any answers which are different and why they might differ.

To facilitate a discussion of the paragraphs, ask the class: Do these paragraphs tell us everything that happened yesterday? Do they give us a second-by-second account of all that happened? Would it be possible for anyone to write a second-by-second account of what all of us did during yesterday's class period? Can these paragraphs nevertheless tell us much about what did occur? How can we account for the fact that not all the paragraphs are exactly the same? Does this mean that only one of the paragraphs is "right"? What, then, does all this tell you about piecing together the history of any people—be it the Jumano Indians, this class, or any other individuals or groups of people?

After completing this lesson, some of your students might also wish to identify groups of Indians or of any other ethnic groups who once lived in your own area and seek out what kinds of historical evidence are now available about them.

This lesson might also be used in a course on American Indian Studies, Minority Group Studies, or any course in which you wish to emphasize the "incompleteness" of history.

Additional References

For more information about Indian history, see Oliver La Farge, "Myths That Hide the American Indian," *American Heritage Magazine*, October, 1956; Jay David (ed.), *The American Indian: The First Victim* (anthology of readings by Indians), William Morrow, 1972, paperback; Peter Farb, *Man's Rise to Civilization as Shown by the Indians of North America from Primeval Times to the Coming of the Industrial State* (a survey of Indian history), Dutton, 1968; Roger C. Owen, James J.F. Deetz, and Anthony D. Fisher (eds.), *The North American Indians* (a sourcebook of articles written by eminent scholars of Indian life), Macmillan, 1967; Stan Steiner, *The New Indians* (a discussion of Red Power), Dell, 1968, paperback; and Ruth M. Underhill, *Red Man's America* (a survey of Indian history), University of Chicago Press, 1953.

If you are interested in anthologies of American Indian folklore, see Cottie Burland, *North American Indian Mythology*, Crowell, 1968; Stith Thompson, *Tales of the North American Indians*, Indiana University Press, 1966. For additional sources on Indian folklore, see Charles Haywood, *A Bibliography of North American Folklore and Folksong*, Greensberg, 1951.

For sources containing illustrative materials on Indian life, see *The American Heritage Book of Indians*, Simon and Schuster, 1961; Norman Feder, *American Indian Art*, Abrams, 1965; and "Our Indian Heritage," *Life Magazine*, July 2, 1971.

For a report on the need for more Indian involvement in the educational system, see "Indian Participation in Public Schools," *Social Education*, May, 1971, pp. 452–465.

**Student Materials for
"Inquiring about Early American Indian Life: The Jumanos"
follow on pages 29–39**

CARD 1
Questions To Consider for Cards 2-10

For Card 2
1. Where did the farming Jumanos live?
2. Where did the hunting Jumanos live?

For Card 3
1. At one time, about how large was the Jumano population?
2. What were five reasons why the Jumanos ceased to exist?

For Card 4
1. How much do we know about the exact origin of the word "Jumano"?
2. How little do we know about the correct spelling of the term "Jumano"?

For Card 5
1. Who was Cabeza de Vaca?
2. How is it that we are able to know about his visits with the Jumano Indians?
3. How many things can you list about Jumano life just by reading Cabeza de Vaca's account?

For Card 6
1. Who was Perez de Luxan?
2. How many things can you list about Jumano life just by reading Luxan's account?

For Card 7
1. Who was Antonio de Espejo?
2. What was a "pueblo"?
3. How many things can you list about Jumano life just by reading Espejo's account?

For Card 8
1. Who was Hernan Gallegos?
2. How many things can you list about Jumano life just by reading Gallegos' account?

For Card 9
1. Describe what you see in the picture on Card 9.
2. Can modern drawings like this one help us to learn more about Jumano life? Tell why or why not.

For Card 10
1. What is an archeologist?
2. *How* have archeologists learned about early Jumano homes?
3. *What* have archeologists learned about early Jumano homes?

For Cards 2-10
1. How, then, are we able to learn anything about Jumano life?
2. Think back about all you have learned about the now-vanished Jumano Indians. Do you think you now have a complete picture of their life? Tell why or why not.
3. Can you make *any* decisions about Jumano life? Explain why or why not.

CARD 2
A Map Locating the Jumano Indians

Between 1400 and 1800 A.D. the Jumano Indians lived in the areas shown on the following map.

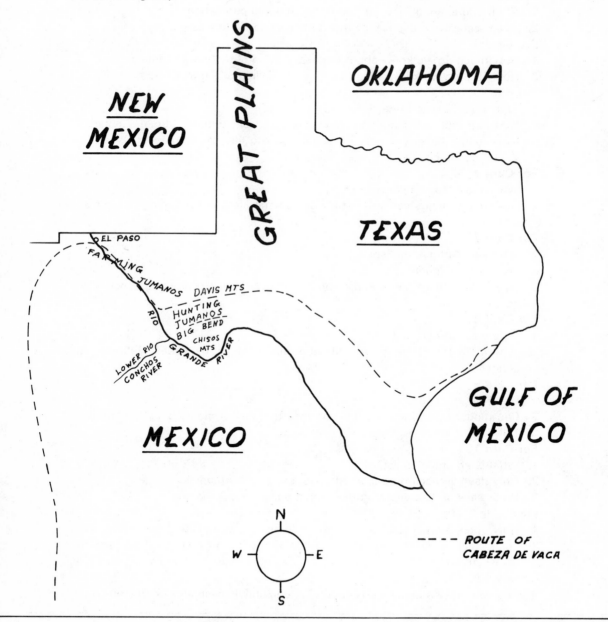

CARD 3
The Jumano Indians

As you can see by the map on Card 2, the Jumano Indians long ago lived either as settled farmers or as hunters. Those who farmed wrestled their living from garden plots between the valleys of the Rio Grande and the lower Rio Conchos Rivers. Jumanos who spent most of their time hunting for a living usually settled between the Chisos and Davis Mountains in Texas. At one time, both of these groups of Jumanos may have numbered as many as 15,000 people.

By 1800, however, all the Jumanos had vanished. Some had been killed by Spaniards seeking Indian slaves to work in Spanish silver mines in Mexico. Other Jumanos died while working in those mines. Some were killed by warlike Apache Indian tribes from the Great Plains. Faced with severe droughts or dry spells and poor crops in the early 1700's, most of the rest of the Jumanos left their lands and were finally absorbed into either the Spanish-Mexican way of life in Mexico or surrendered and became buffalo hunters with the feared Apache tribes of the plains. Thus, by 1800 it became impossible for anyone to be able to locate and identify a full-blooded Jumano. They had simply ceased to exist.

Although gone, the Jumanos nevertheless left behind some evidence about their ways of life. Examples of that evidence are what you will examine on Cards 4-10.

Adapted from W.W. Newcomb, Jr., *Indians of Texas: From Prehistoric to Modern Times*, Copyright © 1961 by the University of Texas Press, pp. 226, 228, 232-235. Used by permission.

CARD 4
The Word "Jumano"

To show how little we are able to know about the Jumano Indians, the exact origin of the word *Jumano* is unclear. No one is quite certain whether it is an Indian or a Spanish term.

Even the correct spelling of Jumano remains a mystery. The Spanish explorers who were the first known Europeans to meet the Jumanos spelled the word many ways. These can be seen in the diagram below.

Different Spanish Spellings of the Word _Jumano_

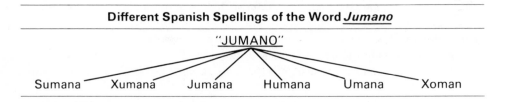

"JUMANO"

Sumana   Xumana   Jumana   Humana   Umana   Xoman

Adapted from Newcomb, *Indians of Texas,* p. 226. Used by permission.

CARD 5
Cabeza de Vaca and the Jumanos

Cabeza de Vaca was one of the best known of the European explorers to actually view Jumano life. He was a member of a Spanish expedition sent to conquer the vast area between Florida and eastern Mexico in 1528. The 300-man expedition went ashore on the west coast of Florida, but then decided to build barges and make their way by water along the coast to Mexico. Before long, however, all the barges were lost in storms. Cabeza de Vaca's barge went aground on the Texas coast. Of the 300 men who began the trip to Mexico, only four arrived there: Cabeza de Vaca, Alonzo del Castillo, Andres Dorantes, and a black named Estevanico. Those four men spent eight years (1528-1536) among the Indians of Texas, sometimes as captives, sometimes as traders, and sometimes as medicine men.

After his arrival in Mexico City, Cabeza de Vaca wrote about his experiences and had them published in a book called a *journal*. The following selection from that journal is an adapted English translation from the Spanish written by Cabeza de Vaca. In this selection Cabeza de Vaca described one part of Jumano Indian life.

The Jumanos fill the half of a large bowl with water, and throw on the fire many stones of such as are most convenient and readily take the heat. When hot, they are taken up with tongs of sticks and dropped into the bowl until the water boils from the heat of the stones. Then whatever is to be cooked is put in, and until it is done they continue taking out cooled stones and throwing in hot ones. They boil their food.

Adapted from Frederick Webb Hodge (ed.), "The Narrative of Álvar Núñez Cabeza de Vaca," *Spanish Explorers in the Southern United States,* Scribner's, 1907, p. 105.

CARD 6
Perez de Luxan and the Jumanos

Perez de Luxan was a member of another Spanish expedition to explore the Southwest. In 1583 he wrote the following descriptions of Jumano Indian life.

Upon our arrival there came to us in procession and singing, more than two hundred Jumano Indians, men and women. They presented us with shawls, tanned deerskins, paints, and ornaments like bonnets with colored feathers which they said they obtained from the direction of the sea.

These people cover themselves with well tanned skins of the buffalo. The women wear some sort of tanned deerskin poncho and other tanned deerskins as skirts, carrying as cloaks tanned skins of the cattle. These people wear their hair long and tied to the head. The men have their hair cut very short, up to the middle of their heads, and from there up they leave it two fingers long and curl it with minium paint in such a way that it resembles a small cap. They leave on the crown a large lock of hair to which they fasten feathers of white and black birds such as geese, cranes, and sparrow-hawks.

The Jumanos tan hides and make them usable by beating them with stones until they are soft.

Adapted from George P. Hammond and Agapito Rey, *Expedition into New Mexico Made by Antonio de Espejo, 1582-1583, as Revealed in the Journal of Diego Perez de Luxan,* Quivira Society Publications, I, 1929, pp. 67, 57-58.

CARD 7
Antonio de Espejo and the Jumanos

Antonio de Espejo came to Mexico as a cattleman but eventually became famous for exploring much of New Mexico and West Texas. As an explorer for Spain, he met the Jumano Indians. In the following account he tells about some parts of Jumano life in 1583. The term "pueblo" as used in this selection was one the Spanish explorers used to describe many of the Indian villages in the Southwest. A description of how the Jumanos made a pueblo home is on Card 8. An illustration of one such pueblo home appears on Card 10.

After we convinced the Jumanos we meant no harm to them, all the people came down within half an hour, making musical sounds with their mouths similar to those of the flute. They kissed the hand of the priest with us, whom we had along. And all, both young and old, offered everyone maize, beans, gourd vessels, buffalo skins, and bows and arrows.

At every pueblo we visited, the Indians kissed the priest's hand and brought presents, and in all these pueblos we were received with much rejoicing and music which they made with their mouths as I have described above. Besides this peaceful and friendly greeting they were treated to dances and other celebrations. They made music by beating their hands while sitting around a big fire. They sing, and in time with the singing they dance, a few rising from one side and others from the opposite, performing their dances two, four, and eight at a time.

Adapted from Hammond and Rey, *op. cit.*, pp. 60, 62, 67. Newcomb, *Indians of Texas*, p. 244. Used by permission.

CARD 8

Hernan Gallegos and the Jumanos

Hernan Gallegos was another Spanish explorer of present-day Mexico and Texas. In 1581 he wrote the following descriptions of Jumano life as he first saw it.

We saw a piece of copper which an Indian carried about his neck tied with some cotton threads. Another carried a copper sleigh-bell. Some of the Indians who came to meet and see us carried white and colored coral shells, although not of fine quality, suspended from the nose; they also had turquoises. Among the things they presented to us were two bonnets made of numerous feathers.

Standing on top of their houses they showed great merriment on seeing us. These houses resemble those of the Mexicans. They build them square. They put up the bases and upon these they place timbers, the thickness of a man's thigh. Then they plaster them with mud. Close to them they have their granaries built of willow, after the fashion of the Mexicans, where they keep their provisions and their harvest of mesquite and other things.

Adapted from George P. Hammond, and Agapito Rey, "The Rodriguez Expedition to New Mexico, 1581-1582," *New Mexico Historical Review*, II, 1927, pp. 257, 260, 256. Used by permission.

CARD 9
A Modern Illustration of Jumano Life

Since we do not have available any paintings done of Jumano life while those people lived, some artists today have tried to recreate what explorers such as Hernan Gallegos had written about those now-vanished Indians. You may recall, for example, on Card 8 that Gallegos had written about the Jumanos: "Standing on top of their houses they showed great merriment on seeing us." An artist recently took that quotation and other early descriptions of Jumano life and drew the following picture. It shows how some Jumano Indians may have greeted those early Spanish explorers.

Illustration from Newcomb, *Indians of Texas*, p. 240. Used by permission.

CARD 10
A Jumano Home—Archeological Finds

As you now know, the Jumanos settled in the area between present-day El Paso and the Big Bend on the Rio Grande River. There they built pueblo-type homes. We are able to know this because of the diggings done by archeologists, scholars seeking to learn more about early people by studying the articles (artifacts) or housing they left behind. The archeologist usually selects a spot where he believes early people once lived and then digs for their remains or searches the ground and caves in that area.

By digging in and around some old Jumano pueblo homes, archeologists were able to learn many other things about Jumano Indian life. An archeologist's reconstruction of pueblo homes of the 1500's follows. It is a reconstruction much like the one the modern-day artist used for the drawing on Card 9.

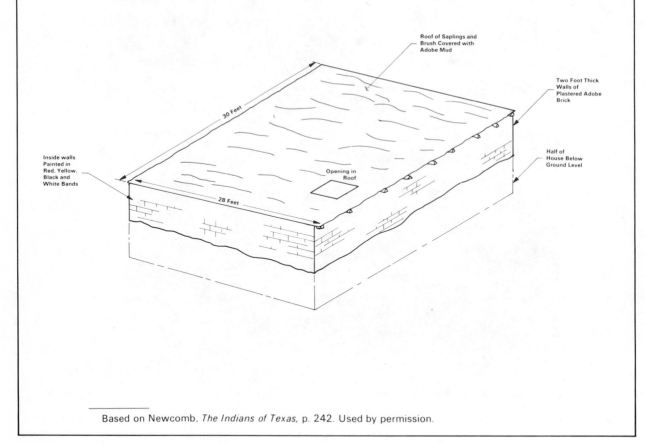

Based on Newcomb, *The Indians of Texas*, p. 242. Used by permission.

STUDENT ASSIGNMENT SHEET
Relating the Materials to Your Own Life

You learned that a history of a people such as that of the Jumano Indians will probably always be incomplete. Yet, how complete is the history of any people or of any person? How complete, for example, is the history of *your* life? Think about this as you consider the answers to the following questions.

1. What sources or kinds of historical evidence are available about your life?

2. Once assembled and examined, could those sources be used to write the *complete* history of your life?

3. If not, does this mean someone should never attempt to write a history of your life?

4. What is meant by the term "interpretation"?

5. Suppose two or more people used that information on the Jumanos and each wrote a history or story about those Indians. Would their *interpretations* necessarily be the same? Explain why or why not.

6. Could two different interpretations about the Jumanos be *different* and yet *valid?* Explain why or why not.

7. If someone wrote a history of your life, *how* would the interpretations formed about you depend on the available evidence?

8. Imagine that two or more people each wrote separate histories or stories of your life. Could they arrive at *different* interpretations about your life? Tell why or why not.

9. If you had two or more histories written about your life, could the interpretations in each be *valid* and yet *different?* Tell why or why not.

10. Is it possible your answers to questions 5-9 could apply to the writing of any history? Explain why or why not.

"Teachers confront inquiry teaching initially and must consider how it 'fits' them, not as new fashion but life style."

O. L. Davis, Jr.

3
Inquiring about the American Experience

Teaching pupils to inquire is tricky—and yet it isn't too.

It's tricky, first of all, because many teachers and pupils and parents understand it to be this season's new fun and games. Or maybe a fresh disguise for the same unsavory issue. Second, it's tricky because inquiry is not just finding out.

Inquiry is real for simple reasons. Pupils who inquire—yes, those who really engage authentic materials and serious questions—*like* to inquire. And that outcome is a happy plus! No matter what else. They also learn, and learning is what most of us understand to be a major purpose of schooling.

Learning through inquiry is not a simplistic notion. It includes dimensions long sought but only infrequently achieved. Some specifics. Pupils should learn substantive knowledge, both facts and relationships, about the topic, period, theme, situation under study. They will also learn important and long accepted procedures of historical study. Thereby, they likely will learn firsthand and in the company of others engaged with history—not only reading and answering queries about someone else's historical conclusions—how historical generalizations and interpretations are made. Crucial to the enterprise is their learning a kind of "habit of mind" about history, its tentativeness, its validity, its sources, its personalness. Pupils will learn something about themselves, quite different from the result of working in only non-inquiry settings. They probably will develop increased personal efficacy and sense of personal work through accomplishment. As a learner, they will have played seriously a significant part of the role of historian.

So much has been written about inquiry in teaching history that a short bibliography would do injustice to the abundance of sources. As you read this yearbook, you will observe clearly that inquiry pervades every section. Each lesson, validated with hundreds of pupils, contains some novel as well as consistent approaches to inquiry teaching. Thus, inquiry teaching is and must be seen as a generalized way of living, a metaphor of strategy and emphasis, rather than any standard formula or technique. So known and practiced by us teachers, inquiry teaching in American history in the schools may have sustained and renewing viability.

Inquiry teaching affects pupils second. Teachers confront it initially and must consider how it "fits" them, not as new fashion but life style. In *addition* a variety of new media, mainly authentic primary sources, is a critical part of the instructional plans. Some of us American history teachers still have little personal experience with such materials in productive study (we have called it "research"). Consequently, we can "work through" the materials in advance of class use or along with the class. Inquiry teaching really does add a luster to our role as teacher: we have no obligation to be the "Answer Man." Rather, our answers are those of a more knowledgeable person who continues to learn. And that is truly an addition to our role! Further, teachers in this setting help to resolve, and often do solve thorny and vexing matters.

Here, one conspicuous concern must be addressed. While this chapter and, really, this yearbook, communicate strongly a commitment to inquiry teaching in American history, the authors do not want to be over-stood. Plainly, as experienced teachers, we are aware of the desirability of pacing, of change of focus, of variety. Just as historians every day do not inquire in the same way, they need to read secondary accounts, to read accounts in different fields or areas from which they direct their principal studies, to talk to colleagues about matters historical and not historical (geographic, artistic, culinary, athletic, etc.), to daydream even. How much more so do pupils need such variety in their school history! So, inquiry teaching, Yes! But not in excess *if* it becomes a dull repetitive process.

A caveat about the inquiry lesson in this chapter. It is neither "teacher-proof" nor "pupil-proof." It carries no guarantee of success, even though it has been used productively with hundreds of pupils. For some classes there will be no pop or sputter at all. On the other hand, it will work beautifully with a number of classes and should serve, at least, as the springboard for hundreds of lessons featuring inquiry in teaching American history.

Sample Lesson for Teaching:
Inquiring about
Conditions of Life During the Civil War

LESSON PLAN

Intended Student Audience	Upper elementary through secondary levels.
Suggested Time for Classroom Use of Materials	3-5 class sessions.
Materials for Classroom Use	Five letters written at the time of the Civil War (pp. 51–55).

Major Objectives for the Lesson

Objectives Within the Cognitive Domain

Upon completion of this lesson the students will:

Knowledge Goals

(a) Know several conditions of life during wartime.
(b) Know that letters communicate symbolically as well as literally and that information obtained from letters must be understood from those vantage points.

(c) Know that data from sources may be checked for validity through re-sort to accepted critical standards.

(d) Know that much of the data obtained from sources is related directly to the questions one asks about the source.

(e) Know that historical sources, while incomplete in a variety of ways, may provide an investigator much information.

(f) Know that interpretations garnered from one set of sources may not be generalized easily to cover all circumstances (in this case, families or even Confederate families).

(g) Know that many of the questions about history cannot be answered with the available evidence, and that incomplete evidence is a neces-sary condition of historical activity.

(h) Know that reasonable interpretations based on the same sources may be quite different.

(a) *Gather* and *interpret* information from original and secondary sources.   ***Skill Development***

(b) Use one's own experience and intelligence to *suggest* ideas, ex-planations and information.

(c) *Formulate hypotheses,* to suggest sources useful to testing these hy-potheses, and to *test the hypotheses* if possible.

(d) *Formulate questions* about the substance of an historical source to guide collection of data.

(e) *Criticize* historical sources using appropriate canons of validity.

(f) *State generalizations* on the basis of data collected and impressions garnered.

(g) *Write* a paragraph(s) constituting an historical account of conditions of life during the Civil War.

(h) *Reflect* and *criticize* both the conclusions and procedures of inquiry.

**Objectives
Within the Affective Domain**

Upon completion of this lesson the students will:

(a) *Empathize* with both the writers and the recipients of the letters.   ***Emphathizing***

(b) *Publicly* state and comment critically on both substantive data and feelings, personal and those inferred from inquiry.   ***Social Participation***

(c) *Participate* both as an individual and as a group member in the inquiry.

(d) Be *receptive* to a range of data about an historical problem, data both complete, and not definitive.   ***Value Clarification***

(e) *Tolerate* ambiguity and possible wide differences in interpretations of data.

Teaching Suggestions

Lesson Overview

This lesson focuses on twin objectives. First, it directs attention to the qualities of living during wartime, the American Civil War, on both home-front and battlefield. Second, it necessitates attention to the nature and conditions of a special type of historical evidence, letters.

The five letters which constitute the basic sources for the lesson are those preserved by three generations of a family. These letters are used with the permission of Mrs. W.D. Price, Route 1, Athens, Georgia. Appreciation is expressed to John L. Davis, social studies teacher, Lampasas (Texas) High School, for his assistance on several matters during the preparation of this chapter. The letters may be reproduced for class use in connection with the lesson developed in this chapter. They have not been published for at least two reasons. They were private and personal to the family, carefully preserved and cherished, the only family material extant from the Confederate years of the family. Also, they seem not specially unlike other letters already published. Perhaps for both reasons, they serve as productive sources for study.

The letters were written at various times during a period of a year by four sons of Prior L. Davis, a farmer near Athens, Georgia. These sons, in order of birth, were James W., Isham J. (Bud), C.W. (Charlie), and W.L. (Willie). They, along with their younger brother, Robert, had enlisted on different occasions and their units were assigned to different Confederate armies. Two of the brothers, Charlie and Willie, died in battle. Following the end of the war, Isham and Robert, two younger brothers, and a widowed sister left Georgia for Texas where they established small farms in Shelby County.

Only these five letters have survived the century. Other letters were written by the soldier sons to their family, and their father wrote to them. No accounts of wartime life were written by any family member and only threadbare reminiscences of their few stories remain as oral tradition in the family. Evidence from U. S. Census records reveals that the father and sons had the rudiments of schooling. Essentially, the five letters provide the only available evidence of lives and conditions of living by this family during the Civil War.

Introducing the Lesson

Most school history accounts of the Civil War direct major attention to the overarching political, economic, and military features of the war. Consequently, to begin this lesson, ask pupils questions such as: Have you wondered as I have about what it was like to be a soldier in this war? Wonder what families at home thought about when their sons were away fighting? What kinds of effects did this war have on people at home? Were the soldiers and families at home concerned about the political and social passions motivating the war? The ensuing discussion likely will yield a range of opinions and personal preferences. Consider each suggestion as important and possible. Later, indicate that such ideas or hypotheses can be verified or tested by recourse to appropriate, authentic sources. Now, the task is to decide what types of sources one would seek. Responses likely will include newspaper articles, diaries, photographs, memoirs, letters, and official records. As sources are suggested, write them on the chalkboard or overhead projector transparency in a column. Continue the discussion by determining which of the types of sources might be considered closer to or further from the individual. A newspaper article, for example, might be the account of an observer or a narrative written by an individual. A third column might indicate a consensus judgement about the accessibility of the sources named.

Distribute the mimeographed letters, making sure that pupils do not receive the set in the same order. At *this* time tell pupils that this collection of letters has been held by generations of the same family since the Civil War. These letters, of all that were written by family members during that war, are the only ones that survived. Tell them, also, that the family home was a small farm near Athens, Georgia.

Then, ask pupils to read the letters for impressions of life during wartime. After a first reading, ask them to list those impressions on a sheet of paper.

The key purposes of this introduction are to motivate pupils to inquire behind the interpretive generalizations in historical accounts, to recognize a problem for inquiry and confront some problems in the inquiry process. Also important is for pupils to recognize that their ideas are important, to themselves and to the group.

Predicted Outcomes

Impressions of the letters may be predicted to vary widely. Accept all the impressions proffered and list as many as you can on the chalkboard. Impressions invariably include ones like: the father surely didn't write to his sons; the letter writers sure were stupid (or couldn't spell); the letters don't contain anything historical; one son apparently was going blind. With older pupils and ones who have more experience with such tasks, you may want each pupil to make a personal list of impressions. After a number of responses are available, ask the class to review the list. Do all impressions "go together"? What was the original assignment? Likely, individuals will recognize at least two groupings of impressions: Those having to do with life during wartime (the assignment) and those reflecting personal judgements about the sources, the letter writers, the times, and the war itself. After grouping impressions according to categories like those above, ask pupils to save the list for reference, to add to and/or delete from. Note with them the value of both types of impressions.

You may find it productive to have pupils discuss their impressions of life in wartime with two or three others in a small group. Following the discussion, ask pupils to write a paragraph about conditions of life during the

Civil War using evidence from the letters. Paragraphs should have topic sentences and contain at least two other sentences.

By this time, pupils will be well into this inquiry. Some probably will say they have too much to work with. Others will lament too few facts to state a generalization. Still others will be asking questions about the letters, their form and contents.

The list of impressions and the paragraph constitute two types of *first* or *tentative* accounts (or hypotheses). Both signal the importance of identification of evidence *prior* to preparation of an account or a set of interpretive statements or generalizations. They are both seen as *tentative* and, thus, may be altered as other evidence becomes available. Further, this activity signals that *interpretations* are sought as a major *product* of the study. Pupils should save those paragraphs in their notebooks after they have discussed them with others in small groups and/or in the entire class.

Implementing the Lesson

As this lesson develops, you may well decide to use an instructional plan that provides a number of occasions for pupils to work in small groups of three or four. Such a plan has been particularly useful when ideas are to be generated and accounts are to receive a first critique. Individual preparation of working papers/documents is deemed essential for personal use throughout the study.

Important early in the study is formulation of questions about the letters. One set of questions inevitably has to do with the validity of the evidence. Another is concerned with information desired to make understanding more complete.

Validity should not be taken lightly, but neither should it consume most of the instructional time. Do plan time for assessing validity with respect to both *external* and *internal* criteria. External criticism, having to do with judgements about the source's genuineness, should include attention, among other things, both to the composition and form of the letters. For example, the misspelling of many words and the spelling of words according to pronunciations rather than a dictionary confirm the level of schooling known to have been held by the letter writers. Also, the form of each salutation seems consistent with the understood formality of written address of sons to fathers. One example appropriate to *external criticism* is the nature of the letters. Each appears to be a personal letter, perhaps written under hasty as well as rustic circumstances. None, therefore, attempts military reports (e.g., as from a scout to a field commander) even though some information of possible military value is included.

Very useful to the lesson development is the formulation of questions about the letters, the answers to which are believed to add information. This task has been initiated fruitfully as a homework assignment. Individual lists can be expanded by both small groups and the entire class. Like other productive thinking activities, some individuals will generate long lists, others few questions. Some questions will concentrate on locations

(Where is Natchitoches, Louisiana?), on relationships (Is C. W. the same as Charlie?), on behavior (Why don't the boys write their mother?), on actions (Why did the boys not ask about crops?). With lists of questions begun, two other steps are important. Pupils should give attention to possible sources useful to answering the questions. A list of sources and their symbols might be class-developed and pupils could use the appropriate symbol to designate their judgement. Also, as the study proceeds, pupils should list by the question any answer(s) determined or located. Some classes have found helpful a chart like the one below:

Question	Possible Source	Answer-Sources
What are "gaunders"? Why would soldiers at front send home cartridges they needed to fight with?	Medical book of period	"jaundice"— class discussion

In some situations, you may want to add another category to the chart labeled "Judgement of Validity of Answer." Pupils will find that a number of their answers are "possible" and ones generated from speculation in the absence of available evidence. In such situations, they should concern themselves with validity; some possibilities are simply more possible than others. Their judgements could range, for example, from "Substantial" to "Doubtful." Other categories could be developed.

As questions are formulated, specific attention should be given to the nature of personal letters. This examination can provide insights into matters of both symbolic and literal communication. Every letter can be studied in this focus and results related directly to understanding some of the conditions of life in this family at the time. For example, in the letter of November 6, 1863, W. L. writes ". . . with the exception of my eyes they are very weak and the Smoke from the camp fires appears to be rank poison to them. so you need not be surprised at any time to hear that you have a blind Son." This passage describes with considerable imagery one dimension of a soldier's camp life. Dramatically, W. L. communicates this unpleasantness. Pupils frequently ask, on the other hand, "Is W. L. really going blind?" Clearly, no evidence is available to respond directly. Careful rereading of the letters, particularly at the beginning, indicates W. L.'s loneliness from family and frustration at not receiving mail from home. These feelings seem to be underscored by the reference to blindness which may have been an exaggeration to describe the campfire, to contrast his good health with that of his brother, and to elicit sympathy and a letter from his family. This speculation does not invalidate the possible literalness of the blindness passage. Nevertheless, it suggests a symbolic interpretation of the communication as possibly more powerful than the literal understanding. In treating this concern, discuss with pupils how they write personal letters. Do they write descriptions of events? describe feelings? Do they ask for love, empathy, understanding? The letter writers were vast distances from home in terms of time and facilities to transmit mail. (Some pupils may want to investigate mail and transportation service in the South and North during those war years. Such projects could add to the overall inquiry.) How might pupils write their parents to communicate feelings like those held by the letter writers?

Predicted Outcomes

Through the foregoing activities, pupils will have generated more, rather than less, ambiguity. They probably will have more questions unanswered than answered. They very well should possess more specific knowledge and generalizations about conditions of life of soldiers and families at home than they held prior to study. They will have used procedures for examining historical sources that they will find useful in subsequent inquiring.

Concluding the Lesson

Several class meetings before the final session of this study, assign the writing of a paragraph about other conditions of living during the Civil War. The paragraph should be available for the final class study session. Take care to remind pupils of the necessity for each paragraph to have a topic sentence and several other sentences. Depending on the age and writing experience of the pupils, you may want to require the inclusion of evidence to support their generalizations, either in the text or as footnotes.

During the discussion of the *interpretations* (paragraphs), be sure to comment and elicit pupil reactions to interpretations presented. Comments should relate to such matters as relationship of evidence to generalization, the adequacy and applicability of the generalization, and the inconclusiveness of the account. A particularly important concern is the differentiation between appropriate speculation and projecting fiction. Pupils should expect questions such as these from you and classmates: "Why did you say that?" "Didn't you go beyond the evidence?"

Then, referring to the account written early in the study, ask pupils to compare their second version with the first. Individually or in small groups, they can list similarities and differences. In the subsequent discussion, ask them to state explanations for these differences. Emphasize the continuing tentativeness of interpretations, contributions of extended inquiry (both answers and unanswered questions), and changed and/or substantiated impressions as study continued.

Convenient to review and summary of the lesson is an extended discussion about conditions of life during Civil War. You can ask questions like: Which conditions of living did we not learn about? How can we explain why we didn't learn about these? How might we learn about them? Are the conditions of living we learned about applicable to other families and situations in the South? in the North? in other wars? How could we verify our ideas?

These concluding activities should facilitate pupils' intellectualizing about (or reflectively examining) their experiences in inquiry. The final account or history they prepare is personal evidence about the generalizations they stated, the evidence they amassed and analyzed, and the feelings they have about the inquiry. Their comparison of first and second accounts helps them review impressions, substantive matters, and inquiry procedures. They should also be able to recognize some impressive values as well as shortcomings of letters as historical evidence and of the historians' need for additional sources and viewpoints. Much classroom evidence of such outcomes will be manifest as pupils talk openly throughout the inquiry, particularly in the final session, about their own feelings about what and how they are learning. Pupils are helped to identify how, in every study, they learn substantive material as well as about themselves, their adequacy, competence, and power.

Some individuals may find productive the process of beginning to edit these letters. Using published letters, singly or collections, in historical journals, they can note elements in these letters which merit comment, explication, and identification. Using some standard and easily available secondary sources (e.g., atlas, accounts of the Civil War), they should be able to make a good start. For items they believe should be explained and for which they have no information, they should be encouraged to indicate the type of source they believe would be particularly helpful.

A beneficial discussion may be based on the relation of these wartime letters to letters from soldiers to family (and friends) in other wars or times of extreme stress (e.g., expedition to Antarctica). What types of information and feelings would pupils expect to find in other personal letters in other wars? Why? How might these hypotheses be tested (sources, procedures)?

To extend their study, some individuals could read other collections of Civil War letters, both North and South, from soldiers as well as family members. These letters could serve as further tests of generalizations as well as provide additional evidence for other generalizations about conditions of living.

Some pupils may enjoy further speculating about the family back home to whom the Davis boys write. What might the family have been like? What did they do during the War? What might they have written to their soldiers? How might they have kept up with the conduct of war operations?

Additional References

Many of the good secondary accounts of the American Civil War contain information about conditions of life on battlefronts and at home, both North and South. Standard and popular references to soldier life are Bell I. Wiley's *The Life of Johnny Reb*, Bobbs-Merrill, 1943, and *The Life of Billy Yank*, Bobbs-Merrill, 1951. The Wiley volumes heavily use soldiers' letters as sources for interpretations. Also useful are Philip Van Doren Stern, *Soldier Life in the Union and Confederate Armies*, Indiana University Press, 1961; Bell I. Wiley's *The Plain People of the Confederacy*, Louisiana State University Press, 1943, and *Embattled Confederates*, Harper and Row, 1964; and George W. Smith and Charles Judah, *Life in the North During the Civil War*, University of New Mexico Press, 1966.

As additional general background, you may find informative works like E. B. Long, *The Civil War Day-by-Day, An Almanac 1861-1865*, Doubleday, 1971; Paul M. Angle, *A Pictorial History of the Civil War Years*, Doubleday, 1967; Mary Elizabeth Massey, *Ersatz in the Confederacy*, University of South Carolina Press, 1952; and Mary Elizabeth Massey, *Bonnet Brigades*, Alfred A. Knopf, 1966. Useful specialized studies can also be helpful, including volumes such as Paul E. Steiner, *Disease in the Civil War*, Charles C. Thomas, 1968, and Robert C. Black, *The Railroads of the Confederacy*, University of North Carolina Press, 1952.

Many Civil War letters from soldiers have been edited and published in both monographs and state and local history journals. Such sets of correspondence provide added background to study of other collections of letters. Examples of edited letters are: from a Confederate soldier, Seymour V. Conner (ed.), *Dear America*, Jenkins Publishing Co., 1971, and from a Union soldier, Margery Greenleaf (ed.), *Letters to Eliza*, Follett, 1970.

An additional exercise to complement this one could focus on how Black slaves felt during the Civil War. Here the amount of available evidence is severely limited by the fact that most slaves were not allowed to learn to read and write. However, material on this subject is available in R. Ethel Dennis, *The Black People of America: Illustrated History*, McGraw-Hill, 1970; John Hope Franklin, *From Slavery to Freedom: A History of Negro Americans*, Third Edition, Knopf, 1967; Langston Hughes and Milton Meltzer, *A Pictorial History of the Negro in America*, Third Revised Edition, Crown, 1968; and Charles Crier Sellers, Jr., "The Travail of Slavery," in *The Southerner as American*, University of North Carolina Press, 1960. Especially see James A. Banks, "Teaching Black Studies for Social Change," in *Teaching Ethnic Studies: Concepts and Strategies*, 43rd Yearbook, National Council for the Social Studies, 1973.

**Student Materials for
"Inquiring about Conditions of Life During the Civil War"
follow on pages 51–55**

LETTER #1

May the 18—1863

    Dear Father—I have written to you again and again—Still it Seems impossoble for me to here from you through the placies from which I wrote are now all in the hands of the Yankeys I have nothing of interes to communicate I am well and getting along very well I belong to the C. S. Light Batery as you know if you got my last letter—
We are encampted near Grant Ecore Lousisianna though we expect to move back towards Alexandria in a few days. We had Several days of hard fighting Since I wrote to you last Capt. O. J. Semmes our cammander was captured near Franklin.
If you receive this pleas write immediatly and let me know where all the Fooks are So that I may write to them all, More if I can once here from you and know that you get My letters I can then write you Something historical—
Direct yours to me Care Semmes' Batery near Nachetoches Louissianna
Yours as ever

      J. W. Davis

LETTER #2

Nov 6th 1863
Camp.Milledge artillery
Culpeper county, Va.

Mr. P. L. Davis

My Dear Father. after waiting a very long time for an answer to my last letter to you I have come to the conclusion to write again. knowing your disposion and exactly how you are about writing I wish you to understand that I do not feel offended in the least at your delay. but at the Same time I think you could afford to write to me onced in every three or four months, for my *Dear* Father, I can assure you that there is nothing, that affords me with more pleasure, than to receive a letter from you. and will you not increase my pleasure by writing to me oftener than you have heretofore. I received a letter from Charley not very long Since he was near Atlanta when he wrote to me but I have heard through other communication that he moved near chatanooga. I also heard that he had been Sick but was geting well. poor fellow I fear he will have a hard time out there in enfentry I much rather he had joined some artillery Company I think artillery is much lighter Surfice than enfentry. and I have tried bouth. I have not heard from Isham personly Since he left home the last time. I am thinking that he will have a hard time also with his many diseases. as to myself I am as sound to day as I was when I joined the army. with the excepion of my eyes they are very weak and the Smoke from the camp fires appears to be rank poison to them. so you need not be surprised at any time to hear that you have a blind Son. I think that there is a chance for me to come home between this and next febuary and if there is even a half a chance I certainly will make us of it. a good posion of our army are building huts for winter quarters but we have not commenced yet nor I do not know how loing before we will we are in camped near culpeper courthouse we have had Some very bad weather this fall I do not think that we will have much more fighting to do in Va until next Spring. you will give my love to ma and all the children. nothing more but
     remain your ever Dear Son
      W. L. Davis

LETTER #3

Feb 20th 1864

Camp. 66th Ga Regt Near Dalton Ga

Mr. P. L. Davis.

Dear Father again I make it conveint to write to you, I am feeling better this morning than I have felt in some time, though I think I am taking the Gaunders, which is, & have been very comon here. Pa I have just taken another march, we left here last wednesday morning, & went some near twenty miles, for to work on the Road, we worked all day Thursday & then marched back that night; There has A good many of the soldiers left from around here for Alabama, I think we will Leave soon for Mobeil Ala; at least all I see look in favor of it. I hope you have recd. my Letter Stating all about the other march; Pa W. W. Brooks & I is going to send A box home in which I sent an old pair of shoes, & a little Bag of cartridriges, these roped up in a peice of News paper you can tare up & use the Balls & pouder, those in brown paper please save for me; & my old shoes I wishe you would have fixed up for me, & keep them untill I call for them; I have nothing more to write, that will enterest you. the Box you & Ma sent me was a great treat; Give my love to Ma & all of the Chrildren, tell ma to Remember me to little sister nothing More, only I Remain

P.S. Direct yours   Your Devoted Son
to Stephens Brigade instead   Charlie
of wetson's

P.S. Isham Sends his love Tender mine to all my friends.

LETTER #4

Feb 25th 1864

Camp on the hillside at Dalton, Ga.

Mr. P. L. Davis.

 Dear father in or- to let you know where I am, & what is doing, I write this; we left our Winter quarters Tuesday, & have been here on the side of A mountain ever since; we are now cooking up 8 days rations, & expect as soon as we get them cookid we will leave; the fight is, & has been going on all the week, at least skirmishing, I hear different reports concerning it, therefore I donot now know who is geting the best of it. we have heard the reports of the cannons ever since we have been here, The fireing is much plainer to day than it has been; it seems by that, that our men is falling
Back.
If we meet them I think they will get A licking. The men are all in good spirits, & have Great confidence in old Joe, I hope we will whip them Good. I am Black & dirty, we are on a red clay hill, & it is very dusty only at night then the smoke is so thick that you cant see any distance at all. nothing more, My love to all. Isham is with the wagon train about 10, or fifteen, miles below here. My speccial Love to Ma;

 in great hast Your Devoted Son
  C. W. Davis.

LETTER #5

March, 7st 1864

Dear Father my ink had hadly dried on my letter when we received ordirs to report on the front lines immediately. So we made the necessary preparations and moved off as Soon as posible and after Staying out there two days we have returned to our old camps without any fight, the exitement arisen from a cavelry raid made by the yankie cavelry. They wase badly whiped and driven back like Sheep, We are exspecting the Spring campaign to open in these quarters Soon, nothing more

Yours

Bud

P.S. the case of Small pox that I spoke of prove to be a very bad case. it has been seened to the hospital, no one else has taken it yet

"For the student, development of any concept means
to elaborate on the many definitions which apply to it."

Cathy Lyn Domann and Mary Lee Wright

4
Teaching the Big Ideas

Today's fast-paced world with emphasis on condensation of everything from foods to news to history represents the antithesis of sound concept development in the classroom. This seems especially true when we try to have students identify the many interpretations associated with development of any concept. It is a process which requires adequate time for anyone to discover how concepts can signify a variety of related meanings, depending on how they are used with a particular set of events or issues.

To illustrate one way for taking the necessary time to develop a concept or "big idea" in the history classroom, we have chosen the concept of "liberation." It is one with relevant and political, economic, social, and historical connotations. Liberation is a term which also has been used often by historians to describe and summarize the very meaning of our past. Its use in the lesson plan and student materials which follow will focus on (1) how "liberation" has been interpreted by many Americans of our present decade who associate it with the Women's Equal Rights Movement and (2) how this concept can be applied and how it can be developed further with an examination of similar liberation movements throughout American history.

Sample Lesson for Teaching:
What Is Liberation? A Closer Look at the Women's Equal Rights Movement

LESSON PLAN

Advanced upper elementary and secondary levels.

Intended Student Audience

1–2 class periods (50–100 minutes).

**Suggested Time for
Classroom Use of Materials**

Two sets of data cards (pp. 65–79).

Materials for Classroom Use

Major Objectives for the Lesson

**Objectives
Within the Cognitive Domain**

Upon completion of this lesson the students will:

Knowledge Goals

(a) Know representative arguments made by those opposed to the Women's Equal Rights Movement of the 1970's.
(b) Know representative arguments made by those favoring the Women's Equal Rights Movement of the 1970's.
(c) Know that the concept "liberation" can be applied to many movements throughout American history.
(d) Know that "liberation" can have different interpretations.

Skill Development

(a) *Read, compare,* and *recall* information about the Women's Equal Rights Movement.
(b) *Recognize a problem:* Can the concept of "liberation" have more than one meaning or interpretation?
(c) *Form hypotheses* about whether the concept "liberation" can have more than one meaning or interpretation.
(d) *Test the validity of the hypotheses* by examining available evidence in which the term is used or implied by those who oppose or support the Women's Equal Rights Movement.
(e) *Form a more definite conclusion* about how the term "liberation" can be interpreted.

**Objectives
Within the Affective Domain**

Upon completion of this lesson the students will:

Empathizing

(a) *Empathize* with those opposed or favorable (or both) to the Women's Equal Rights Movement.

Social Participation

(b) Be *willing to participate* in group discussions while examining a relevant and historical topic.

Value Clarification

(c) Be *willing to attempt to analyze* objectively their own values and those held by others.

Teaching Suggestions

Lesson Overview

Even before the Seneca Falls Declaration of 1848, many women participated in movements whose primary objectives were attainment of equal economic, social, and political rights with men. At times those movements succeeded in meeting their objectives. This has been apparent with (1) adoption of the Nineteenth Amendment to the Constitution, which granted women the right to vote, and (2) recent Supreme Court decisions, which barred discrimination against women by local, state and national legislators (1971), and which upheld the legality of abortions for women who sought them (1973).

Many people seeking more comprehensive legislation in the area of women's liberation have staunchly supported ratification of the proposed Equal Rights Amendment (see Card 5 in Set I). Critics of that proposed amendment, however, often attach a different connotation to the liberation associated with it. This lesson will focus on representative samples of some views sympathetic to and some views opposed to the Women's Equal Rights Movement of the past decade. This lesson will also emphasize (1) different meanings which can be attached to the concept of liberation, (2) ways in which the term "liberation" can be developed more fully, and (3) examples of other liberating movements in American history.

Student examination of views which support and oppose the Women's Equal Rights Movement of the past decade will involve use of two sets of data cards.

Cards in Set I include background material and views opposed to the Movement: *Data Cards: Set I*

Card 1—Questions which can guide student inquiry through Cards 2–6.

Card 2—An account by J. H. Plumb in which he describes how women by 1971 had managed to liberate themselves socially, economically, and politically.

Card 3—An excerpt from an account by Elsieliese Thrope in which she argues that women are more liberated than men.

Card 4—Part of an account by Jacqueline Himelstein in which she argues that the Women's Lib Movement is having adverse effects on older housewives.

Card 5—A description of the proposed Equal Rights Amendment to the Constitution.

Card 6—An argument by Phyllis Schlafly in which she states her main reasons for opposing adoption of the Equal Rights Amendment.

Cards in Set II include background material and views supportive of the Movement: *Data Cards: Set II*

Card 1—Questions which can guide student inquiry through Cards 2–9.

Card 2—Another account by J. H. Plumb in which he describes what liberation from household duties has done for many middle-class women.

Card 3—Recent data depicting general economic and political statistics on the female population of the United States.

Card 4—Present data depicting specific examples of female employment in the United States.

Card 5—A description by a working Black woman in which she relates some of her problems.

Card 6—An account about problems facing many Mexican-American working women.

Card 7—A brief essay depicting the problems of many Indian-American women.

Card 8—Advice from Shirley Chisholm about what role women should play in politics.

Card 9—An argument by Bella S. Abzug in which she states her main reasons for support of the proposed Equal Rights Amendment.

Introducing the Lesson

Before the students examine information about the current Women's Equal Rights Movement, ask the class for a definition of the concept "liberation." (For example, the process of providing new liberties to someone or freeing something from previous controls.) Then ask if the term has received any widespread or popular usage with any recent or current movements. Here some of your students might mention the Black civil rights movement of the 1960's, student unrest during the past decade, the growth of Chicano groups, the American Indian Movement (AIM), and especially the Women's Equal Rights Movement, sometimes referred to as Women's Lib. Conclude this part of the discussion by asking how people today might define the term "liberation" when associating it with the Women's Equal Rights Movement. Would everyone attach the same meaning to it? In other words, could a person's opinion of the Women's Equal Rights Movement affect how he or she might interpret the term "liberation."

Whatever the students' response, they should have *recognized a problem for inquiry* (Can the concept of "liberation" have more than one meaning or interpretation?) and *offered some hypotheses* or tentative answers (Perhaps meanings associated with that concept depend on a person's view of the issue associated with it.).

Implementing the Lesson

Then tell the students that they will now examine representative samples of how many Americans recently viewed the Women's Equal Rights Movement. They will also read about the proposed Equal Rights Amendment.

As the class examines the cards in each set, you may wish to have your students work in six groups. You may want to duplicate both sets of cards and perhaps dry-mount and laminate them so that each group can have complete copies. Depending upon the make-up of your class, you may want each group to contain representative proportions of what you regard as slow, average, and bright students and allow each group, once formed, to select a leader to report group findings.

Once each group has selected a leader, remind the students that they have already offered some tentative answers about how people might interpret the term "liberation," especially as it applies to the recent (and present) Women's Equal Rights Movement. Now the class will examine examples of how some Americans have interpreted that Movement, beginning with the information on cards in Set I.

Emphasize that while seeking answers to the questions on Card 1, group members should feel free to express different points of view. Once the students have answered those questions, each group leader should be prepared to report group findings to the remainder of the class.

To facilitate student discussion of group findings about information on the cards in Set I, ask what seemed to be the major arguments of those opposed to the Equal Rights Movement. Are there any other arguments the students can list in opposition to the Equal Rights Movement? List all arguments on the board under the category of "Arguments Opposed to Equal Rights."

If some students note that the military draft mentioned on Card 6 is no longer in effect, ask if it is possible we will again have a draft system in the future. If so, how might this affect women with passage of the Equal Rights Amendment? Here too you may also wish to tell the class that today more women are volunteering for military service and many are now becoming policewomen—high risk occupations which in the past were usually reserved for males.

Then ask if any members of the class are opposed to legislation such as the Equal Rights Amendment. Ask if any are opposed to the Equal Rights Movement in general. Ask the students to give reasons for their views. Are there any new meanings or interpretations they can now add to the term "liberation"?

Once your class has completed a discussion of cards in Set I, introduce Set II to the students. Before the groups examine information on those cards, emphasize that this set of cards will contain arguments in support of the Equal Rights Movement. As they consider those arguments, the students are to decide (1) if the views expressed on the cards can add other interpretations to the term "liberation" and (2) how those views differ from opinions expressed on the cards in Set I.

To facilitate student discussion about information on the cards in Set II, ask what seemed to be the major arguments of those favoring the Equal Rights Movement. Are there other arguments you can list in support of the Movement? List all arguments on the board under the category of "Arguments in Favor of Equal Rights."

Concluding the Lesson

Ask if any members of the class would oppose any of those arguments. How many would agree with them? Did any new interpretations of the term "liberation" emerge from the information on these cards—new meanings which you can now add to your original listing? In addition to the information on the cards in both sets, are there any new meanings which the students can now think of to add to that listing? How many meanings do they now think can be applied to the term meaning of "liberation"?

In completing this part of the lesson, the students will have *tested the validity of their earlier hypotheses* (by determining if other interpretations could be added to their original ones for "liberation") and, finally, will have arrived at a *broader generalization* (by forming a more comprehensive definition about what the term means).

If you use a lesson such as this one early in the school year, the students should be prepared to determine how the concept of liberation applies to other areas of American history. For example, how does "liberation" apply to conquest of our first Native Americans, the American Revolution of 1776, the slavery question prior to 1860, the Civil War, or labor union and massive immigration movements of the nineteenth and early twentieth centuries? With each of these areas the students could consider: (1) Would an American Indian have defined "liberation" the same as a European conquistador or later Anglo settlers or missionaries? (2) Would an American rebel of 1776 have interpreted the term "liberation" in the same way as King George III? (3) Would an American Black slave have interpreted "liberation" in the same manner as a slave owner? (4) Would a staunch member of the Confederacy who supported the doctrine of secession have defined "liberation" the same way Abraham Lincoln did? (5) Would organizers of our early labor unions have interpreted "liberation" the same as did our early business tycoons and proponents of Social Darwinism? (6) Would an Asian-American living in California in 1880 have interpreted "liberation" the same as those legislators who drafted laws restricting immigration from the Far East? (7) Would newly arrived Jews, Italians, Irish, Czechs, Poles, and Scandinavians to the United States around 1900 have interpreted "liberation" the same as the city ward bosses who soon controlled many of their lives? (8) Would non-English-speaking Cubans who immigrated here during the late 1950's have defined "liberation" the same as "established" residents then living in Florida? (9) Could the same be true of Puerto Ricans who have moved to New York City during the past twenty years? (10) Would an integrationist of the 1960's have defined "liberation" the same way a segregationist would have defined it? (11) Would a Chicano living in the Southwest interpret the concept in the same manner as members of the ruling landed aristocracy? (12) Would many students now define "liberation" in the same way as their parents? Is it possible that all these kinds of people may have had different interpretations of the same term? What, then, can this signify about the interpretation of *any* concept or "big idea"?

Additional References

For additional information concerning the *frontier woman*, see William W. Fowler, *Woman on the American Frontier* (biographical accounts of frontier life). Bancroft, 1884; Nancy Wilson Ross, *Westward the Women*, Knopf, 1945; Shirley Sargent, *Pioneers in Petticoats* (a survey of Yosemite's Early Women from 1856–1900), Trans-Anglo, 1966; Helena Huntington Smith, "Pioneers in Petticoats," *American Heritage Magazine*, February, 1959; and Edwin Tunis, *Frontier Living*, World, 1961.

For sources containing information on the *women of the Roaring '20's and the Great Depression*, see Bruce Crawford, "Whose Prosperity?", *The Reader's Digest* (an article describing the inequality of wealth found in the American society of the 1920's), August, 1929; Doris Faber, *Petticoat Politics* (survey of women fighting for the right to vote from the 1840's until 1920), Lothrop, Lee, and Shepard, 1960; John Anthony Scott (ed.), *Brother, Can You Spare a Dime? The Great Depression 1929–1933*, Knopf, 1969; and Dorothy Thompson (Mrs. Sinclair Lewis), "Is America a Paradise for Women?—No," *The Reader's Digest*, August, 1929.

If you are interested in additional information concerning *women during World War II*, see LaVerne Bradley, "Women at Work," *The National Geographic Magazine* (excellent portfolio of women in occupations created by the war), August, 1944; LaVerne Bradley, "Women in Uniform," *The National Geographic Magazine* (another excellent portfolio of women working in occupations demanded by wartime), October, 1943; and Mattie E. Treadwell, *The Women's Army Corps*, U. S. Government Printing Office, 1954.

For additional information concerning roles of *women today*, see Caroline Bird, *Born Female*, McKay Company, 1968; Sara Davidson, "An 'Oppressed' Majority Demands Its Rights," *Life*, December 12, 1969; Elisieliese Thrope, "But Women *Are* the Favored Sex," *The Reader's Digest*, May, 1972; Anne Grant West, "Women's Liberation, or Exploding the Fairy Princess Myth," *Senior Scholastic*, November 1, 1971; "Who's Come a Long Way Baby?", *Time*, August 31, 1970, and "Galluping Attitudes," *Saturday Review*, February 17, 1973, pp. 41–42.

For sources containing *illustrative materials* on the role of *women since the frontier days*, see William Cole and Florett Robinson, *Women Are Wonderful!* (a history of women in cartoons since the mid-1800's), Houghton, Mifflin, 1956; Agnes Rogers, *Women Are Here to Stay* (historical portfolio of women since the turn of the century), Harper, 1949; Cynthia Frichs Epstein, *Woman's Place* (numerous graphs illustrating the role of women within society), University of California, 1971; and George P. Shultz (ed.), *1969 Handbook on Women Workers* (statistical guide on women workers), U. S. Government Printing Office, 1969.

If you are interested in additional *songs about women's liberation*, see John Greenway, *American Folksongs of Protest*, University of Pennsylvania, 1953.

For more information about how women have been presented in *social studies programs*, see Janice Law Trecker, "Women in U. S. History High School Textbooks," *Social Education*, March, 1971; Janice Law Trecker, "Teaching the Role of Women in American History," in *Teaching Ethnic Studies: Concepts and Strategies*, 43rd Yearbook, National Council for the Social Studies, 1973; and Elizabeth Burr, Susan Dunn, and Norma Farquhar, "Women and the Language of Inequality," *Social Education*, December, 1972, pp. 841–845.

For more information about selected ethnic minority cultures, see Lowell K. Y. Chun-Hoon, "Teaching the Asian-American Experience," James A. Banks, "Teaching Black Studies for Social Change," Carlos E. Cortes, "Teaching the Chicano Experience," Jack D. Forbes, "Teaching Native American Values and Cultures," and Francesco Cordasco and Diego Castellanos, "Teaching the Puerto Rican Experience," all in *Teaching Ethnic Studies: Concepts and Strategies*, 43rd Yearbook, National Council for the Social Studies, 1973. For additional information on American Jews, see Anita Libman Lebeson, "The American Jewish Chronicle," and Moshe Davis, "Jewish Religious Life and Institutions in America," in Louis Finkelstein (ed.), *The Jews: Their History, Culture, and Religion*, Third Edition, Vol. I, Harper and Row, 1960. A highly readable volume for secondary-level students is Ruth Gay, *Jews in America*, Basic Books, 1965.

Student Materials for
"What Is Liberation?
A Closer Look at the Women's Equal Rights Movement"
follow on pages 65–79

SET I—CARD 1
Questions to Consider for Cards 2-6

For Card 2
1. According to this account, what was life like for many women in 1733?
2. According to the author of this account, what two factors have brought about the liberation of women?
3. How does the author of this account seem to define the term "liberation"?

For Card 3
1. What were some reasons the author of this account gave for believing women are the favored sex?
2. How does the author of this account seem to define the term "liberation"?

For Card 4
1. According to this account, what has the Women's Liberation Movement done to many older housewives?
2. Does the author of this account seem to feel this is a form of liberation?

For Card 5
1. What is the proposed Equal Rights Amendment to the Constitution?
2. What are some things this proposed amendment would eliminate?
3. Can the term "liberation" be applied to this amendment? Explain the reasons for your answer.

For Card 6
1. According to this account, what would the proposed Equal Rights Amendment do to women?
2. Do you think all this is a form of liberation? Explain the reasons for your answer.

For Cards 2-6
1. According to the information on all these cards, how is the term "liberation" used?
2. Is this the same as your use of the term? Tell why or why not.

SET I—CARD 2

In 1733 everything preservable, from pigs to mushrooms, had to be preserved. Fruits were jammed and crystalized. There were no mixers, no shredders, no liquidizers. Nor was it only food that the women prepared. Even a young boy's shirts and nightgowns were made at home or by a gentlewoman who lived ten miles away and was noted for her splendid needlework. And, of course, his sisters' petticoats and dresses were made by themselves or by their mother.

There were worse chores. The streets and the roads of the countryside were in bad weather a mess of mud and water, women could only keep their houses clean by getting down on their knees and scrubbing. They finished late in the day. We can scarcely imagine the hard work that went into maintaining even a small household: water had to be fetched from wells, candles made, lamps filled, and firewood carried. Except in the highest classes, women worked, perhaps slaved would be a better word, in their houses.

The terrible fate of many women was still more terrible by the fact that marriage was so closely bound up with the giving over of their property to their husbands. Naturally, some women sought escape. A few succeeded in trade, either by sheer business ability or by obtaining their release from drudgery through the death of a husband or father.

This was but a hundred years ago. Although women still cry for liberation, and links of their old shackles still chain their lives, the freedom, the opportunities, and the range of experience now open to women border on the incredible. This change is one of the most outstanding and the most remarkable of modern times.

Such liberation as women have enjoyed up to this time is usually explained by two factors: the spread of education, and the dedicated fighting spirit of women themselves, especially those significant suffragettes who, in order to achieve passage of the Nineteenth Amendment in 1920, chained themselves to railings, threw themselves under the hooves of race horses, or starved themselves in prison to the point of death. These heroic women certainly helped their cause, but only because the tide had already turned toward the gaining of their feminist goals.

What is still hard for people to see is that the technological and scientific revolution in which mankind has been involved with ever-increasing speed during this past century has greatly affected every social and personal relationship, no matter how seemingly private. It is a process whose end is nowhere in sight. Scientifically-based industry had brought wealth and freedom—even to the poor and the disadvantaged.

This wealth, and the personal freedom it creates, springs from two sources: the rise in the value of labor and the growth of the consumer society. Go to the most wretched slum in urban America or to a desolate village in Appalachia and there you will find canned goods of every description, wrapped and sliced bread, packaged meats, and vegetables, not to mention refrigerators, vacuum cleaners, running water, and heat. Move from the ghettos to middle-class suburbs and the ease of household management becomes even more marked—with washing machines, dishwashers, and electrical gadgets for quick preparation of food.

Adapted from J.H. Plumb, "Up From Slavery," *Horizon*, Summer, 1971, pp. 80–81. Used by permission of J.H. Plumb.

SET I—CARD 3

If Women's Libbers don't stop their commotion, their rumblings of discontent and pleas for equality, we might end up getting what they are asking for. And who wants equality when we women are doing so much better now?

Biologically, legally, temperamentally and just about every other way that matters, we women are the favored sex. Physically, males have several strikes against them. . . Men suffer from more ulcers, more heart trouble, and die younger.

We women have things going for us in other areas, too. From the moment Baby Girl appears on the scene, she will have it soft. Someday, if she chooses, she can find herself a man to look after her. She may or may not choose to have children. Or she may want to go to work and support herself. Whatever, she has a choice. . .

Legally, I think we women have things going for us in a big way, too. When we get married we are saying to this man that he will have to look after us, support us, pay life and hospital insurance for us and take care of whatever children we may produce together. What's more, if the marriage does not work out, he will be required, in most cases, to continue to support us and the children—and if he doesn't, he will go to jail.

Today, I can work full-time, part-time, or not at all. I can get civic-minded, work on the problems of air pollution, help the Red Cross, or just play bridge if I am so inclined. I can go into politics or write magazine articles. Men don't have all lovely options. And you know what worries me? Unless we stop making equality noises, men might wake up and realize what they have been missing.

Adapted from "But Women *Are* the Favored Sex," by Elsieliese Thrope. *The Reader's Digest*, May 1972. Copyright 1972 by The Reader's Digest Assn., Inc. Used by permission.

SET I—CARD 4

The privilege of remaining a nonworking wife in the years past middle age is fast disappearing, and thus the choice that women have traditionally enjoyed of staying home or working will soon almost vanish.

The main push of Women's Liberation has been toward increasing women's choices—particularly in the job market. They've pushed for equal status and equal pay for women.

The sad thing is that a lot of women in these older age groups might really prefer to remain at home because the kinds of jobs available to them are not very exciting.

And it's very likely that we're going to find a lot of pretty unhappy older women around.

Jacqueline Himelstein, "Women's Lib Pushing Many Older Housewives Out of Home," *National Enquirer*, April 29, 1973, p. 3. Copyright: *National Enquirer*, Lantana, Florida. Used by permission.

SET I—CARD 5

Progress toward passage of a constitutional amendment to eliminate all forms of discrimination against women was a major goal of many Americans in 1973. The proposed amendment, which has been considered by Congress since 1970, was finally passed by both the House of Representatives and the Senate in 1972. However, the proposed amendment will become the law of the land only if three-fourths (38) of the state legislatures ratify it within seven years. In its final form, the amendment, if accepted by the required number of state legislatures, will:

(1) Wipe out state laws that impose special limits on the types of jobs women may take and the number of hours they may work.
(2) Eliminate laws limiting women's rights in some states to handle property and start businesses on an equal basis with men.
(3) End discriminatory admissions practices by state colleges and graduate schools, and bar discrimination against women in hiring and promotions in public schools and colleges.
(4) Forbid discrimination against women in state and local government jobs.
(5) End laws treating women more harshly in a number of criminal situations—for example, one state statute which permits women to be jailed for three years for continual drunkenness but men for only 30 days.
(6) Abolish state laws that give women less favorable treatment than men in the handling of their children's property, and more favorable treatment in cases of child-support and child-custody.

In its proposed form, the Equal Rights Amendment reads as follows:

Section 1. Equality of rights under the law shall not be denied or abridged by the United States or by any State on account of sex.
Section 2. The Congress shall have the power to enforce, by appropriate legislation, the provisions of this article.
Section 3. This amendment shall take effect two years after the date of ratification. . . . .

SET I—CARD 6

The ERA (Equal Rights Amendment) will take away from women their most important rights—the right NOT to take a job, the right to care for their own babies in their own homes, and the right to be financially supported by their husbands.

The laws of every state now require a husband to support his wife and children and to provide a home for them to live in.

The ERA will remove this obligation and make his wife equally responsible to provide a home for the family and half their financial support.

If the ERA is ratified, a non-working married woman will no longer be able to get credit because stores and banks would have no assurance of being repaid.

The ERA will make women subject to the draft and for combat duty on an equal basis with men.

The ERA will wipe out all the protective labor legislation designed to safeguard and benefit women who do manual labor and industrial work.

Most women want to preserve our "right to be a woman." The ERA would be a step down for American women.

Phyllis Schlafly, "The ERA Will Take Away from Women Their Most Important Rights," *National Enquirer* (June 3, 1973), p. 10. Copyright: *National Enquirer*, Lantana, Florida. Used by permission.

SET II—CARD 1
Questions to Consider for Cards 2-9

For Card 2

1. According to the author of this account, what problems has the Industrial Revolution created for many middle-class married women?
2. Could these problems be a form of "liberation"? Explain the reasons for your answer.

For Card 3

1. According to these data, how has the status of women compared to that of men since 1970?
2. What did the President's Commission on Population Control conclude about the status of women?

For Card 4

1. According to these data, how has the status of women recently compared to the status of men in the area of jobs?
2. How do you suppose the author of this account would define the term "liberation"?

For Cards 5, 6, and 7

1. According to these sources, what are some problems many Black, Mexican-American, and American-Indian women face? Do the problems differ?
2. Do these problems seem to contradict any arguments presented on cards in Set I?

For Card 8

1. What problems had Shirley Chisholm encountered as a woman-politician?
2. What did she recommend women do to improve their status in life?

For Card 9

1. According to the author of this source, why should women support adoption of the proposed Equal Rights Amendment?
2. Does this author seem to contradict any arguments presented in the cards in Set I?

For Cards 2–9

1. According to information on all these cards, how is the term "liberation" used?
2. Is this the same as your use of the term? Tell why or why not.

SET II—CARD 2

The Industrial Revolution has steadily provided women of all classes with more leisure. For the middle-class married woman, however, this new freedom has created almost as many problems as it has solved. With commercial, technical, and professional activities still male-dominated, with their lives still cluttered with the vestiges of household duties and motherly cares, and still, alas, the victims of social beliefs that regard women as essentially decorative or domestic, many of them are faced with the boredom of ever-increasing leisure. Indeed, one might argue that middle-class women are now the victims of liberation. They have been freed from their age-old tasks, from their constant toil within the basic social unit, the family, yet have been given little in exchange.

The freedom of women from their burdens owes more to cheap electricity and the supermarket than it does to those women seeking the right to vote before 1920.

Adapted from J.H. Plumb, "Up From Slavery," *Horizon*, (Summer, 1971), p. 81. Used by permission of J.H. Plumb.

SET II—CARD 3

On April 1, 1970, the total population of the United States was 203,211,926. There were 98,912,192 males and 104,299,734 females. Female children born in 1971 were expected to live more than seven years longer than male children born in the same year. And, according to doctors and scientists, women were not only expected to live longer than men, they were also found to be healthier during their lifetimes.

Yet, despite the fact that they are a majority in this country, in 1973 there were no women senators, and only 14 women representatives out of a total of 435.

Nearly half of all American women work at jobs outside the home. And more than half of all working women are the sole support of a family. They are usually paid less than men for the same work, and they are barred from certain jobs by old-fashioned state and local laws. Generally, they have less chance for advancement in their jobs even when they have worked for long periods of time. Minority women have suffered the greatest discrimination in jobs.

Additional information about the status of women in the United States resulted from a study several years ago, when the President and Congress established a Commission to study the growth of our population and the impact such growth will have on the American future. The Commission examined nearly every aspect of life in the United States. In its final report it made the following comments on women in the United States.

. . . Women in the United States occupy a separate and unequal status under the law. Under most laws women were allowed few rights, and our *Constitution was drafted on the assumption that women did not exist as legal persons.* The legal status of women has improved in the past century with the adoption of the Nineteenth Amendment, which gave women the right to vote, alteration of some laws, and passage of some positive legislation. *But equal rights and responsibilities are still denied women in our legal system.* We believe this should be remedied. The right to be free from discrimination based on race, color, or creed is written into our fundamental document of government. We believe the right to be free from discrimination based on sex should also be written into that document.

Population and the American Future: The Report of the Commission on Population Growth and the American Future, The New American Library, Inc., 1972, p. 156.

SET II—CARD 4
Working Women: Problems They Face

Recently, three social scientists at the University of Michigan surveyed American workers on many of the problems they faced, their job satisfaction, and their working conditions. Much of their study focused on women workers. The following selection shows what they discovered about the problems faced by working women.

Many of us are now aware that the average American working woman earns less than the average working man. To be exact, she earns only 58 percent of what an equally qualified man would make. . . . women do *not* receive pay and benefits commensurate with their achievement. They are far worse off than equally qualified men. . . .

We found, overall, that the average woman earned $4,372 less than the average man. . . . We further found that the median woman would have to earn 71 percent more than her current salary to equal the income of a man with her achievement scores.

The discrepancies between a woman's expected income and her actual salary were often extraordinary. . . .

For example . . ., for the past two years (Miss W, 29) worked as one of two heads of a major department in a large discount store. She gets very good fringe benefits, but a salary of $3,120—$6,477 less than a man with her supervisory responsibilities. . . .

Mrs. G., age 26, is employed as a house director at a college dormitory: she works 45 to 50 hours a week ("night and day," in her words) with no scheduled days off. . . . She has completed college and some graduate training, but thinks that her job demands only a high-school education. Because her income is inadequate to meet monthly expenses, she will probably try to find another job soon. . . . Mrs. G. earns $3,000 a year. . . . Her salary is $11,832 less than that of a man of comparable experience and skills.

Miss B has been a secretary for some 30 years, working 40 hours a week in a brickyard. She has a college degree, for which she makes $3,600 a year—or $7,613 less than a man with her skills and experience. . . .

It turned out that fully 95 percent of the women were earning less than they deserved. . . .

Teresa E. Levitin, Robert P. Quinn, and Graham L. Staines, "A Woman Is 58% of a Man," *Psychology Today* (March, 1973), pp. 89–90. Quoted from *Psychology Today* Magazine, March, 1973. Copyright   Communications/Research/Machines, Inc.

SET II—CARD 5
A Black Woman Speaks Out

In the following selection Margaret Wright, a Los Angeles community leader, speaks out on some of the problems facing some black women in the United States.

Black women have been doubly oppressed. On the job, we're low women on the totem pole. White women have their problems. They're interviewed for secretarial instead of the executive thing. But we're interviewed for mopping floors and stuff like that. Sometimes we have to take what's left over in Miss Ann's refrigerator. This is all exploitation. And when we get home from work, the old man is wondering why his dinner isn't cooked on time.

Margaret Wright, "I Want the Right To Be Black and Me." from *Black Women in White America: A Documentary History*, Random House, 1973, p. 607, cited in "Storming the All Electric Dollhouse" by Mary Reinholz, in the West Magazine, *Los Angeles Times*, June 7, 1970.

SET II—CARD 6
The Chicanas

The following account reflects some of the problems that Mexican-American women face today.

Many Mexican-American women or *Chicanas* must deal with even more problems than do the men of their race. These women have been forced to serve in capacities which require them to be wives, mothers, and, along with their husbands, breadwinners as both cope with the problems of providing a family with enough clothing, minimum medical care, a more balanced diet, and decent housing.

Consider, for example, a typical weekday in the life of a *Chicana*. It begins before sunrise when she must prepare breakfast and get the older children ready for school. After breakfast, she must leave her preschool-age children in the care of a nearby neighbor or relative. More often than not, she must then travel a lengthy distance across town by bus to perform housework for very low wages at the home of an affluent family. This is because she probably had to drop out of school after the eighth or ninth grade in order to help support her own younger brothers and sisters. While at work, she continues to worry about her own children —especially those who will arrive home from school and be unsupervised for at least two hours prior to her arrival. Once home again that evening, she must also contend with the problems of a husband frustrated because he too was a school dropout and had failed to acquire skills which would have prepared him for a better paying job. Such a life allows the *Chicana* little time or money for her own entertainment.

Based on interviews conducted by Allan O. Kownslar, April, 1974.

SET II—CARD 7
American Indian Women Today

American Indian women have also taken steps to gain equal rights and improve their condition. The following selection, from *The New Indians*, by Stan Steiner, describes some of the efforts they have made to assert themselves as women and as Indians.

Tens of thousands of Indian women have come into the cities. For the last decade they have been leaving the reservations in growing numbers, not to seek their fortunes . . . but to find a fuller, freer life for themselves. Many have made the trek to the cities simply to find the poorest of jobs.

More often than the tribal men, these tribal women have been able to cross the cultural divide from rural to city life without losing their way. The men often leave, unnerved by the hectic pace of urban life, the ghettoes of crowded rooms, the smoggy sky, and the humiliation of unemployment lines.

In the cities, the power of the women has been recognized by the various Indian committees. Election of tribal women to the leadership of these urban Indian centers has been a wonder in modern Indian life. The San Francisco Indian Center, for instance, had four women on its board of directors and one man. Of the seven officers of the California group, three were women. The Indian Center of Chicago had three women on its board of directors and one man.

Los Angeles, Minneapolis, and New York City clubs of urban Indians all have women among their leaders. So do the Indian centers in other cities, almost without exception.

"We adapt like crazy," said Mary Lou Payne of the young Indian women. The women, especially the younger women, are more resilient and flexible, more accepted and accepting, more capable of outward change and inner stability than their husbands are at times. "No one adapts like an Indian, if given half a chance," the Cherokee girl said.

Stan Steiner, *The New Indians*, Harper & Row, 1968, p. 224. Used by permission.

SET II—CARD 8
Women and Politics: Representative Shirley Chisholm

Shirley Chisholm represents a Brooklyn, New York, district in the Congress of the United States. She is the first black woman ever elected to the House of Representatives. In 1972, she ran for the Democratic nomination for the position of President. In addition to her duties as a congresswoman, she is also active in the movement to change and improve the status of women in the United States. The following selection is taken from a speech made by Representative Chisholm at a conference on women's employment held in Washington, D.C., in 1970.

I'm a politician. I have been in politics for 20 years, and in that time I have learned a few things about the role of women in power. And the major thing that I have learned is that women are the backbone of America's political organizations. They are the letter writers, the envelope stuffers, the telephone answerers; they're the campaign workers and the organizers. Perhaps it is in America, more than any other country, that the . . . proof of the old saying, "The power behind the throne is a woman" is most readily apparent.

The harshest discrimination that I have encountered in politics is anti-feminism, both from males and brainwashed females. When I first announced that I was running for the United States Congress, both males and females advised me, as they had when I ran for the New York State Legislature, to go back to teaching—a woman's vocation—and leave the politics to the men.

I believe that women have a special contribution to make to help bring order out of chaos in our nation today because they have special qualities of leadership which are greatly needed today. And these qualities are the patience, tolerance, and perseverance which have developed in many women because of suppression. And if we can add to these qualities a fund of information about the techniques of community action, we can indeed become effective bringers of change . . .

In a speech made a few weeks ago to an audience that was mostly white and all female, I suggested the following, if they wanted to create a change. You must start in your own homes, your own schools, and your own churches. I don't want you to go home and talk about integrated schools, churches, or marriages if the kind of integration you're talking about is black and white. I want you to go home and work for, fight for, the integration of women into American society.

Hearings Before the Special Subcommittee on Education and Labor, House of Representatives, 91st Congress, 2nd Session, United States Government Printing Office, 1970, pp. 909–915 *passim.*

SET II—CARD 9

The common myth is that women belong at home taking care of the kids. Let's get one thing straight: For every woman at home, there are dozens working in kitchens, in laundry rooms, in dirty back-breaking jobs, in work beneath their abilities. They are exploited and underpaid.

For years we women have been told that we can't balance our checkbooks, even though we do most of the consumer buying. We're told women are fragile, though it's perfectly all right for us to lift children, lug home groceries and move furniture.

We hear opponents of women's rights ask: "What more do women want?"

What we want is what we still haven't got—full equality with men in our social, legal, economic and political institutions.

If the women who oppose the ERA (Equal Rights Amendment) understood what it really meant in terms of their own lives and dignity, they would be out demanding its passage.

Bella S. Abzug, "We Want Full Equality with Men . . . We Still Have a Long Way to Go," *National Enquirer* (June 3, 1973) p. 10. Copyright: *National Enquirer*, Lantana, Florida. Used by permission.

"If teachers are to have students pretend, let them role play in a situation which reveals that questions in the game have something to do with them."

Virginia M. Rogers and Ronald K. Atwood

5
Can We Put Ourselves in Their Place?

In this age of rapid transportation and instant mass communication, isolation of a culture is a rare phenomenon. Successful interaction among persons in contact on a day-to-day basis—perhaps even the survival of the United States as a free nation—depends on the ability of each American to understand other Americans with cultural differences. A study of history can provide data and facilitate experiences to help develop the needed understanding, or empathy.

As we come to understand people who live by different values or under pressures we have not experienced, possibly separated by time and/or distance, it is likely that we begin to view and respect them as individuals, rather than members of groups. In the process we develop a better understanding of ourselves and our peers, and we become more humane. Also, developing empathy, "the capacity for participating in another's feelings or ideas,"[1] should help us cope with our future cultural change. A more traditional but important outcome is the development of a better understanding of historical times and characters.

The development of the ability to empathize should not be entrusted to chance. Rather, systematic instructional efforts utilizing a variety of data sources and instructional techniques should be employed. Within the discipline of history there are many cultures, individuals, and periods of time which qualify for study. The focus of this chapter is contemporary United States history. The choice is based on the authors' assumption that contemporary United States history represents the most easily understood and the most functional phase on the basis of both location and chronology. It also represents a phase of American history most likely to be neglected because of the usual emphasis on a chronological approach that seldom seems to reach the contemporary period. Before considering more specific content and instructional strategies, it seems appropriate to state additional assumptions.

The developmental psychology of Jean Piaget is highly relevant in considering the prospective learner. It is assumed that most elementary school children are concrete operators and must be provided concrete activities for meaningful learning beyond the level of memorization to occur. Many middle school or junior high students are also concrete operators and need the same kind of experiences. Many senior high students prefer instructional opportunities that include concrete components. Thus, the activities suggested in this chapter are largely concrete in nature.

There are some promising instructional strategies consistent with the previously stated assumptions. Role-playing is a technique long used to make historical events more meaningful and historical characters more real.[2] Recently, simulation games, which go beyond typical role-playing activities in imposing a reality structure, are being utilized in an increasing number of instructional situations.[3] Teachers should be aware of the advantages and disadvantages of each of these instructional tools, especially their potential for developing empathy.

As educators we have too frequently lacked creativity and imagination in utilizing data sources other than textbooks and encyclopedias. For contemporary United States history, teachers need access to copies of documents, letters, diaries, tapes or recordings of speeches and news telecasts and broadcasts.[4] Family photo albums also have potential as a source for learning about people and developing empathy for them. While primary data sources are often difficult to obtain, there are some good commercial suppliers.[5] Still, greater efforts are needed to increase the pool of primary data sources and to develop some kind of mechanism for sharing successful attempts with the teaching profession at large.

It would likely be fruitful for students to examine and perhaps use artifacts from a particular culture while studying that culture. For example, one could better participate in the feelings of a pioneer woman if one churned but-ter, ironed a nonpermanent press garment with a flat iron, spun yarn, and/or made lye-soap.

Since the vast majority of young people are interested in contemporary music, it is really astounding that we have not utilized this data source to a greater extent. Students can gather data, useful for empathizing with members of a culture, from the popular music of the culture. Folk music, whether modern or traditional, is an especially fruitful source.

The interview is an interesting technique, the success of which is illustrated by the publication of *The Stoop*[6] and *Foxfire*.[7] One can think of administrative difficulties in student-conducted interviews as a school experience. However, many interviews can be conducted after school hours and preserved by inexpensive cassette recorders. In general, more use could and should be made of technology. An entire class could interview an individual by phone, communication satellite or similar medium.

Comparisons of accounts from old textbooks with more recent ones provide insight into how the times influence interpretations of the past. The examination of old textbooks, magazines and catalogs also provides information about beliefs, technology, economics, customs, and events of a particular period in history, which can be used for developing empathy.

Considering the assumptions previously stated and some promising instructional schemes identified herein, specific examples of instructional activities for "putting ourselves in their place" have been organized around the following two suggested lessons for classroom use:

(1) Initial activities for developing empathizing skills.

(2) A simulation game, Appalachian Coal Miners, as a strategy for developing empathizing skills.

These sets of activities, or lessons, are largely non-graded. However, the first set does require less experience and maturity than the second. Instructions for utilizing the first set have been aimed at the primary level of an elementary school program; minor modifications in the instructions can be easily made and the same activities used in working with older, more mature students. Appalachian Coal Miners is a simulation game which would likely be most beneficial to the more mature middle school, junior and senior high students. It is suggested that a teacher review the objectives and suggested activities for each of the lessons and use his professional judgment to determine the appropriateness of one or more of these activities, making whatever modifications that seem appropriate.

FOOTNOTES

[1]*Webster's Seventh New Collegiate Dictionary*, G. and C. Merriam Co., 1969.

[2]Fannie R. Shaftel, and George Shaftel, *Role-Playing for Social Values*, Prentice-Hall, Inc., 1967.

[3]Virginia M. Rogers and Marcella I. Kysilka, "Simulation Games—What and Why," *The Instructor*, LXXIX, No. 7, 94–95 (March 1970).

[4]See for example "The Sound of 50 Years." Coordinator: Tony Simon. Source: *Scholastic Magazine*, Copyright 1970, Columbia Broadcasting System.

[5]Richard C. Brown (ed.), *The Human Side of American History*, Ginn and Company, 1970.

[6]*The Stoop*, The Fourth Street Brigade in Action, 136 Avenue C, New York, New York 10009.

[7]*Foxfire*, Rabun Gap, Georgia, 30568.

Sample Lesson for:
Developing Empathizing Skills

LESSON PLAN

Primary level and above.

Intended Student Audience

10 to 30 minutes for each activity.

Suggested Time for Classroom Use of Materials

Selected pictures and tapes.

Materials for Classroom Use

Major Objectives for the Lesson

Upon completion of this lesson the students will:

Objectives Within the Cognitive Domain

Skill Development

(a) *State* two to five observations based on a picture, a series of pictures, or a tape.
(b) *Describe* two to five differences in individuals shown in two different pictures or heard on two different tapes.
(c) *Orally predict* an action which might follow a situation represented by a picture or tape.

Objectives Within the Affective Domain

Upon completion of the lesson the students will:

Empathizing

(a) *Orally infer* specific feelings or emotions of people shown in the pictures or heard on the tapes.
(b) *Verbally infer* the cause(s) of an emotion or action.

83　　*Can We Put Ourselves in Their Place?*

In addition to these behavioral outcomes, another purpose of the activities is to develop a caring attitude.

As used in this chapter, the term "observation" refers to a perception using any of the senses (not just sight). An "inference" is a tentative conclusion based on limited observations.

Teaching Suggestions

Lesson Overview

In order for individuals to be able to empathize with one another, they must be good observers; they must be able to infer feelings or emotions based on their observations; they must be able to infer differences in values; they must understand that individual actions are influenced by their values; and, they must be able to infer cause and effect relationships relative to emotions. The activities in this lesson focus on these fundamental process skills and ideas.

Four short activities are suggested rather than one large block or unit of instruction. The activities will require (a) the analysis of pictures and/or tapes, and (b) the ordering, or sequencing, of events.

Introducing, Implementing, and Concluding the Activities

ACTIVITY 1: The first set of activities can be led by the teacher, or directions may be written out so that individual students or small groups of students may participate independent of the teacher. If the teacher is working with the students, the students should respond orally rather than in writing.

Select a number of magazine pictures which focus on individuals or small groups of individuals. The pictures should include easily observed clues that can serve as a basis for inferring an emotion or situation. Some pictures may show only the face of an individual; others may show one or more persons in a setting. Select pictures exhibiting a variety of emotions, such as anger, fear, compassion, anxiety, joy, surprise, thoughtfulness, and depression. For ease of handling and care, the pictures might be dry-mounted and/or laminated. If students are to respond to the questions in writing, put an identifying numeral or letter on the back of each picture.

Ask the students to carefully look at a particular picture and then respond to questions that include or are similar to the following:

1. How do you think the individual(s) is (are) feeling?
2. Why do you think this? (Encourage students to be specific about observations from which they infer emotions. Distinguish between observations and inferences.)
3. Might the person(s) be feeling a different emotion than the one you inferred? Give an example.
4. Have you ever felt this way? Why?

5. What do you think might happen next to this person?
6. If you inferred an unpleasant emotion, what possible action might the person(s) take in order to feel better?

Repeat the procedure for other pictures.

ACTIVITY 2: Ask the students to select pictures from magazines or to draw pictures that show an individual expressing an emotion specified by the teacher. Students should be asked to defend their choices. Can a particular facial expression reflect more than one emotion? Consideration might also be given to the practice of exhibiting one emotion while hiding the way we really feel.

ACTIVITY 3: The teacher tapes several short segments for students to hear. These segments might include two people arguing, a person crying, a person laughing, or a person expressing self-doubt, insecurity or fear. After listening to each segment, questions like those in Activity 1 could be considered.

ACTIVITY 4: Facility with the basic process of ordering, or sequencing, events can serve as an intellectual tool to aid students in inferring cause and effect relationships, which can be useful in developing empathy. To help develop this process at the elementary level a teacher can select groups of pictures, for example, from magazines, comic strips, or old student workbooks that have sequencing possibilities. Three to five pictures per group are usually adequate; it is helpful to place an identifying numeral or letter on each picture in a group and clip them together or place them in an envelope to keep the groups separate. Ask the students to examine the pictures in a group and order the pictures; that is, line them into a row so that the order (sequence) tells a story or shows how something happened. For some groups of pictures more than one sequence may seem logical to the students. Encourage the student to explain what is happening in his sequence. Any seriously given explanation that is reasonable to the student can surely be accepted by the teacher. Students might compare their sequence with a different one and discuss the possible consequences of things happening in the different orders. This activity might also be discussed relative to understanding school-day events such as a dispute or accident on the playground. In these and similar cases the order of events would likely be important, but would unlikely be agreed upon by all principals and witnesses.

For this activity a comic strip divided into separate pictures might be a good place to start. Variety and complexity can be introduced as desired from this point of almost certain success. Some students, for example, may wish to make their own comic-type frames to be sequenced and interpreted by a peer.

Lesson Plan for:
Appalachian Coal Miners: A Simulation

LESSON PLAN

Intended Student Audience

Middle school, junior and senior high and college.

**Suggested Time for
Classroom Use of Materials**

3 to 6 hours.

Materials for Classroom Use

Role Cards, Ledger Sheets, Fixed Costs Sheets, Expenditure Rules, Chance Cards, Bank Loan Transaction Poster, Product Poster, Spinner, and a mail order catalogue (Student Materials pp. 93–111).

Major Objectives for the Lesson

**Objectives
Within the Cognitive Domain**

Upon completion of this lesson the students will:

Skill Development

(a) *Describe* four to eight economic conditions of mining families in Appalachia.
(b) *Describe* four to eight social conditions of mining families in Appalachia.
(c) *Compare* these conditions to their own.
(d) *Infer* cause and effect relationships regarding social, emotional and economic problems common to Appalachian mining families.

**Objectives
Within the Affective Domain**

Upon completion of this lesson the students will:

Empathizing

(a) Describe how one might *feel* if placed in circumstances common to an Appalachian mining family.

Teaching Suggestions

Lesson Overview

Coal mining camps have largely disappeared from the Southern Appalachians, and the lives of contemporary miners have become more diverse and difficult to characterize and understand. However, the importance of better understanding an important element of an often studied but poorly understood region prompts us to proceed, utilizing a simulation game as a mechanism.

Introducing the Lesson

Prior to playing the game, the teacher should duplicate the following materials in the indicated amounts for a single class. Teachers with multiple sections should multiply the number of ledger sheets by the number of sections.

```
Role Cards (one copy of each)
Ledger Sheets (15)
Fixed Costs Sheet (15)
Expenditure Rules (15)
Chance Cards (number indicated on master list)
Bank Loan Transaction Poster (1)
Product Poster (1)
Spinner (1)
```

Pair the students. One student can work alone if the class is smaller than 30 students, or three can work together, if the class is larger than 30.

Verbally present some information included in the following *Introduction* but do not read the Introduction to your class or attempt to tell them everything in it.

Many factors have operated to prevent Appalachia from sharing fully in the economic growth of the world's wealthiest nation. One of the most obvious factors is the geography of the region. The rugged terrain for many years formed an isolating barrier which only recently has been pierced by good highways.

The earliest settlers of the Southern Appalachians were freedom-loving, highly independent individuals. Feeling no great need to associate closely with other persons, they rejected the frontier settlements where people clustered in greater numbers. They were fair hunters and farmers.

As generations passed, the progress in agriculture and education made in many other parts of the country was not generally shared by Appalachia. Children in mountain families tended to marry and locate in the immediate vicinity of their parents, often in another part of the same hollow. This practice reduced the already small acreage of tillable land.

For generations many outsiders who came into the mountains did so to exploit the mountaineer. This practice made him wary of interaction with the outside world. It also tended to confirm his belief that the outside world was basically corrupt, and he saw no value in joining it.

Mountain families most often live in small frame houses which are built near or into the side of a steep hill. Typically, the house has four rooms, one of which is a kitchen. It is sometimes difficult to differentiate among the other three, since each may contain a bed, if that much space is needed.

A mountaineer tends to be fatalistic in his outlook. A common attitude is: Things are not too good now, but they very well may get worse. There is an attitude that whatever happens was meant to be, and is likely the will of God. Although statements such as the latter are common in Appalachia, relatively few mountaineers have a religious conviction to the point of being active in a church.

As a matter of fact, mountaineers are generally not joiners. They typically do not plan very far ahead and do not want to commit themselves for future endeavors. It has been suggested that a mountaineer does not work as much to "get ahead" as he does "to live." Of course there are many exceptions to this generalization as well as others made in this Introduction.

Possibly one of the strongest contemporary links with the outside world is television. Almost all families, no matter how humble the house and furnishings, have a television. In this mountainous area a television set must be connected to a cable system for good reception. The cable service requires a monthly expenditure of funds.

Coal mining in the region has greatly changed during the past 20 years. Mining companies have taken advantage of technological advances so that the labor force requirements are much smaller for each unit of coal removed. Mining is still the most hazardous major occupation in this country, although recently enacted legislation appears to have the potential of improving mine safety somewhat. With the technological advances, the skills required of workers have changed drastically. A man proficient in handling a pick and shovel might be very poorly equipped for operating or maintaining a complex piece of mining machinery. Thus, many individuals who spent several of their younger years as miners are poorly qualified to work in a modern mine. In recent years strip mining has become a common method of removing coal from the ground. In 1972 more coal was removed in Kentucky by strip mining than was taken from underground mines. For the same year, almost half of the coal mined in West Virginia was removed by stripping.

The development of more and better hard-surfaced roads into the region has made it possible for individuals in the area to work elsewhere, while frequently driving back to their cultural base. Miners may drive 25 miles or more one way to work. Some mountaineers live and work in large industrial cities, driving back to their homes in the mountains on weekends.

While a strip miner is not as likely to be seriously injured or killed as a miner in an underground mine, the work is still quite hazardous. The fatalistic attitude of the miner likely enables him to function effectively in a deep mine day after day. It provides him with the attitude, when your time is up, it's up, and there's nothing you can do about it.

Workers at some mines are unionized while others are not. Deep underground mines are usually unionized; strip mines tend to be non-union. Strikes, the weather, available transportation, earth slides, cave-ins and the price of coal are some of the major factors which influence the regularity with which mines operate.

(Note to the teacher: A miner would not typically prepare a written budget. In this game the student will be provided a *Ledger Sheet* which will influence him to prepare a short-term budget. This bit of structure is thought to be mechanically necessary for playing the game. This element of the game should be discussed during the Debriefing Session.)

Implementing the Lesson

Distribute *Role Cards* (character sketches); have one student of each pair identify "himself," his job, and tell the class at least two other things about "himself." (Discourage the student from reading everything on the *Role Card* aloud to the class.)

Distribute *Ledger Sheets.*

Read the following rules to the students:

Miners in this game are paid twice monthly. Each pay period, i.e., two weeks, will constitute a round. We will play ten (10) rounds, i.e., five (5) months. For ease in computing salary, the game uses a five-day work week and ten days for each full pay period. We begin the game on October 1. It is fall; the weather has been good, and the mines were open all ten work days during the previous two weeks. Multiply your daily take-home pay by ten to calculate your income for this pay period. Foremen already have their total pay determined.

Your take-home pay is your gross earnings minus Social Security, income taxes and hospitalization. It might be noted here that medical coverage for a union worker is quite comprehensive for all members of the family, while coverage for a non-union worker and his family typically provides for hospital and emergency care only, paying about 95% of that cost.

As in reality, every family has a multitude of expenses too small and numerous to include on the *Ledger Sheet*. Items such as lunch money, school supplies, linens, postage, some minor clothing articles, and tobacco are lumped together in a Miscellaneous category on the *Ledger Sheet*. At least ten dollars ($10.00) must be allocated for this purpose each month.

Distribute *Fixed Costs* sheets and the *Expenditure Rules* and tell the class:

Read the *Expenditure Rules* before making decisions about how to spend your money. Try to make decisions that the character you are playing would make. You should note that some bills are due monthly while others may be paid bimonthly. You will receive another check on October 15; the amount will be determined by how many days you work during the next two-week period. You may add categories or items to the *Ledger Sheet,* if it is helpful to your record-keeping.

(Depending on the age of the participants, the teacher might need to go over the *Expenditure Rules* or answer questions pertaining to them.)

When your students have had an opportunity to allocate their earnings for October 1, they should be instructed to enter these amounts on their *Ledger Sheet*, under Oct. 1.

Request one partner to check the other's computations to insure that all money is accounted for. Any unspent money should be entered as "Savings Account," although in reality the cash might be kept at home rather than deposited at a bank. This money may be drawn upon at any time.

Announce that round one is completed. Allow questions at this point to make sure participants understand the rules of the game and have their *Ledger Sheets* completed for round one.

Read Round Notice for October 15:

There is a special fall sale on kitchen appliances. Stoves, refrigerators, and freezers can be bought for 30% off during the next two weeks.

Then read or paraphrase the following:

The mines seldom operate as regularly in the late fall and winter as in the summer and early fall due to inclement weather. Strikes, equipment breakdowns and other problems can affect mine operations anytime. To determine how many days the mines will operate during the next two weeks, Frank "Bubba" Howard, foreman for Big Sandy, and J. T. Bowers, foreman for Smokey Ridge, will each spin the *Spinner*. (The teacher should record the results for the October 15 pay period on the board for each mine.)

As in reality, unforeseen events can affect our income and expenditures. Each miner must draw a *Chance Card* to see if such an event has affected him during the Oct. 1–Oct. 15 pay period. (Have participants read their *Chance Cards* aloud for this round only.)

Calculate your income based on the chance elements and the number of days the mine was open. Enter your expenditures on your *Ledger Sheet*.

(Allow plenty of time for partners to consider their situation, negotiate loans, calculate income, etc. Display charts of *Bank Loan Transactions and Products* and a *catalog* containing general merchandise to use as a pricing source.)

Sequence for subsequent rounds:

(1) Teacher reads Round Notice (not necessary for all rounds). Those Notices are:

November 1: There is an opening at Smokey Ridge #1 for an explosive setter. No experience necessary. This is a union job and pays $40.00 a day before deductions. (Note for teacher: Take-home pay for a man with four dependents would be $33.00. See *Fixed Costs* sheet if miner had other than four dependents.)

December 1: There are just 23 shopping days left until Christmas. At this time, you will have 20 minutes to make out your shopping list and decide what gifts, if any, you want to purchase this month. (Note for teacher: The teacher can either have several Christmas catalogs available for students to use or he can make a chart with specific items and prices listed.)

January 1: The annual inventory sale is now in progress. You can purchase a brand new color television for one-third off the original price.

February 1: After many months of negotiating, leaders have announced this morning that there will be an increase in wages amounting to $2.00 per day take-home pay for union members.

(2) Foremen spin for number of work days.

(3) Miners draw Chance Cards.

(4) Miners fill out Ledger Sheet.

The game should not advance from one round to the next, however, until all miners have completed their calculations. Allow time for bank transactions, pricing of articles, or transactions among miners. Occasionally miners may negotiate between themselves to buy or sell second-hand automobiles or appliances or for services, such as a ride to work. If needed, the teacher can be the final judge of the validity of a transaction. After each two or three rounds, the teacher should collect the *chance cards* and shuffle the stack.

Concluding the Lesson

At the end of the game a debriefing session is held where some of the following questions may be discussed by the students. It is important that the teacher accept all seriously given responses, especially when students express their feelings about a situation.

If the teacher will write down a few ideas that seem important to the players or teacher while the game is being played, it may help in selecting questions for the debriefing that are appropriate to the students' reactions to situations in the game.

The teacher should allow students to discuss freely questions of interest about the game. All the questions included here need not be considered; neither must the questions that are used be asked in any particular order. The teacher should try to build on the feelings and the interests of the students.

1. What were your goals in the game?
2. What feelings did you have as you played the game? Viewed the movies/pictures? Read the books/articles?
3. Which aspects of the game did you think were realistic/unrealistic?
4. Which role would you rather play? Why?
5. How would you describe Appalachian coal miners in general, based on the game? How can we find out if our descriptions are accurate?
6. What does "poverty" mean?
7. Could these people make a living doing something else? Why or why not? If they could, why don't they?
8. How might the life of a coal miner in other parts of the country/world differ from that of an Appalachian coal miner?
9. What forces work against the miner? In his favor?
10. What are some of the positive aspects of the life of Appalachian miners? The negative aspects? What solutions can you suggest to resolve the negative aspects?
11. Does age or family responsibilities of the miner affect his ability to get ahead?
12. If you played the game for more rounds, do you think it would make a difference in your situation? If so, in what respect?

The following questions might be used if students are going to do additional research on Appalachia.

13. What is the background (heritage) of the people of Appalachia?
14. What caused the poverty of Appalachia? Are all Appalachians poor? (Check economic conditions of Pike County, Kentucky for example.)
15. Has a large percentage of mountaineers of Appalachia always mined? If not, what means of livelihood did they previously have?
16. What occupations other than mining are now prevalent in Appalachia? How do other occupations compare with mining economically?
17. What effect does mobility or lack of mobility have on these people?
18. Do you see any remnants of frontier life? If so, what are they?
19. Can you think of similar situations (or possibilities of similar situations) in other parts of the world where industrial society invades or disrupts rural people?

The teacher might suggest some additions to the game such as building in the alternative of a strike, roles of teen-agers with the option of going to school or working in the mines, welfare or food-stamps, or writing roles for family members and playing in family groups. Follow-up activities might build on the interests of the students in finding out more about miners, mountaineers, Appalachia, poverty in the United States, and perhaps comparing the life of an Appalachian miner with a person living in a ghetto or on a small farm. A student might do library research on the Appalachian coal miner, and then make up a more complete story about the role he played, based on his research.

Additional References

We have attempted to capsulate minimum information for participation in this simulation. Additional background reading before, during, or following the game would make the study more meaningful. Your library may have some helpful materials on this topic. Listed below are references that we have found to be especially beneficial. One of the films might be shown to the class prior to participating in the game.

Books: Jack E. Weller, *Yesterday's People,* University of Kentucky Press, 1966; and Harry Caudill, *Night Comes to the Cumberlands,* Little, Brown and Company, 1963.

Films: "Appalachia: Rich Land—Poor People"; 59 minutes, $8.00, #3626; Audio-Visual Service; University of Kentucky; Lexington, Kentucky 40506. The following films can be rented from the Community Film Workshop Council of Appalachia, Box 332, Whitesburg, Kentucky 41858. "Whitesburg Epic"; B-W, 10 minutes; $20.00; "UMWA 1970: A House Divided"; B-W, 15 minutes; $30.00; "Coal Miner: Frank Jackson"; B-W, 12 minutes; $25.00; and "Appalachia Genesis"; Color, 30 minutes; price upon request.

Other references: "Region Made by Problems," *Regions of the United States* from *Our Working World,* Elementary Social Studies series, Science Research Associates, 1973; Kirby and Rich Kline, "They Can't Put It Back." Recorded by David Portugal, Capon Bridge, W. Virginia: Killion Run Records; R. Garry Shirts, "Simulations, Games, and Related Activities for Elementary Classrooms," *Social Education*, March, 1971, pp. 300-304; and Virginia M. Rogers and Audrey H. Goodloe, "Simulation Games As Method," *Educational Leadership,* May, 1973, pp. 729-732.

**Student Materials for
"Appalachian Coal Miners: A Simulation"
follow on pages 93–111**

ROLE CARDS

[*Duplicate each character sketch on a separate sheet and give each pair one Role Card.*]

Role Card for
Mark Walton

You are 26 years old and live with your wife and three young children. You have a high school education and have lived in the same community, except for an unpleasant two-year period of factory work in a large city. You rent a four-room frame house for $55.00 per month and own an eight-year-old automobile which costs an average of $15.00 per month for repairs. You are a union coal cutter in Smokey Ridge #1 with a take-home pay of $33.00 per day. You are making payments of $20.00 per month on a color television set with eight payments remaining.

Role Card for
James E. Smythe

You are 37 years of age and a non-union bulldozer operator at the Big Sandy Strip Mine. You live with your wife and five children in a five-room frame house which you rent for $60.00 per month. Your take-home pay is $29.00 per day. You own with no debt a six-year-old and an eight-year-old automobile. However, repairs on these automobiles average $30.00 per month. You are buying a new refrigerator with payments of $22.00 per month (12 payments remaining) and a black-and-white television with payments of $10.00 per month (four payments remaining).

Role Card for
J. T. Bowers

You are 45 years old and a foreman at Smokey Ridge #1, an underground mine. You have advanced in the mine, beginning as a driller when you finished high school. Except for four years in the service, you have worked in the mines since you were 18. You have a wife and five children, one of whom is married but separated, has a small baby, and lives with you and your family. You are paid twice a month with a take-home salary of $375.00. Mine shutdowns of less than a month's duration do not affect your salary. Two of your children have eye disorders; the eight-year-old has just gotten a pair of glasses for which you owe $25.00 and the seven-year-old needs them also. Your oldest son, J. T. Bowers, Jr., is presently working at a drive-in restaurant in a nearby town and contributes $20.00 per month for household expenses. Your family lives in a six-room frame and log house eight miles out of town. Mortgage payments are $70.00 monthly. You own an eight-year-old pickup truck for which maintenance costs run about $10.00 per month and a two-year-old automobile with payments of $75.00 per month (12 payments remaining). Your refrigerator does not work well and upkeep on your old black-and-white television costs an average of $5.00 per month.

Role Card for
David Lee Carter

You are 48 years of age. You have a wife and an adolescent living with you; a grown son works in a factory in Detroit. You have been a miner for 27 years, and have just recently completed a three-year rest period for tuberculosis. You load coal deep in a union mine, Smokey Ridge #1, and your take-home pay is $32.00 a day. You have an eighth-grade education. Your family has lived in this area since the coal boom of the early 1900's, and you now live in a four-room frame house on the edge of town. You have a second mortgage on the property, which when combined with the regular mortgage payment totals $85.00 per month. You own an eight-year-old automobile which requires an average of $15.00 per month for repairs. Your wife has arthritis and requires medication, which is completely covered by your union insurance. You own an old black-and-white television.

Role Card for
James Justin McDermit

You are completing 17 years as a union coal loader at Smokey Ridge #1, an underground mine. You are now 35 years of age and live with your wife and six children. Your take-home pay is $34.00 per day. You are renting a four-room frame house ($55.00 monthly) which is located up a hollow about twelve miles from the mine. One child is severely allergic and has to have weekly injections which are covered by your union insurance. Another child has a learning disability and has been recommended for a special school, which would require transportation by the parents over a distance of 28 miles (round trip) at an additional expense of $8.00 per week (excluding depreciation of the automobile). The family television (color) is two months old with monthly payments of $20.00 (17 payments remaining). You have a nine-year-old automobile which is worn out and will not run. You are about to choose between buying a three-year-old used car with monthly payments of $50.00 for 24 months or a new car with payments of $90.00 per month for 36 months. A down payment of $300.00 and your old car will be required to swing either deal.

Role Card for
John David Martin

You are in charge of equipment maintenance at Smokey Ridge #1, an underground union mine. You are 38 years old and have worked with equipment in deep mines since you were 16. You have worked in other mines prior to your present job and have lived in this community all of your life. Your father, an uncle and a brother were killed in a mine explosion three years ago. Your wife died of tuberculosis last year, and you are left to care for six children. The oldest child is a girl, sixteen years of age, who has dropped out of school to take care of the house and the other children. Your take-home pay is $34.00 per day. You now rent a five-room frame house for $60.00 per month. You lack two payments of $10.00 each on a refrigerator and ten payments of $25.00 each on a color television. You would like to buy or rent a larger house and hire a housekeeper so that your daughter could complete her junior and senior years in high school. The housekeeper would cost $15.00 per week. Rent on a six-room frame house would be $65.00 per month and mortgage payments on a three-bedroom brick ranch-style house would be $140.00 per month.

Role Card for
Jimmy Dan Hardin

You are 22 years old and have two years of college. You worked summers in a non-union mine until you were 20. By that time you were quite frustrated with college, and you greatly missed the peace and quiet of the mountains. You, therefore, quit college and began working full time at Smokey Ridge #1, an underground union mine, where your take-home pay is $32.00 per day. You married a woman from a large city while in college, and you have one child. However, because your wife became very unhappy after you moved back to this community, you have recently divorced. Your ex-wife has moved with the child to a nearby urban area, and you pay $75.00 per month for child support. You are a fireboss and were injured last year while inspecting a worked-out portion of the mine for accumulated gas. Your father worked in the deep mines for 45 years; he has black lung disease and can no longer earn a living. You help supplement his retirement check by giving him $20.00 per month. You are sending $40.00 per month to a younger sister who is attending a nearby college. You are living in an unfinished three-room cabin that you are building near the top of the area's tallest mountain. You have borrowed $8,000.00 from a bank for this venture and are paying it back at $100.00 per month, including interest. You are driving a four-year-old convertible for which you owe two more payments of $68.00 each. You have purchased a minimum quantity of used make-shift furniture and have no television.

Role Card for
Claude Thomas Bowers

You moved to this community to begin mining during an economic boom of World War II and have since lived here with your wife and mother-in-law. You are 62 years old; you are an active member of your church; you work as a maintenance man in Smokey Ridge #1, an underground mine, where you earn a take-home pay of $27.00 per day. You own a new pickup truck, a new television set, and modern kitchen appliances and furniture throughout your ranch-style brick house. You owe only for the pickup truck with monthly payments of $85.00 (20 payments remaining). Your mother-in-law has a bad heart, and medical expenses for her average $40.00 per month.

Role Card for
Harry V. Hardin

You are 54 years old and, as a non-union worker, operate a gigantic power scoop shovel at the Big Sandy Strip Mine. You have 35 years' experience in mining and were once trapped for two days in an underground mine cave-in. You have a recurring respiratory problem which causes you to miss an average of one day of work per month. You have unpaid medical bills of $100.00 and own a two-year-old automobile for which you make payments of $70.00 per month (12 payments remaining). You, your wife and your mother live in the downstairs portion of a two-story frame house. Your take-home pay is $27.00 per day. All of your seven children are married and live away from home, except for one daughter. She is married and lives upstairs with her husband and three children. Since your son-in-law is unemployed, his family depends on you to pay the total house rent of $90.00 per month and utilities of $35.00 per month. You also help buy school clothes and other necessities for their children, which averages $15.00 per month. Your mother sells hand-sewn quilts through a cooperative souvenir shop in the nearby town for which she receives an average of $20.00 per month. You are making payments of $15.00 per month on a new refrigerator (14 payments remaining) and you recently sold your old television set to pay a $29.50 traffic fine your son-in-law received.

Role Card for
Frank "Bubba" Howard

You are 35 years old and a non-union foreman at the strip mining operation of Big Sandy. Your take-home pay is $330.00 each pay period and that income is not affected by mine shut-downs of less than two weeks. Your mortgage payments are $85.00 per month on a three-bedroom stone and frame home, where you live with your wife and three children. You have a three-year-old pickup truck and are making payments of $70.00 per month on a two-year-old automobile (eight payments remaining). Your family owns debt-free all of the modern appliances in the home, including a new color television.

Role Card for
Robert Gene Mosely, Jr.

You are a 42-year-old non-union truck driver, loading at the Big Sandy Strip Mine. Your income is variable, depending on how much coal you haul, but you average $45.00 per day above expenses related to truck payment, maintenance and taxes. Except for a three-year stint in the Army, you've spent your working years driving a coal truck. Initially you drove for another person, but now you are in the process of buying your own vehicle. Your wife is a school teacher and her take-home pay is $520.00 per month, September through June. You have four children, all of whom are in school. You are buying a modern three-bedroom brick home with mortgage payments of $160.00 per month. You are also buying a one-year-old automobile with monthly payments of $92.00 (12 payments remaining). The family television, which is black and white, is quite old and doesn't work well; you spend an average of $5.00 per month for repairs on it. Mrs. Mosely would like to buy a home freezer as soon as possible.

Role Card for
Billy Joe Hardin

You are 19 years old and operate a coal-cutting machine in an underground union mine, Smokey Ridge #1, where your take-home pay is $34.00 per day. Your father was killed in a mine accident and you now support your family, which consists of your mother and five younger brothers and sisters. You have a tenth-grade education, having quit school when your father was killed. You did odd jobs for two years until you were old enough to work in the mine. You have lived in the same house in this community all of your life. The house is a five-room frame structure which is owned by the family. You own a one-year-old automobile with payments of $82.00 per month (26 payments remaining). You also make payments of $25.00 per month for a color television (10 payments remaining). Several of your younger brothers and sisters do odd jobs after school and on Saturdays and earn enough to contribute an average of $10.00 per month to help with household expenses.

Role Card for
Laddie P. Points

You are a 28-year-old non-union truck driver, loading at the Big Sandy operation. You drive a truck owned by someone else and earn a take-home pay of $17.00 per day for the support of your mother and yourself. You are renting a four-room trailer for $60.00 per month and make payments of $62.00 per month on a two-year-old automobile (12 payments remain). A drinking problem keeps you in trouble with the law and causes you to miss an average of one day of work per month.

Role Card for
Stephen John Truman

You are a 41-year-old power shovel operator (non-union worker) at the Big Sandy Strip Mine. Your left knee scarcely bends as the result of an accident in an underground mine, but it does not affect your operation of the power shovel. You have a recurring respiratory problem which causes you to miss an average of two days of work per month. You rent a four-room frame house for $55.00 per month for your wife and teen-age son. You have two other children in college (living away from home) who depend on you for a minimum of $20.00 per month. Your take-home pay is $28.00 per day. The family is making payments of $42.00 per month on a five-year-old car which you bought used; six payments remain. The family owns few modern appliances, but those are paid for with the exception of a used portable black-and-white television set. You still owe $15.00 for that set.

Role Card for
Jessie Lynn Howard

You operate an auger at the non-union Big Sandy Strip Mine. You are 24 years of age and have been a miner for six years. Your take-home pay is $29.00 per day. You live with your wife and four small children in a four-room frame house renting for $55.00 per month, and you are making payments of $85.00 per month on an automobile that is one-year-old (20 payments remaining). You are also making payments of $33.00 per month on a color television with five payments remaining.

LEDGER SHEET

		Oct. 1	Oct. 15	Nov. 1	Nov. 15	Dec. 1	Dec. 15	Jan. 1	Jan. 15	Feb. 1	Feb. 15
Rent/Mortgage	1										
Utilities	2										
Food	3										
Insurance	4										
	5										
	6										
Clothing	7										
Medical Expenses	8										
	9										
	10										
Television	11										
Cable Fee	12										
Automobile	13										
	14										
	15										
Appliances	16										
	17										
	18										
Union Dues	19										
Savings Account	20										
Church Tithe	21										
Gifts	22										
	23										
	24										
Bank Note	25										
	26										
Miscellaneous	27										
	28										
	29										

FIXED COSTS

(This information should be duplicated and made available to each pair by the teacher at the beginning of the first round. It should be used in conjunction with the Expenditure Rules.)

Utilities: 4-Rm. House, $25.00 monthly
6-Rm. House, $30.00 monthly
Ranch Style, $35.00 monthly

Phone is additional $8.00 per month; not required.
Cable T.V. is additional $5.00 per month; not required.

House rentals: 4-Rm. Frame House, $55.00 monthly
6-Rm. Frame House, $65.00 monthly
2-Story Frame House, $80.00 monthly

Food Costs: Each 2-week Pay Period

No. of Persons	Minimum Subsistence	Average Subsistence	Above Average
1	$15	$25	?
2	25	45	?
3	33	57	?
4	41	69	?
5	49	81	?
6	57	92	?
7	65	102	?
8	73	112	?
9	81	122	?
10	89	132	?

Wages: (Take-home pay)

Union	Non-Union	No. of Dependents
$31.00	$26.00	1
32.00	27.00	2
32.00	27.00	3
33.00	28.00	4
33.00	28.00	5
34.00	29.00	6
34.00	29.00	7
35.00	30.00	8
35.00	30.00	9
35.00	30.00	10

EXPENDITURE RULES

[*Questions may arise pertaining to rules not listed here. The teacher should make up a rule that he feels is realistic. Games usually run smoother if the students are not forced to remember too many rules. Experimenting with various options is considered a valuable learning experience.*]

1. Rent/mortgage must be paid on the first of the month.
2. Utility bills are due on the first of the month. If they are not paid by the 10th an overdue charge of $2.00 will be added to the bill. If the total, including the penalty, is not paid by the 10th of the next month, the utilities are turned off. The full amount due plus a $15.00 service charge must be paid before they will be turned back on.
3. The minimum food bill must be paid each pay period. The minimum amount is considered bare subsistence. If a miner wants his family to be healthy, he cannot pay only the minimum for very long.
4. Hospitalization is paid monthly by non-union workers or it is discontinued with no coverage. Union workers and their families are completely covered with no direct cost to themselves. Rates for non-union workers are:
   Single, $14.00 per month; Family, $22.00 per month.
5. Car maintenance is on a cash basis. If it is not paid, the miner and his family must pay for a ride with another miner. The cost of this must be negotiated with another miner in the game.
6. Union dues of $8.00 must be paid each pay period or membership is dropped and the miner loses his job.
7. Money can be borrowed from the bank if the miner has the equivalent in collateral or normally earns the equivalent in one month. If the note is not paid as agreed, the items mortgaged will be confiscated by the bank or his wages will be garnisheed. A new house may not be purchased during the game; money may be saved toward a down-payment.
8. To obtain a clear television picture in this area the set must be connected to a cable system. The cost is $30.00 for the initial hookup and $5.00 per month for service. If your character sketch indicates that you own a television, you may assume the connection fee of $30.00 has already been paid.
9. If you are making payments on a car, insurance is included. Otherwise, insurance is $6.00 per month for liability only, $10.00 per month for both liability and collision ($100.00 deductible on one's own car).

CHANCE CARDS

You have been promoted to an area supervisory position (non-union) over three mines. This promotion means that you will receive a steady net income of $425.00 every two weeks and mine shut-downs of less than 30 days will not affect your income.

For deep miners only: A large coal rock fell from overhead near the working face and resulted in a bad bruise and cracked bone in your foot. As a result of this injury, you lose two weeks of work. Workmen's compensation pays 80% of your expected salary for this period. All medical expenses are covered.

For deep miners only: While attempting to board a moving man-trip, you fell and suffered a broken arm. You will be unable to work for three months beginning with the next pay period, but receive workmen's compensation equal to 80% of your expected salary for this period. All medical expenses were covered.

For strip miners only: A defective explosive injured six men at your mine. You suffered a concussion and severe bruises. You lose two weeks of work for the current pay period and one week of the next. However, you receive 80% of your expected salary from workmen's compensation during this period.

A heavy piece of equipment overturned killing two men and injuring several others. You are fortunate to have only sustained a wrenched back. You lose the two weeks of work for this pay period and will lose two days during the next pay period. You receive 80% of your expected salary through workmen's compensation for the lost time.

One of your children has to have an emergency appendectomy. The total bill is $400.00. If you are a non-union worker but have hospitalization insurance, it covers $325.00. If you are a union worker, all expenses are covered.

Two members of your family are struck by influenza. The total doctor and drug bills are $20.00 for non-union workers. Union workers' families are fully covered.

A member of your family has to have an impacted wisdom tooth cut out. Your dental bill is $50.00. Non-union workers must pay $15.00 of this amount; union workers pay nothing.

A member of your family has to have an infected foot lanced. The office calls plus antibiotics cost $12.00 for non-union workers, nothing for union workers.

For deep miners only: Medical tests have just revealed that you have black lung. You are not eligible for workmen's compensation; however, you are eligible for a disability pension of $200.00 per month. *(Disregard this chance card if you are under 45 years of age.)*

Congratulations! Your wife has just given birth to another child. Remaining medical expenses of $50.00 must be paid within the next 90 days if you are a non-union worker. All expenses are paid for a union worker.

The transmission of your automobile has gone out. Repairs of $75.00 will be required in addition to your regular maintenance costs. If your car is less than one year old, the warranty will cover this expense.

An appliance store in a neighboring town is having a sale of color televisions. You can buy a console for $400.00 or a portable for $250.00. This sale is good for this two-week pay period only.

You ran over a sharp rock in the road and ruined a good tire. Warranty on this tire covers half of the cost; you have to pay the other $15.00.

If you have outstanding medical, automobile, or appliance bills of over $200.00, you must pay a minimum of $30.00 this pay period or face a law suit.

Your mortgage payments are increased $5.00 beginning this month. *(Disregard this card if you are not buying a home.)*

A freak accident at home caused you to knock over your television set and burst the picture tube. Repairs will cost $145.00 if you own a color set or $50.00 if you own a black-and-white set.

Your television set is not working properly. If the set is less than a month old, the warranty will cover the repairs; otherwise, it will cost you $20.00 to repair it.

A member of your family sold two hand-sewn quilts. Add $60.00 to your income for this period.

A member of your family sold two home-cured hams; add $45.00 to your income for this pay period.

You worked two Saturday afternoons to help your boss build an addition to his house. He paid you $20.00 which should be added to your income for this pay period.

Your boss paid you $10.00 for helping him build a shed in back of his house. Add this amount to your income for this pay period.

You worked overtime one day this week; add $15.00 to your income for this pay period.

You worked overtime one day this week. Add $10.00 to your income.

You worked overtime two days this week; add $20.00 to your income.

You have been sued for non-payment of an old debt; you may settle out of court for $80.00 or you may have the case tried in court. If you decide to go to court, flip a coin. Heads you win and must pay only a lawyer fee of $50.00; tails you lose and must pay the $80.00 plus costs and fees of $90.00.

You made a trip to a nearby town to visit relatives and discovered a big sale. You may purchase any household item for 20% off the list price. Good for this pay period only.

You may purchase any household item for 10% off the list price. This card is good for two pay periods.

You may purchase any household item for 30% off the list price. This card is good for the current pay period only.

A close relative died and you had to buy a new suit for the funeral. This cost $55.00.

You need new work clothes. Pay $25.00 for them during the current or the next pay period.

You need a new pair of heavy work gloves; pay $5.00.

One of your children needs a new winter coat; pay $20.00.

One of your children needs a new pair of shoes; pay $8.00.

You were caught speeding one morning when you were late for work. Pay a fine of $29.50 and subtract $5.00 from this pay period for arriving late to work.

Heavy rains caused a mud-slide which demolished your house but injured no one. Insurance covers the loss, but you must move to other quarters until it is rebuilt. *(Applies to homeowner or renter.)*

Property taxes are due in the fall; if you are a property owner, your taxes are $55.00 and must be paid by December 1 to avoid penalty. If not paid by that date, the penalty is an additional 1% per month. *(Disregard this card if drawn after December 1.)* [**2 cards**]

Nothing happened. [**6 cards**]

School clothes for your children cost $30.00 during the current pay period. *(Disregard this card if you have no school-age children.)* [**2 cards**]

For deep miners only: You have been switched to an evening shift for the next month. Your take-home pay will increase $10.00 per week for that month. [**2 cards**]

Heavy rains caused a mud-slide which damaged your home. Insurance covers repairs but you and your family have had to remove a lot of mud and debris. [**2 cards**]

Traveling at a high rate of speed you rounded a curve on a narrow mountain road and met a loaded coal truck. While your car (or pickup truck) was "totaled" when you were forced to run off the road, you escaped with only minor bruises and two cracked ribs. Subtract two days pay for recovery. If your vehicle was insured, a replacement will cost only $100.00; if it was not insured, you receive no compensation for the loss. [**2 cards**]

BANK LOAN TRANSACTIONS

[*The following information should be put on a poster and displayed in front of the class during the game.*]

12-month Cash Loans

PRINCIPAL	MONTHLY PAYMENTS
	(Interest, Service Charge, Principal)
$100.00	$10.00
200.00	19.00
300.00	28.00
400.00	37.00
500.00	46.00

36-month Automobile Loan (with trade-in)

Compact	$76.00
Intermediate	88.00
Full size	98.00
Half-ton pickup truck	88.00

PRODUCTS POSTER

Here the teacher should construct a poster which includes pictures (possibly from magazines) and the cost of various items that students might want to purchase during the game. The poster might include a television, car, stove, refrigerator, freezer, dishwasher, washer-dryer, vacuum cleaner and boat. The teacher should list a good approximation of the current retail prices for these items.

SPINNER

Construct a spinner with the "face" as shown. Construction paper and a round-head paper fastener can be used. Care should be taken to insure that the spinner is turning freely and is unbiased. Numerals indicate the number of days the mine is open during a two-week period.

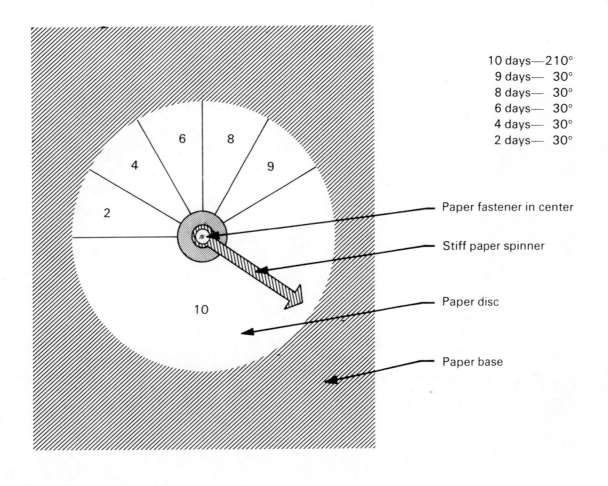

10 days—210°
9 days— 30°
8 days— 30°
6 days— 30°
4 days— 30°
2 days— 30°

Paper fastener in center

Stiff paper spinner

Paper disc

Paper base

"Historical myths exist precisely because they so effectively embody human values that they influence our perceptions of reality and the way we at least say we behave."

6

What Can Be Done with Myths?

By "myth," as I use the word here, I do not mean an idea that is simply false, but rather one that so effectively embodies men's values that it profoundly influences their way of perceiving reality and hence their behavior. In this sense myths may have varying degrees of fiction or reality.

Richard Hofstadter in
The Age of Reform

Myths, social scientists tell us, are an integral part of the character and culture of a people. In historical terms myths provide a romanticized version of the past, a view of antiquity not entirely as it was, but rather as it should have been—or perhaps as we need to remember it. Often myths are fanciful bits of folklore—such as Parson Weems' tale of George Washington and the cherry tree—which may serve to endow national heroes with superhuman powers. Or they may provide an often needed escape mechanism, allowing us to reminisce about the "Good Old Days" when, we are certain, life was much simpler and times were much better. But myths can also function as insidious masks, hiding the "closed" areas of social problems and perpetuating simplistic and outdated interpretations of the past and present. Only when the South was confronted by the civil rights movement of the

1960's, for example, did it begin to question its *Gone with the Wind* self-image of beautiful plantations, Scarlett O'Hara womanhood, and happy slaves. And many Americans still cling tenaciously to the Horatio Alger myth of personal efficacy and its converse, that this nation's poor continue in their state of poverty because of shortcomings in their character.

Because historical myths tend to be accepted at face value and because they are not frequent subjects of classroom investigation, teaching about myths in American history presents some rather involved problems. As Hofstadter suggested in the quote at the beginning of this chapter, historical myths exist precisely because they so effectively embody human values that they influence our perceptions of reality and the way we at least say we behave. Because reality exists only as we construct it in our minds, it is difficult to argue didactically that one reality construct is more valid than another. Certainly if our goal is to provide students with the skills to "debunk" the myths imbedded in their value systems, it is logically improbable that they will oblige us by now automatically and spontaneously questioning long-standing beliefs. Heightened awareness of the factors involved in value systems based on myth and an increased understanding of alternative ways to perceive reality require both adequate amounts of time and appropriate teaching strategies.

The three lessons that follow form a continuous teaching unit rather than the discrete, self-contained lessons found in some of the other chapters. The pattern of the unit is inductive, with the first two lessons presenting a case study of the formation of a historical myth and the application of that myth to a specific group as a means to test its validity. The third lesson, though brief, offers the teacher an opportunity to have students generalize from the case study of the specific myth to larger generalizations, in terms of having students establish criteria for detecting and checking historical myths for validity.

The example-myth offered for "debunking" in these lessons—that American society was and is a "melting pot" for the various cultures and ethnic groups living in this country—offers some noteworthy instructional opportunities. A study of this topic should be interdisciplinary in nature, as many of the sources and concepts involved—such as "assimilation" and "cultural pluralism"—are derived from the fields of sociology and anthropology as well as history. Also, given the premise that a historical myth involves human values that are not consistently operationalized, these lessons offer opportunities for value-clarification exercises. And, finally, there is the opportunity to encourage students to apply the methods of rational inquiry to still-controversial social problems.

Sample Lesson for:
Inquiring about the Development of a Myth: The Melting Pot

LESSON PLAN

Intended Student Audience   Upper secondary level.

**Suggested Time for
Classroom Use of Materials**   1–2 periods (50–100 minutes).

Materials for Classroom Use   Five "evidence sheets" (pp. 131–135) containing descriptions of the melting pot ideal during different periods in American History.

Major Objectives for the Lesson

**Objectives
Within the Cognitive Domain**   Upon completion of this lesson the students will:

Knowledge Goals

(a) Know that the belief that a broad variety of peoples could be assimilated into American society developed early in this nation's history.
(b) Know that this belief has persisted, in approximately the same form, for the entire existence of the United States.

(c) Know that the belief in the melting pot ideal has included the belief that all groups, regardless of their race, religion, or ethnic origins, could be assimilated into American society.
(d) Know that the melting pot ideal has included the belief that a unique, homogenous American culture would develop from the fusion of many different cultures.
(e) Know that the melting pot theory has been accepted by many Americans over a long period of time because it seems to express a basic American value—faith in the democratic ideal.

(a) *Analyze* and *interpret* information from primary source readings.
(b) *Formulate a hypothesis* about the values of Americans by examining evidence contained in their writings.
(c) *Pose questions* to consider in determining whether the values expressed in these writings were carried out in practice.

Upon completion of this lesson the students will:

(a) *Be willing to publicly state and defend* their agreement or disagreement with the values expressed in the melting pot ideal.
(b) *Be willing to participate in group discussions* on the analysis and interpretation of pieces of historical evidence.

Teaching Suggestions

The myth of the melting pot offers one example of the way selective interpretations of historical processes become commonly accepted as valid explanations of the past and present. This occurs, as the Hofstadter quote suggested, because these idealized interpretations or myths effectively embody the values of a people. From its beginning this country appears to have been plagued by an identity crisis. Especially during the years following the Revolution, there is evidence that many citizens of the new nation consciously asked themselves what Americans were. Were they merely transplanted Europeans, still bound culturally by the ways of the old country, or were they a new entity, a product of the condition in the new land? Most Americans seem to have opted for the latter choice, justifying their distinctiveness by claiming that a new culture had been created from the fusion of various European backgrounds. In time this supposedly unique ability of the American culture—to strengthen itself by "melting" the customs and traditions of diverse peoples into a common heritage—came to be prized as an expression of the democratic nature of American society and resulted in the adoption of the melting pot as an official national value; witness, for example, the proud statements of almost every

President that America is "a nation of immigrants" and the double meaning of the national motto, *E Pluribus Unum.*

The student materials to be used in this lesson represent expressions of belief in the melting pot ideal through almost two hundred years of America's history. Separately, each evidence sheet is an example of one individual interpreting a social and historical process according to his own value system. Collectively the evidence sheets demonstrate the development and perpetuation of a historical myth. Brief descriptions of each evidence sheet and its role as an illustration of the development or perpetuation of the melting pot myth follow:

Evidence Sheet 1

J. Hector St. John Crèvecoeur (Krev-coor'), a Frenchman, expressed the optimism of many new Americans who found themselves in a society with no formal class structure in the early national period. Note that the evidence for his predictions of "a new race of men" is derived from observation of intermarriage among people of different nationalities. The "ingredients" in the melting pot here are all northern Europeans.

Evidence Sheet 2

Ralph Waldo Emerson, writing over half a century later, includes Africans and Polynesians in the ingredients of his "new race," even though slavery was still spreading and nativist sentiment against immigrants was rising. Like Crèvecoeur, Emerson's faith was in the future, rather than the present, and his belief was that a new culture as well as a new society would be created. Unlike Crèvecoeur, Emerson offers no evidence to support his belief, but rather supports his assumptions by the analogy of the Corinthian Brass.

Evidence Sheet 3

Frederick Jackson Turner's most significant contribution to American history was, of course, his thesis of the importance of the frontier in the development of America. This passage from Turner's paper indicates the degree of common acceptance of the myth of the Melting Pot as he uses the myth to support his claims for the role of the frontier.

Evidence Sheet 4

By 1909, as these excerpts from Israel Zangwill's play indicate, the myth of the melting pot was being celebrated as God's own handiwork. *The Melting Pot* opened in New York in 1908, at the height of the "new" immigration from southern Europe, and played to large audiences all over the United States for five years.

Evidence Sheet 5

175 years after Crèvecoeur first expressed his faith in the melting pot of America, Arthur Schlesinger underscored the strength and longevity of the myth by ranking it fifth in a list of ten American contributions to world civilization. Here the cycle of the myth has come full circle, from Crèvecoeur's faith that the melting pot would determine the course of the future to Schlesinger's assertion that it did, in fact, explain much of America's past.

Since this lesson and the two that follow form a unit dealing with the expression of a belief on a national level and the testing of that belief for validity, you may want to begin by posing some general questions about values and beliefs and their ability to explain reality. Before you distribute the evidence sheets, ask the students such questions as: What is a value? Do all people have values? Are all people's values alike, or do some people operate under different sets of values? From where do we get our values? How do values affect the way we behave or act? Can a country have values, just as an individual does? What are some of the values you think the United States has as a country? How might a country acquire its values? Do the values expressed by a whole nation affect the way it acts?

Introducing the Lesson

The goal of the lesson introduction is to have students recognize some *key problems* for inquiry, which include: (1) How does a nation acquire its values? and (2) What is the relationship between a generally accepted ideal or value, and the way a nation such as the United States acts?

Students should also suggest some *tentative answers or hypotheses* to be tested, such as: (1) A nation may originally acquire its values by adopting those held by a large portion of its citizens; (2) These values are then transmitted by one generation to the next; (3) Values or ideals influence the way nations act just as they influence the actions of individuals; and (4) Nations, like individuals, tend to *believe* they act according to their stated values, regardless of how they actually do behave.

Predicted Outcomes

The introduction to this lesson dealt with very general and perhaps even vague concepts, with the goal of having students state hypotheses, or tentative answers, to the questions. In this section, students should test their hypotheses about the expression and development of national values by working with a specific example, the ideal of the melting pot. You may wish to have your class work on this assignment in groups, duplicating a set of evidence sheets for each group. As there are five evidence sheets, a group of five may be the most convenient, with one student in each group responsible for the questions relating to a particular evidence sheet. When the groups have formed and students have had time to look over the evidence sheets, write questions like the following on the chalkboard or a transparency, or distribute dittoed copies of the questions to each group. Questions are given that relate to each evidence sheet as well as to the group assignment.

Implementing the Lesson

1. What did Crèvecoeur believe would happen to individuals coming to America?
2. What evidence, if any, did he give to support his statements?
3. What is meant by the term "values"?
4. How do you think Crèvecoeur felt about the process he described? What statement can you make about his own values?

Questions for Evidence Sheet 1

Questions for Evidence Sheet
2

1. What did Emerson believe was happening in America?
2. What evidence, if any, did he give to support his statements?
3. What did Emerson believe would happen to the cultures of the groups he describes?
4. What do you think his personal feelings about this process were?

Questions for Evidence Sheet
3

1. What process did Turner describe in this paragraph?
2. What did he believe caused this process to happen? What evidence, if any, did he give to support his claims?
3. How do you think Turner felt about the process he described?

Questions for Evidence Sheet
4

1. Describe the phenomenon Zangwill believed was happening in America. What did he call it?
2. What did Zangwill believe was causing this process to happen? State reasons for your answer.
3. What is the tone of this passage? How do you think Zangwill felt about the process he described?

Questions for Evidence Sheet
5

1. What term did Schlesinger use to characterize America? What are the characteristics of the process he described?
2. What evidence, if any, did Schlesinger give to support his claims?
3. What do you think his personal values were with regard to the process he described?

Questions for Evidence Sheets
1-5

1. What definition or definitions of the term "melting pot" seems to emerge from these readings?
2. Do the five authors seem to regard the melting pot idea as an actuality or more as an ideal to be achieved?

When each student has answered these questions, ask the groups to share their information and prepare a one sentence summary of the melting pot theory as seen through the eyes of these five men. In preparing their summary you may wish to have the groups consider other questions in addition to those posed previously. For example, it may be desirable for students to consider such factors as the time span covered by the group of writings and to speculate on the nationality or ethnicity of the authors as indicated by their last names. Then have each group report its summary sentence, justifying it to the rest of the groups.

By this point the students will have analyzed evidence and contributed to the production of a summary sentence regarding the melting pot theory. They should now have a grasp of the factors involved in the melting pot ideal and some feelings for the value system implied in the writings.

Once the groups have reported their summaries of the melting pot theory and those summaries have been discussed, the lesson may be concluded in two phases. First, ask the students to express and defend their *own* values with regard to the melting pot ideal. Finally, as a transitional exercise to the next lesson, ask the students to pose key questions which would allow them to test the validity of the melting pot ideal as expressed in the writings on the evidence sheets. Examples of these questions might include: If the melting pot theory is a reality, how would a foreign visitor expect American society to look? What things would he look for? What patterns would the visitor expect to see: all Americans speaking the same language, playing the same games, and laughing at the same kinds of jokes? What, in other words, would be the result of a true "melting pot"?

Concluding the Lesson

The preceding questions are only examples. Your students will undoubtedly think of different ones—and perhaps better ones. However, the specific questions your students use are not as important as their realizing that questions such as these play a vital role in the process of historical inquiry. As historians, they have been confronted with generalizations about the melting pot theory of history that have been asserted, but not tested for validity. Before they can verify or debunk the theory, they must know what to look for, and it will be the questions they pose that guide their inquiry.

Predicted Outcomes

**Evidence Sheets 1–5 for
"Inquiring about the Development of a Myth:
The Melting Pot"
are on pages 131–135**

Sample Lesson for:
Inquiring about the Validity of the Melting Pot Theory: The Case of Black Culture

LESSON PLAN

Intended Student Audience	Upper secondary levels
Suggested Time for Classroom Use of Materials	4 or 5 class periods (200–250 minutes).
Materials for Classroom Use	Film "Black History: Lost, Stolen, or Strayed." Selected articles and poems (Evidence sheets pp. 136–143).

Major Objectives for the Lesson

Objectives Within the Cognitive Domain

Upon completion of this lesson the students will:

Knowledge Goals

(a) Know that many Blacks and other minorities have been systematically excluded from full participation in American society.
(b) Know that exclusion from full participation in American society caused many Blacks to develop a unique culture of their own.
(c) Know that America is a culturally pluralistic society instead of a monolithic society or a melting pot.

Skill Development

(a) *Gather and analyze* information about how many Blacks have been excluded from American society.
(b) *Gather and analyze* data about the effects of these exclusionary policies and practices, and how many Blacks have responded to them.
(c) Know how to *distinguish* between myths and realities of American history and culture with regard to many Black Americans.
(d) *Recognize and/or identify* problems involved in distinguishing myths from realities in American life, history, and cultures.
(e) *Formulate hypotheses* about identifying myths in American life, history, and culture relative to many Blacks.
(f) *Test the validity of the hypotheses* by examining data which attest to the exclusion of many Blacks from mainstream society and their responses to this exclusion.
(g) *Formulate generalizations* about the use of laws, articles, personal commentaries, poetry, etc. as historical evidence about the invalidity of the melting pot theory for many Americans.

Upon completion of this lesson the students will:

(a) Begin to *empathize* with those Blacks and people from ethnic groups who have been denied full participation in American society.

(b) *Clarify and/or modify* racial attitudes and values relative to many Blacks in American society.

(c) *Consider* the advantages and disadvantages of *participating* in efforts to end discriminatory and exclusionary policies and practices used against many Blacks.

Teaching Suggestions

The film, articles, and poems suggested for use in teaching this lesson are designed to show the "myth" of the melting pot idea relative to the position and treatment of many Black Americans.

The film "Black History: Lost, Stolen or Strayed" by CBS News presents a summary of how many Blacks have been ignored in American history, the effects of this exclusion, and Black responses to it. The film can be purchased for $575.00 or rented for $35.00 from BFA Educational Media, 2211 Michigan Avenue, Santa Monica, California, 90404.

The articles (see Evidence Sheets pp. 136–141) present four different points of view which illustrate how or why many Blacks have been systematically excluded from full participation and unqualified acceptance in American society. They illustrate institutionalized discriminatory practices which have reflected the attitudes and beliefs of the American majority. These beliefs say, in effect, that people of color are inferior to whites and ought to be relegated to an economic caste system and a position of second-class citizenship. The first article, written in 1883, deals with racial discrimination against Blacks. The second presents a list of state laws passed between 1876 and 1945 which were designed to enforce racial distinctions and separation by prohibiting interracial marriage. The third article, written in 1919, argues that most Blacks are "unknown" to white Americans, yet knowledge of them is a prerequisite to the realization of social equality. The fourth article is concerned with "what it meant to be Black" in American society in 1962.

Poems by Black authors, Langston Hughes, Claude McKay, and Paul Lawrence Dunbar, illustrate (1) the effects of the exclusion of Blacks from unqualified entry into mainstream society; and (2) the kinds of responses Blacks have made to this exclusion. (Evidence Sheets pp. 142–143.)

Introducing and Implementing the Lesson

Show the film, "Black History: Lost, Stolen, or Strayed." This film will serve as a means of orienting the students or creating a frame of reference from which to proceed to an analysis of why the melting pot idea has not worked in the past for most Black Americans. It explains how numerous cultural contributions of Blacks have been ignored in telling "America's Story"; the formulation and perpetuation of stereotypic images of Blacks, especially through motion pictures; the effects of the dehumanization and degradation of many Blacks on their own self-concept and the attitudes of many White Americans toward Blacks; and how some Blacks began to counteract the negative influences of prejudicial and discriminatory attitudes and actions.

After the students have seen the film, ask them: (1) What is "prejudice"? (2) What is "discrimination"? (3) Do the two terms differ in meaning? Then have them:

(1) Discuss their general reactions to the film.
(2) Identify ways mainstream America had closed its door to Blacks which were evident in the film.
(3) Discuss how Black Americans have been stereotyped according to the film.
(4) Explain the process much of white America used to create and project an "image of Black Americans" which violated the principles of the melting pot idea.

Ask:

(a) Do you think social conditions of Blacks have changed drastically in America since this film was produced? Explain why or why not.

(b) Do you think we are closer to or farther away from realizing a true melting pot than when this film was made in 1967?

Predicted Outcomes

As a result of viewing, discussing, and debriefing this film, the students will have:

(1) Become sensitized to analyzing weaknesses in the assimilationist theory.
(2) Witnessed specific illustrations of how Blacks were systematically denied rights of total entry into American society.
(3) Experienced or gained some insights into the process of formulating hypotheses, collecting and analyzing data, and testing the validity of hypotheses.
(4) Begun to develop empathy for and understanding of how and why Blacks developed negative concepts of self.
(5) Begun to understand why America is, in reality, a culturally pluralistic society.

If you are unable to obtain "Black History: Lost, Stolen, or Strayed," have the students take whatever time seems necessary to consider the following questions before they examine the selected articles and poems in this lesson.

(1) What is "prejudice"?

(2) What is "discrimination"?

(3) Do the two terms differ in meaning?

(4) What is meant by "assimilation"?

(5) Based on what you already know about American Blacks, do you think they have been assimilated into American society? Tell why or why not. (You may later change your answer if you wish.)

(6) What kinds of evidence can you cite which show that the melting pot idea *has* existed for many people in American history?

(7) What kinds of evidence can you cite which might prove that a melting pot does *not* exist or has not existed for some people in American history? (Here the students might offer evidence which applies not only to many Blacks but to other racial or ethnic groups as well.) For responses to question 7, student suggestions might include:

(a) Stereotypes of Blacks, Chicanos, Native Americans, Asian Americans, or Puerto Ricans.

(b) Ideas about superiority and inferiority.

(c) Previous discriminatory practices against people of color in law, politics, education, economics, religion, and social activities, such as:

(1) Denial of citizenship rights in the nineteenth century to Chinese by the California Constitution.

(2) Blacks being barred until the 1960's from voting by poll taxes, literacy tests, and "grandfather clauses."

(3) Laws prohibiting interracial marriages.

(4) Segregated schools prior to 1954.

(5) Japanese placed in concentration camps during World War II.

(6) Lynchings, riots of the "Red Summer of 1919" and treatment of "freedom riders," marchers and boycotters during the late 1950's and early 1960's.

(7) Existence of reservations, ghettos, barrios, Chinatowns, and "Little Japans" across the country.

(8) Previous laws prohibiting Blacks and other people of color from testifying in court or serving on juries.

(9) Police brutality against some ethnic minorities.

Secondly, students might be asked to list some ways in which Blacks and other ethnic groups have responded to being closed out from enjoying the benefits of mainstream America. They may suggest that some groups have, in varying degrees:

(1) Passively accepted their lot as inferior, second-class citizens.
(2) Actively protested discrimination and oppression by marches, boycotts, sit-ins, voter registration, riots, etc.
(3) Written protest poetry and prose, sung protest songs, etc.
(4) Developed alternative institutional structures, norms, mores, and values—that is, *cultures*—to satisfy their needs and regulate their lives.

Furthermore, they might be asked to locate resources that could be used to find supportive evidence to corroborate or refute their opinions and ideas.

Predicted Outcomes

Students will have begun to *recognize several problems for inquiry*, such as:

(1) How to go about identifying, compiling, classifying, and analyzing data which document the existence of cracks in the melting pot theory.
(2) How to go about interpreting and understanding the effects of the inconsistencies between theory and practice of American life on Blacks and other ethnic groups.
(3) How to determine whether the responses of ethnic groups to being barred from full participation in American life are legitimate and viable.

They will also have *begun the process of formulating hypotheses* about how to proceed to answer these questions or find solutions to the problems. (We might be able to learn why the melting pot is a myth and the responses of Blacks to this myth by examining personal commentaries, diaries, laws, economic practices, poetry, prose, and songs, political activism, and cultural characteristics or life styles of Blacks, and other ethnic groups, who live on the periphery of mainstream America.

Next, explain to the class that two sets of data by which to test the validity of the melting pot idea as it was relative to Blacks will be examined next. The first set (Evidence Sheets 1–4, pp. 136–141) discusses exclusionary practices. The second set (Evidence Sheets 5–6, pp. 142–143) illustrates Black poetry in response to being excluded from total acceptance into mainstream society.

Ask the students to also consider several general questions when reading the selected articles and poems. These may be written on the chalkboard or dittoed so that each student will have a copy of them. The questions are: (1) What are the general principles underlying the theory of the melting pot? (2) Do these selections document the nonexistence of a melting pot relative to many Blacks? (3) Do these selections help to explain the true nature of American society? (4) Do these selections help to explain how many Blacks have responded to being excluded from full participation in American life? (5) Has it been possible for Blacks to fulfill their human needs—physical, social and personal needs for love, respect, security, or acceptance—and regulate their lives?

Additional questions accompanying each selection appear as a means of further stimulating class discussion.

Concluding the Lesson and Predicted Outcomes

Discussion of the articles and poems should focus on whether or not, both overtly and covertly, individual and institutional means have been used to exclude many Blacks from mainstream society. Here the students should be willing to question whether the melting pot idea has ever been a reality for most Blacks. The students should also consider why most Blacks established separate sets of cultural rules and norms to govern their lives. The students should also be able to form generalizations about the similarities between the Black treatment and response, the reaction of other ethnic groups, and whether America for many became a culturally pluralistic society rather than a melting pot.

> **Evidence Sheets 1–6 for**
> **"Inquiring about the Validity of the Melting Pot Theory:**
> **The Case of Black Culture"**
> **are on pages 136–143**

Sample Lesson for:
Drawing Conclusions about Myths

LESSON PLAN

Intended Student Audience	Upper secondary levels.
Suggested Time for Classroom Use of Materials	1–2 class periods (50–100 minutes).
Materials for Classroom Use	Two question sheets and one process-application form (pp. 144–146).

Major Objectives for the Lesson

Objectives Within the Cognitive Domain

Upon completion of this lesson the students will:

Knowledge goals

(a) Know that myths have central themes, and that these themes are expressions of human values and often national values.
(b) Know that myths, when they begin, are based on observable evidence.
(c) Know that myths are examples of generalizations that will not withstand verification with objective evidence.

Skill development

(a) *Hypothesize* about the characteristics of historical myths.
(b) *Test hypotheses* about myths by reviewing evidence on the myth of the melting pot.
(c) *State generalizations* about the characteristics of myths on the basis of evidence.
(d) (Optional) *Apply* the criteria for recognizing and testing a myth by investigating a historical myth of the student's choice.

Teaching Suggestions

Lesson Overview

The first two lessons in this unit presented evidence about development of the theory of the melting pot—and materials that challenged the validity of that theory as it applied to Black Americans. In general terms, the lessons provided a case study in myth analysis; students first described the parameters and analyzed the assumptions underlying the myth of the melting pot as romanticized by various authors through centuries of time; this was followed by an analysis of discrepant reality. The overall goal of this concluding lesson is for students to generalize beyond the specific example contained in the first lessons and establish criteria for detecting any historical myth. Materials for this lesson consist of two analysis sheets and one process-application sheet (pp. 144–147), each containing a series of questions designed to guide student thinking. The first analysis sheet deals with means for describing the characteristics of a suspected myth. These include, again in Hofstadter's terms, a description of the values implied by the suspected myth, the length of time, in historical terms, that the suspected myth has existed, and a list of behaviors that students would expect to find if the suspected myth actually describes what has occurred. The second analysis sheet asks students to relate the kinds of evidence they would expect to find to either verify or debunk the suspected myth, to determine what kinds of sources they should seek, and to describe the criteria they would use to decide whether a piece of evidence supports or contradicts the assumptions implied in the suspected myth. The process-application sheet provides, in outline form, guidelines for investigating a suspected myth.

Introducing and Implementing the Lesson

Before you distribute the analysis and application sheets, ask your students to recall the discussion on values and their relationship to behavior that preceded the first lesson in the unit. Then ask the students to consider whether the process they used to test the validity of the myth of the melting pot might be used to test other suspected myths in American history. After this introduction, distribute the student materials for use either by individuals or in groups, as before. When the individuals or groups have arrived at tenable answers to the questions on the sheets, have them share their answers with the rest of the class, with the goal being to have the class reach consensus on a set of criteria for describing and testing a suspected myth.

Predicted Outcomes

To repeat, the goal of this lesson is to have students describe the general process involved in recognizing and testing a suspected myth. To do this, students must abstract the steps in this procedure from the specific case study of the first two lessons. Finally, the students should be able to apply the process to a suspected myth other than that of the melting pot. To accomplish these steps successfully, students should recognize the following when working through their materials:

(a) A myth is an interpretation of a past event or historical process that embodies the expression of human or national values. Though the myth was originally based on factual evidence, it tends to become increasingly fictional with the passage of time. Though myths become more fictional as they are repeated through the years, they become more and more accepted as fact because the belief in the values expressed in the myth continues to persist, and common acceptance of the myth serves to justify continued belief in the earlier values.

(b) It is possible to test whether a suspected myth is true or not by carefully asking what we would expect would have happened if the myth is accurate. Then we can seek evidence to determine whether the expected occurrences did, in fact, occur.

This process of "myth-debunking" is closely related to the procedures of the historical method, as indicated on the process-application sheet. On this sheet, students are first asked to state the suspected myth to be tested. This important first step should point the way for succeeding steps. As an example, take the myth of the innate goodness of outlaws such as Jesse James or Bonnie and Clyde. These are examples of the recurring pattern of the Robin Hood myth, where an essentially good-hearted person is forced by circumstances beyond his control to turn to a life of crime. The outlaws then continue to exhibit their justness by robbing only selected rich banks or men and by then sharing their loot with others less fortunate. A hypothesis for testing the validity of this myth might include the statement, "If Jesse James (or Bonnie and Clyde) really were good-hearted souls, then they must have given large amounts of their money to people who were poor." This "if . . . then" statement suggests the kind of behavior that would result if the value assumption underlying the statement is correct. Following the statement of the hypothesis, the next step is to search for evidence to corroborate or reject the hypothesis. Here several important considerations involved in the historical method come into effect. These have to do with the validity of evidence. Two kinds of criticisms are employed by historians to check evidence. The first of these is *external criticism*. External criticism attempts to ascertain whether the piece of evidence is real or not. That is, if the source is supposed to be a letter written by a certain person, is it reasonable to believe that it is? If, for example, the letter was supposed to have been written by a semi-literate backwoodsman, and it contained no misspelled words or incomplete sentences and was written in the elaborate style of Victorian prose, it would be reasonable to doubt its authenticity. The second type of criticism is *internal criticism*. Internal criticism asks: Can we believe what the document says? If, for example, we find a letter from Jesse James to his mother stating that he gave a large sum of money to pay a widow's rent, his statements would be questionable, in that people often falsify information about themselves. The final step in the process is to reach a generalization, or conclusion, about the suspected myth based on the evidence gathered in the preceding steps.

Concluding the Lesson

As a final step in the unit, you may wish to test the students' ability to apply the process of "myth-debunking" to a new myth. American history is full of examples of myths of varying degrees of difficulty and interest. Many of these have to do with people, as in the cases of Jesse James, Bonnie and Clyde, and Wyatt Earp; or in the cases of George Washington,

Andrew Jackson, or Davy Crockett. Others concern more global processes, as with the melting pot, the Horatio Alger myth, or the myth of peaceful progress, which asserts that the history of this country is one of continual progress marked by an absence of violent upheavals. Some concern myths which have emerged about different peoples—Native Americans, Asian Americans, Jewish Americans, Puerto Ricans, and Mexican Americans—as well as the many myths associated with American women and with American men. Whatever the case, interpreting our people's past by examining beliefs about ourselves offers a challenging, if controversial, means for studying American history.

**Student Materials for
"Drawing Conclusions about Myths"
are on pages 144–146**

Additional References

To provide a clearer and more workable understanding of the concepts and teaching strategies presented in these lessons, a variety of sources may be consulted. For the context and an elaboration of Richard Hofstadter's ideas on myths in the American past, see his *The Age of Reform: From Bryan to F.D.R.*, Random House, 1955. The quote used at the beginning of this chapter appears on page 24. For more on the myths in American history, see W. J. Cash, *The Mind of the South*, Alfred A. Knopf, 1942, and Henry Nash Smith, *Virgin Land: The American West as Symbol and Myth*, Harvard University Press, 1950.

The melting pot theory receives direct treatment in Milton M. Gordon's *Assimilation in American Life: The Role of Race, Religion, and National Origins*, Oxford University Press, 1964; Nathan Glazer and Daniel P. Moynihan, *Beyond the Melting Pot*, M.I.T. Press, 1963; and Melvin Steinfield's *Cracks in the Melting Pot: Racism and Discrimination in American History*, Glencoe Press, 1970. Gordon's work explains the concepts of assimilation and acculturation, while Steinfield's contains many useful primary sources adaptable for student use. An invaluable source for understanding the effects of the "melting pot" on immigrants is Oscar Handlin's classic *The Uprooted*, Grosset and Dunlap, 1951.

The theory and strategies of value clarification may be found in a variety of places, including Louis E. Raths, Merrill Harmin, and Sidney B. Simon, *Values and Teaching*, Charles E. Merrill, 1966; and Lawrence W. Metcalf, editor, *Values Education*, the 41st Yearbook (1971) of NCSS. Additional sources relating to the melting pot and inquiry strategies are available in a number of textbook series as well as in anthology texts like William E. Gardner, *et al.*, *Selected Case Studies in American History*, Allyn and Bacon, 1970.

You will find Otto Lindermeyer's book, *Of Black America; Black History: Lost, Stolen, or Strayed*, Discus Book, 1970, a useful supplement to use in conjunction with the film, "Black History: Lost, Stolen, or Strayed."

For additional information and more detailed explanations of discrimination against Blacks, and their responses to this treatment, as explained through primary documents, see: Richard Resh's *Black America: Accommodation and Confrontation in the Twentieth Century*, D. C. Heath and Company, 1969; Joanne Grant's *Black Protest: History, Documents, and Analyses 1619 to the Present*, Fawcett Publishers, 1968; Thomas Frazier's *Afro-American History: Primary Sources*, Harcourt, Brace, and World, 1970; George Ducas and Charles Van Doren's *Great Documents in Black American History*, Praeger Publishers, 1970; Lettie Austin, Lewis Fenderson and Sophia Nelson's *The Black Man and the Promise of America*, Scott, Foresman and Company, 1970; and Langston Hughes and Arna Bontemps' *Book of Negro Folklore*, Dodd, Mead and Company, 1958, and *Poetry of the Negro: 1946–1970*, Doubleday and Company, 1970.

If you wish to expand this study to include other ethnic groups as well as Blacks, consult these references for materials: Bruce Glasrud and Alan Smith's *Promises to Keep: A Portrayal of Nonwhites in the United States*, Rand McNally and Company, 1972; Melvin Steinfield's *Cracks in the Melting Pot: Racism and Discrimination in American History*, Glencoe Press, 1970; William Ryan's *Blaming the Victims*, Pantheon Books, 1971; James Zanden's *American Minority Relations*, Ronald Press Company, 1966; and Kathleen Wirth's *The Other Americans: Minorities in American History*, Fawcett Publications, 1969.

Any examination of how myths have plagued other ethnic groups should also include Geneva Gay, "Racism in America: Imperatives for Teaching Ethnic Studies"; David Ballesteros, "Social Justice and Minorities"; Barbara A. Sizemore, "Shattering the Melting Pot Myth"; and Larry Cuban, "Ethnic Content and 'White' Instruction," all in *Teaching Ethnic Studies: Concepts and Strategies*, 43rd Yearbook, National Council for the Social Studies, 1973.

Evidence Sheets 1–5 for
Inquiring about the Development of a Myth:
The Melting Pot
appear on pages 131–135

EVIDENCE SHEET 1

What is the American, this new man? He is either an European, or the descendant of an European, hence that strange mixture of blood, which you will find in no other country. I could point out to you a family whose grandfather was an Englishman, whose wife was Dutch, whose son married a French woman, and whose present four sons now have four wives of different nations. *He* is an American who, leaving behind him all his ancient prejudices and manners, receives new ones from the new mode of life he has embraced, the new government he obeys, and the new rank he holds. He becomes an American by being received in the broad lap of our great Alma Mater. Here individuals of all nations are melted into a new race of men, whose labors and posterity will one day cause great changes in the world.

J. Hector St. John Crèvecoeur, 1782

From *Letters from an American Farmer*, Albert and Charles Boni, 1925, reprinted from the original edition, London, 1782, pp. 54–5.

EVIDENCE SHEET 2

Well, as in the old burning of the Temple at Corinth, by the melting and inter-mixture of silver and gold and other metals a new compound more precious than any, called Corinthian brass, was formed; so in this continent,—asylum of all nations,—the energy of Irish, Germans, Swedes, Poles, and Cossacks, and all the European tribes,—of the Africans, and of the Polynesians,—will construct a new race, a new religion, a new state, a new literature, which will be as vigorous as the New Europe which came out of the smelting pot of the Dark Ages, or that which earlier emerged from the Pelasgic and Etruscan barbarism.

Ralph Waldo Emerson, 1845

From Emerson's *Journal,* quoted by Milton M. Gordon, *Assimilation in American Life: The Role of Race, Religion, and National Origins,* Oxford University Press, 1964, p. 117.

EVIDENCE SHEET 3

The frontier promoted the formation of a composite nationality for the American people . . . In the crucible of the frontier the immigrants were Americanized, liberated, and fused into a mixed race, English in neither nationality nor characteristics. The process has gone on from the early days to our own . . . the tide of foreign immigration has risen so steadily that it has made a composite American people whose amalgamation is destined to produce a new national stock . . . It is not merely that [the West] was growing rapidly and was made up of various stocks with many different cultures, sectional and European; what is more significant is that these elements did not remain as separate strata underneath an established ruling order, as was the case particularly in New England. All were accepted and intermingling components of a forming society, plastic and absorptive. Thus the . . . West was teaching the lesson of national cross-fertilization instead of national enmities, the possibility of a newer and richer civilization, not by preserving unmodified or isolated the old component elements, but by breaking down the line-fences, by merging the individual life in the common product—a new product, which held the promise of world brotherhood.

Frederick Jackson Turner
American historian, 1893

Frederick Jackson Turner, *The Frontier in American History*, Henry Holt and Co., 1920, pp. 22–3, 190, 350–51.

EVIDENCE SHEET 4

America is God's Crucible, the great Melting Pot where all the races of Europe are melting and re-forming! Here you stand, good folk, think I, when I see them at Ellis Island, here you stand in your fifty groups, with your fifty languages and histories, and your fifty blood hatreds and rivalries. But you won't be long like that, brothers, for these are the fires of God you've come to—these are the fires of God . . . Germans and Frenchmen, Irishmen and Englishmen, Jews and Russians—into the Crucible with you all! God is making the American . . . Yes, East and West, and North and South, the palm and the pine, the pole and the equator, the crescent and the cross—how the great alchemist melts and fuses them with his purging flame! Here shall they all unite to build the Republic of Man and the Kingdom of God. Ah, Vera, what is the glory of Rome and Jerusalem where all nations and races come to worship and look back, compared with the glory of America, where all races and nations come to labour and look forward.

Israel Zangwill
American playwright, 1909

Israel Zangwill, *The Melting Pot*, The Macmillan Co., 1909, pp. 37, 199.

EVIDENCE SHEET 5

America has been, in the best sense of the term, a melting pot, every ingredient adding its particular element of strength. Many other peoples, it is true, are also of mixed origin; but the American achievement stands alone in the scale, thoroughness, and rapidity of process and, above all, in the fact that it has been the outcome not of forcible incorporation but of peaceful absorption.

Arthur M. Schlesinger
American historian, 1959

From Arthur M. Schlesinger, "Our Ten Contributions to Civilization," *The Atlantic Monthly*, March, 1959, quoted in Melvin Steinfield (ed.), *Cracks in the Melting Pot*, Glencoe Press, 1970, p. xvi. Used by permission of Mrs. Arthur M. Schlesinger and the publisher.

Evidence Sheets 1-6 for
**Inquiring about the Validity of the Melting Pot Theory:
The Case of Black Culture**
appear on pages 136-143

EVIDENCE SHEET 1

Report of the Committee on Grievances at the State Convention of
Colored Men of Texas, 1883

While reading the article on page 137, think about possible answers to these questions:

(1) According to the report, what were the reasons which account for Blacks (called colored people) being denied their citizenship rights?

(2) What were four examples of discriminatory practices discussed in this article?

(Evidence Sheet 1 continued)

Mr. Chairman and Gentlemen:

We, your Committee on Grievances, beg leave to make the following report: We find that the denial to the colored people of the free exercise of many of the rights of citizenship is due to the fact of there being such great prejudice against them as a race. This prejudice was engendered from the belief which underlay the institution of slavery, and which kept that institution alive, and built it to the enormous proportions which it has attained; that is, the belief that the Negro was intended by the Divine Creator as servants and menials for the more favored races; hence, was not to be accorded the rights and privileges exercised by other races . . .

Free Schools: The Constitution, and laws made in pursuance thereof, make provisions for the education of the youth of the State, without regard to race or previous condition . . . .

What we complain of is, that notwithstanding the Constitution, laws, courts, and the Board of Education have decided that provision. of each race must be equal and impartial. . . . Many cities make shameful discrimination because the colored people do not own as much property on which to pay taxes as the white people do, in proportion to the number of children in each race. They utterly refuse to give colored schools the same provision as to character of buildings, furniture, number and grade of teachers as required by law. The result of this discrimination is that the white schools of such cities show good fruit, while the colored show poor fruit or none at all . . . .

Railways, Inns and Taverns: The criticisms and censures of many, that colored persons in demanding admission to the first class cars are . . . unjust and unwarranted. For those who censure know that if the companies were to furnish accommodations for colored passengers holding first class tickets, equal to the accommodations furnished white passengers holding the same, though such accommodations be in separate cars, no complaint will be made. But selling two classes of passengers the same kind of tickets, at the same time and price, certainly sell to them the same accommodations and privileges. The colored people, like any other class of citizens, will contend for the right in this matter as long as our Constitution reads, "all men when they form a social compact have equal rights," and even longer.

As for accommodations at public inns, taverns and hotels, we have the same right as other races to be accommodated on equal terms and conditions, though we cannot compel them to accommodate us in the same room, at the same table or even in the same building, but the proprietor can be compelled to make provision as good . . . .

Adapted from *Proceedings of the State Convention of Colored Men of Texas, Held at the City of Austin, July 10–12, 1883,* as quoted in Thomas R. Frazier (ed.), *Afro-American History: Primary Sources,* Harcourt, Brace and World, 1970, pp. 178–183. Original *Proceedings* in the University Library, University of Michigan, Ann Arbor.

EVIDENCE SHEET 2
Other Racial Distinctions in State Law

These samples of racist laws were accurate when compiled. On June 12, 1967, the United States Supreme Court ruled that states cannot outlaw marriages between whites and nonwhites. Although some laws have been repealed, the following table describes the legal situation only a decade ago. As you examine this summary of laws, ask yourself: (1) For whom are these laws primarily intended? (2) Do these laws illustrate America as a Melting Pot?

Statutes Which Prohibit Miscegenation (marriage between people of different races)

STATE	EXPLANATION
Alabama	Marriage between whites and Negroes prohibited. Marriage of person of Caucasian blood to Negro, Mongolian, Malay, or Hindu void.
Arkansas	Marriage between white and Negro or mulatto illegal.
Delaware	Marriage between white and Negro or mulatto void.
Florida	Marriage between white and Negro or mulatto illegal.
Georgia	Marriage between white and person of any other race void.
Indiana	Marriage between white and Negro void.
Kentucky	Marriage between white and Negro or mulatto void.
Louisiana	Marriage between white and person of color void.
Maryland	Marriage between white and Negro, Negro and Malayan, or white and Malayan illegal, punishable by up to ten years.
Mississippi	Marriage between white and Negro or Mongolian void.
Missouri	Marriage between white and Negro or Mongolian void.
Nebraska	Marriage between white and Negro, Japanese, or Chinese void.
Nevada	Marriage between white and person of black, brown, or yellow race prohibited.
North Carolina	Marriage between Negro and white prohibited.
Oklahoma	Marriage of person of African descent to anyone who is not African prohibited.
South Carolina	Marriage of white to Negro, Indian, mulatto, or mestizo void.
Tennessee	Marriage of white and Negro prohibited.
Texas	Marriage of person of Caucasian blood and person of African blood void.
Utah	Marriage between white and Negro, mulatto, or quadroon void.
Virginia	Marriage of anyone who is not white or part white and part American Indian prohibited.

From Melvin Steinfield, *Cracks in the Melting Pot: Racism and Discrimination in American History*, Glencoe Press, 1970, pp. 208–210. Reprinted with permission of the publisher.

EVIDENCE SHEET 3

Views of a Negro During the Red Summer of 1919: A Letter from
Stanley B. Norvell

The letter on page 140 was written by Stanley B. Norvell to Victor F. Lawson, editor and publisher of the *Chicago Daily News* and member of the Chicago Commission of Race Relations. The commission was created to study the causes of the Chicago riot of July, 1919, and recommend solutions to the problem.

In the midst of the Great Migration and after the First World War came what James Weldon Johnson called the Red Summer of 1919. During the Red Summer—so called because of the blood that flowed in the streets—there were race riots in at least twenty-two United States cities, and seventy-four Blacks were lynched.

After the Chicago riot of July, 1919, the governor of Illinois created the Chicago Commission on Race Relations, composed of six Blacks and six Whites, to study the causes of the riot and make suggestions for avoiding future disturbances. The Commission's report, published as *The Negro in Chicago*, was a telling indictment of Chicago whites. Unfortunately, its suggestions for the most part were ignored.

Victor F. Lawson, the white editor and publisher of the *Chicago Daily News*, received the letter shortly after being appointed to the Commission. The Black author of the letter, Stanley B. Norvell, wrote to inform Mr. Lawson and the Commission that there was a "new Negro" in Chicago. No longer were Blacks going to sit back and be acted upon. They were going to take the initiative and strive actively for the justice due them.

While reading Norvell's letter, think about possible answers to these questions: (1) Why did Blacks know Whites but Whites did not know Blacks? (2) What reasons were given for the growing tensions between Blacks and Whites? (3) What recommendations were suggested for improving Black-White relations? (4) Are this author's viewpoints useful for understanding Black-White relations in modern-day America? Tell why or why not.

(Letter by Stanley B. Norvell on next page)

(Evidence Sheet 3 continued from page 139)

My Dear Mr. Lawson:

. . . Few white men know the cause [of the riots], for the simple reason that few white men know the Negro as an entity. On the other hand, I daresay that almost any Negro that you might meet on the street could tell you the cause, because Negroes have become highly suspicious of white men, even such white men as they deem their friends ordinarily. The Negro has always been and is now largely a . . . dependent upon the white man's generosity and charity for his livelihood, and for this reason he has become an expert cajoler of the white man and a veritable artist at appearing to be that which he is not. . . . "Conning" the white man has become his profession, his stock in trade. Take for example the Negro in Chicago—and Chicago is fairly representative—sixty per cent of the male Negro population is engaged in menial and servile occupations such as hotel waiters, dining car waiters, sleeping car porters, barbershop porters, billiard room attendants, etc., where "tips" form the greater part of their [wages]. Thirty per cent are laborers and artisans, skilled and unskilled, governmental and municipal employees; while the remaining ten per cent are business and professional men. . . .

The white man of America knows just about as much about the mental and moral calibre, the home life and social activities of this class of colored citizens as he does about the same things concerning the inhabitants of the thus far unexplored planet of Mars. . . .

The five hundred thousand Negroes who were sent overseas to serve their country [in World War I] were brought into contacts that widened both their perceptions and their perspectives, broadened them, gave them new angles on life, on government, and on what both mean. They are now new men and world men, if you please. . . .

What the Negro wants and what the Negro will not be satisfied with until he gets is that treatment and that recognition that accords him not one jot or title less than that which any citizen of the United States is satisfied with. He has become tired of separate but equal rights. He wants the same rights. . . .

We ask not charity but justice. . . .

. . . .We have surely proven by years of unrequited toil and by constant and unfaltering loyalty and fealty that we are worthy of justice that we ask. For God's sake give it to us!

Adapted from William Tuttle (ed.), "Views of a Negro During the Red Summer of 1919," *Journal of Negro History*, Vol. LI (July, 1966), pp. 211–218. Used Courtesy of The Association for the Study of Afro-American Life and History, Inc., 1407 14th Street, N.W., Washington, D.C. 20005.

EVIDENCE SHEET 4

Louis Lomax argues that there are common experiences shared by all Black Americans, which have caused them to develop a sense of brotherhood.

As you read this selection by Lomax, think about the following questions: (1) What is the main point of the article? (2) What do you think the author meant when he said, "all American Blacks 'pay dues'"? (3) What effects have "paying dues" had on American Blacks?

Despite the absence of a classic culture, the American Negro is a people. There is now a tie that binds us all while yet allowing for the variegated lives we live. We call each other "brother," and we congregate together to eat "soul" food and listen to "soul" music. We are—from Muslim Leader Malcolm X to the United Nations' Ralph J. Bunche—"Lodge Members." Ask a Negro about soul music, soul food, his brothers, and what a lodge member is, and, chances are, he will laugh and walk away. But while laughing and walking he will bump into a fellow lodge member, and they will take off to eat some soul food while listening to soul music. And they will call each other "brother."

All American Negroes "pay dues." "Dues" is the fee one pays for being black in America. If you are a musician, "dues" is the price you pay when you see white musicians take tunes and concepts you created and make millions while you tramp the country on one-nighters; if you are a writer, "dues" is the price you pay for being relegated to "Negro" themes when your real interest could very well lie somewhere else; if you are a college professor, on an "integrated" campus, "dues" are what you pay when students make you a specialist on the Negro and approach you with sympathetic condescension; if you are just a common man—and that is what most of us are—"dues" are what you pay when rents are high, apartments are filthy, credit interest is exorbitant, and white policemen patrol your community ready to crack heads at any moment. In a phrase, "dues" are the day-to-day outlay—psychological and economic—every black American must make simply because he is black. And a "lodge member," as anyone who stopped laughing at Amos and Andy long enough to think should realize, is a fellow Negro who, of course, also pays dues. Soul music and soul food are the mystical oneness with certain rhythms and the cooking we have enjoyed while forging ourselves into a people welded together by common suffering.

Louis Lomax, *The Negro Revolt*, Harper and Row, 1962, pp. 42–43. Used by permission.

EVIDENCE SHEET 5

As you read this poem by Paul Laurence Dunbar, ask yourself:

1. What did Dunbar seem to mean by Blacks wearing masks in American society? Why was this necessary?
2. W.E.B. Dubois once said that Black Americans have a double identity or a dual personality. Is this similar to what Dunbar was talking about in his poem?
3. What effect do you think this attitude and/or behavior may have had on Black-White relations in American society?

WE WEAR THE MASK

We wear the mask that grins and lies,
It hides our cheeks and shades our eyes.
This debt we pay to human guile;
With torn and bleeding hearts we smile,
And mouth with myriad subtleties.

Why should the world be overwise,
In counting all our tears and sighs?
Nay, let them only see us while
    We wear the mask.

We smile, but O great Christ, our cries
To thee from tortured souls arise.
We sing, but oh, the clay is vile
Beneath our feet, and long the mile:
But let the world dream otherwise,
    We wear the mask.

From W.D. Howells, *The Complete Poems of Paul Laurence Dunbar*, Dodd, Mead and Company, 1935, p. 71. Used by permission.

EVIDENCE SHEET 6

While reading these poems, think about these questions:

1. What seems to be the point of the poems by Hughes and McKay?
2. Do you think that the "dream" in Hughes' poem is the same as the "American dream"?
3. How might recent Black reactions to exclusionary practices be considered illustrations of a "deferred dream exploding"?
4. What advice did McKay offer to Black Americans?

IF WE MUST DIE[1]
Claude McKay

If we must die, let it not be like hogs
Hunted and penned in an inglorious spot,
While round us bark the mad and hungry dogs,
Making their mock at our accursed lot.
If we must die, oh, let us nobly die,
So that our precious blood may not be shed
In vain; then even the monsters we defy
Shall be constrained to honor us though dead!
Oh, Kinsmen! We must meet the common foe:
Though far outnumbered, let us show us brave,
And for their thousand blows deal one deathblow!
What though before us lies the open grave?
Like men we'll face the murderous, cowardly pack,
Pressed to the wall, dying, but fighting back!

DREAM DEFERRED[2]
Langston Hughes

What happens to a dream deferred?

Does it dry up
like a raisin in the sun?

Or fester like a sore
And then run?
Does it stink like rotten meat?
Or crust and sugar over
like a syrupy sweet?
Maybe it just sags
Or does it explode?
like a heavy load?

---

[1]Claude McKay, *Selected Poems of Claude McKay*, Bookman Associates, 1953, p. 36, Reprinted with permission of Twayne Publishers, Inc.

[2]Copyright 1951 by Langston Hughes. Reprinted from *The Panther and the Lash* by Langston Hughes, by permission of Alfred A. Knopf, Inc.

Analysis Sheets 1-2 and Process-Application Sheet for
Drawing Conclusions about Myths
appear on pages 144-146

ANALYSIS SHEET 1

In the previous lessons you have examined a myth about the American past, that of the "Melting Pot." Using the characteristics of this myth as examples, see if you can now make some statements about myths in general by answering the following questions:

1. What is a myth?

2. Does a historical myth ever have any basis in fact?

3. Why does a myth come into existence?

4. Why does it continue to exist?

5. What happens to a myth as time passes?

6. If a suspected myth really did explain what actually happened, what kinds of events or behaviors would you expect to find? What kinds of things would you *not* expect to find?

ANALYSIS SHEET 2

On this sheet, state the conclusions you have drawn about the use of evidence to test a suspected myth by answering the following questions:

1. If you suspect that something you have heard or read is not true, what kinds of evidence would you look for to determine whether it is true or false?

2. Where would you go to find the evidence you need? To secondary sources such as textbooks? Why or why not? To primary sources such as newspapers, letters, or autobiographies? How would you know whether to believe what you find there? How can you tell the difference between a fact and an opinion?

3. When you do find evidence related to the suspected myth you are investigating, how will you decide whether the evidence supports or rejects the suspected myth?

PROCESS-APPLICATION SHEET

On this sheet an outline is provided for you to apply the process of checking out a suspected myth. Your teacher will help you with more specific instructions if you need them.

I. Statement of the suspected myth:

II. Hypothesis about the suspected myth to be tested:

III. Evidence that tends to support the myth   Validity of evidence

IV. Evidence that tends to reject the myth   Validity of evidence

V. Generalization: The suspected myth is (true, false) because:

PART THREE

Coping with Future Issues

"Throughout the study of history one can guide students in formulating questions that will serve as handles for analyzing ideas, movements, and developments."

Francis P. Hunkins

7
What To Ask and When

Chapter One indicated that the proper study of American history can aid students in their continued adjustment to the world of tomorrow. Through the study of history one can guide students in formulating questions that will serve as handles for analyzing ideas, movements, and developments. The question is central to learning, and one might define history as the formulating and answering of questions about our past activities in order to more effectively formulate questions relating to the present and the future. Certainly, historical investigation is dependent upon the types and quality of questions raised. In past teaching of history, a major emphasis was upon presenting information, and questions were raised to determine the level of students' attention and comprehension. Today, a shift is occurring in that we are considering questions primarily as tools for advancing knowledge rather than as devices solely for assessing students' understanding. This is not to negate the use of questions as a means of assessment, but rather to indicate that questions can be used more productively as vehicles for advancing students' understandings and skills relating to their world, in particular to the historical dimensions of their world.

This chapter will not expound the values of good questions and the need to involve students in asking effective questions. Rather, the chapter presents a lesson for elementary students, with direct implications for use at the secondary level, to demonstrate ways in which questions can be utilized in the study of American history. The lesson is developed primarily to provide students opportunities to obtain skills in formulating questions and incorporating them into strategies. Also, it is designed to stimulate in students a questioning attitude essential for the study of history.

The sample lesson emphasizes process and content, but the prime emphasis is process, specifically, the process of formulating questions of specific types and incorporating them into productive questioning strategies. The lesson is designed to suggest to students possible types of questions and when they should be formulated. Further, the lesson is developed so that both teachers and students will have numerous opportunities to raise questions. In the lesson students are to assume increasing responsibility for their questions, to be in charge of their learning.

In the lesson students are to confront the fact that all persons raise questions, oftentimes numerous questions, but usually without careful thought. Throughout the lesson the teacher has

149

opportunities to focus students' attention on why people ask questions with consideration being directed to some of the following reasons: to obtain information, to check insights, to uncover relationships, to discover basic assumptions, to formulate conclusions, and to judge whether these conclusions are warranted or useful. Pupils will have opportunities to suggest other reasons for posing questions.

The lesson assumes that students have not received any depth treatment previously about the American city in the nineteenth century. Of course some students will have some background knowledge of the topic, but these students certainly will find opportunities to consider the topic from different vantage points and to generate varied foci for their investigations. Of course, if the majority of students has had prior consideration of the topic, the question types employed in introducing the lessons and the directions and depth of the investigation in response to particular questions will be different from that indicated in the examples. But, one need not feel that the lesson must be taught as specifically indicated in this chapter. Hopefully, readers will be triggered into divergent thinking about ways to teach the lesson and schemes to utilize questions and questioning strategies.

Sample Lesson for Teaching:
The American City in the Nineteenth Century— Questions We Can Ask

LESSON PLAN

Intended Student Audience	Upper elementary levels and lower secondary levels.
Suggested Time for Classroom Use of Materials	5–7 class periods.
Materials for Classroom Use	8 pictures, 2 of each which depict political, economic, social, and cultural aspects of city life. 5 data charts (pp. 162–166).

Major Objectives for the Lesson

Objectives Within the Cognitive Domain

Upon completion of this lesson the students will:

Knowledge Goals

(a) Know the various reasons for the growth of cities in America during the last century. They will be able to list these reasons and to generate arguments as to why these factors facilitated the growth of cities.

Skill Development

(a) *Identify* the various stages in technological growth affecting the American city during the nineteenth century.
(b) *List* the major inventions that affected the growth of cities and will explain, when asked, why these inventions affected the city as they did.
(c) *Summarize* when asked the various working conditions in factories.

(d) Be able to *point out* the several major causes for persons emigrating to this country and migrating to the city.

(e) *Write* reports describing the major living conditions of immigrants and workers in the American city.

(f) Be able to *generate* and *evaluate* four major conclusions regarding the growth of cities in America and the life style of the majority of persons in these cities.

(g) Be able to *gather, interpret,* and *compare* information from several sources of data which include maps, charts, and pictures.

(h) Be able to *respond* to questions at six specific cognitive levels as defined by Bloom's *Taxonomy*.

(i) Be able to *generate* their own questions relating to the topic at the various cognitive levels as defined by Bloom's *Taxonomy*.

(j) Be able to *incorporate* their questions into a questioning strategy that will guide them in processing information in order to arrive at conclusions about the city.

(k) Be able to *employ* various diagnostic schema to judge the effectiveness of the questions raised throughout the study of the history of the rise of the American city.

Upon completion of this lesson the students will:

Objectives Within the Affective Domain

Appreciation

(a) Exhibit, through verbalization, that they *appreciate* the contributions various groups of individuals have made to the growth of American cities.

(b) Value the functions of questioning as a way of learning new data.

Teaching Suggestions

Lesson Overview

This lesson has a dual purpose: first, to assist students in becoming knowledgeable of the types of questions one can generate regarding a topic and also how to respond and utilize these several types of questions in processing information, arriving at conclusions, and judging the appropriateness of these conclusions; second, to provide students with opportunities to employ questions and questioning strategies to arrive at conclusions relating to the rise of the American city in the last century.

A large percentage of the American public lives in cities. Indeed, one can make a sound case that all persons living in the United States are affected by cities whether they live in them or not. Today, many cities are confronted with myriad problems, but these problems cannot be understood without an analysis of them in a time dimension. Cities are continuing to grow with overflow populace spilling into the suburbs. In order to comprehend the current growth and growth patterns of cities, students require opportunities to raise questions about the past growth of cities.

One reason for the focus on American cities in the nineteenth century is because during this time American cities achieved a "take off" point in which necessary and sufficient conditions for rapid growth of urban centers appeared. Through migration and immigration great numbers of people entered the cities creating a labor market as well as affecting demand. Inventions such as steel, the skyscraper, the elevator, the telephone, the electric light, the automobile, and myriad others enabled man to alter the shape and size of his cities. Truly, cities, after a rather slow growth in the eighteenth century, were "off and running" in the nineteenth. Students need to know those reasons and have opportunities to posit questions to assist them in obtaining high-level understandings.

The sample lesson includes the following topics: factories and workers (technology); various ages affecting the growth of cities; inventions assisting the city to develop; the influence of transportation on the city; and migration and immigration as they affected the city's growth. These topics are only suggestive and, as the lesson develops, other related topics could be generated by the students and/or teacher. Also, the materials suggested are for the basic theme and other materials should be provided for the processing of each topic. Additional materials are included in the bibliography at the end of this lesson.

Introducing the Lesson

Before the students begin the lesson, select from available magazines eight pictures, two of each which illustrate political, economic, social, and cultural dimensions of city life. Display these pictures on the class bulletin board and have the students observe the pictures and the phrases "Political Parts of a City" (for pictures A-B), "Economic Parts of a City" (for pictures C-D), "Social Parts of a City" (for pictures E-F), and "Cultural Parts of a City" (for pictures G-H). After observing the pictures and the appropriate phrases accompanying each, have the students record their reactions. Allow ten minutes for this brainstorming, and then ask students to share their reactions with classmates. How many reactions are statements and how many are questions? Record in two columns—on Chart I (p. 162)— the major statements about the city and the major questions about the city. Have students explain their reactions and during the discussion direct their attention to the questions raised, allowing sufficient time for discussion. What types of information will the questions provide? What procedures for gaining answers do these questions suggest? What types of answers do you think you will get if you pursue the implied method of analysis? Are any of the questions asking you to formulate a conclusion? Are any of the questions requiring a judgment as to how livable cities are?

Predicted Outcomes

By focusing attention to their questions, students will be required to react to the questions raised and to begin to consider the implications of posing certain types of questions and how these types can guide their processing of information. Most likely, if the students have not done this before, they will have questions loading up on the knowledge and comprehension levels. Their questions will relate to specific facts such as the number of cities, populations of cities, locations of cities, activities of cities, and what someone has said about cities. Rarely will students without initial guidance raise questions asking for solutions to problems or focusing on key elements or relationships between elements, or asking for generalizations and the evaluation of them at the various cognitive levels as defined by Bloom's *Taxonomy*. Those levels with definitions of each are: *

(1) *Knowledge* (those behaviors and test situations which emphasize the remembering, either by recognition or recall, of ideas, material, or phenomena).
(2) *Comprehension* (those behaviors, objectives, or responses which represent an understanding of the literal message contained in a communication).
(3) *Application* (to apply something which requires comprehension of a method, theory, principle, or abstraction).
(4) *Analysis* (emphasis on the breakdown of material into its constituent parts and detection of the relationships of the parts and of the way they are organized).
(5) *Synthesis* (putting together of elements or parts so as to form a whole—combining parts in such a way as to constitute a pattern or structure not clearly there before).
(6) *Evaluation* (making judgments about the value, for some purpose, of ideas, works, solutions, methods, or materials).

This initial activity can create a receptivity for discovering the types of questions and ways of incorporating them into strategies and can identify student needs for careful use of questions. Also, the activity can set the stage for possible directions for investigating the topic of cities in the nineteenth century.

Implementing the Lesson

With the total class group, emphasize that when investigating any topic one needs to generate questions and that the more carefully thought out the questions the more likely one will uncover meaningful information and formulate useful generalizations. Indicate that this lesson really has a dual purpose: to get them aware of and asking good questions and to learn about the American city in the nineteenth century.

From the list of questions generated in the lesson introduction, select questions that can be classified at the various cognitive levels according to

---

* Benjamin Bloom (ed.), *Taxonomy of Educational Objectives: Handbook 1 Cognitive Domain*, Longmans, Green and Co., 1956, pp. 62, 89, 120, 144, 162, and 185.

Bloom. Most likely the questions will be at the knowledge and comprehension levels which should now become evident to the children. Ask the pupils how they might rephrase some of these questions to get at higher levels of thinking to discover some basic understanding of the city. From this activity questions such as the following might be phrased: What are some of the reasons cities exist? What are some conditions necessary for a city to grow? How does the economic base of a city affect population numbers? What is the relationship between the people living in the suburbs and transportation? How did transportation affect the early growth of cities? Explain how certain inventions affected the growth of cities? How did some inventions adversely affect the growth of cities? What were some of the adverse effects of the immigration movement? What can you tell about how people adapt to their environments? How might man solve problems of the city?

Most of these questions are designed to elicit more than memory, and even those questions at the lower cognitive levels are worded so as to suggest ways in which information might be processed later at a higher level. One would not necessarily identify for pupils the specific cognitive levels at this phase of the lesson, but one can mention that some of these questions ask us to engage in problem solving, others ask us to look for important information, others ask us to form some conclusions, and still other questions require that we judge the worth of our conclusions. Later, the children can learn that these questions can be classified as knowledge, comprehension, application, analysis, synthesis, and evaluation.

At this stage of the lesson, indicate to the class that not only can they ask questions of specific types, but they also can position these questions in various sequences. One productive sequence would be to ask questions focusing on facts, the *knowledge level* (for example, "How many people lived in our city in 1880?"); then some questions asking for understanding, the *comprehension level* ("Do you think people living in our city in 1880 lived a good life?"); then some questions relating to problem solving, the *application level* ("How could you begin to determine if those people lived a good life?"); then some questions dealing with looking at key elements of the city, the *analysis level* ("What aspects of the city in 1880 would have allowed the people to live a good life?"); then some questions dealing with producing a conclusion, the *synthesis level* ("Using the variety of evidence you have available about how people lived in our city in 1880, what can you now conclude about that life?"); and finally some questions asking judgment of their conclusion, the *evaluation level* ("Which part of your answer about those people is a conclusion and which parts are statements of fact?"). Other sequences can be suggested once children become more skilled in question formation.

In group discussion have students generate needs for considering the topic of cities in the last century. These needs can be recorded by each student on *Chart II* (p. 163). On the chart the pupils can record the need, the information to satisfy the need, and a specific example. In analyzing the data chart, students can generate topics they wish to investigate and formulate a key question or questions to trigger their investigation.

Pupils can be teamed with a classmate for analyzing their topics. Before they begin their investigation, they can record possible questions relevant to each topic. These questions can be placed on *Chart III* (p. 164) indicating possible directions of investigation. A sample of how a student might arrange his questions in relation to the topic follows on page 156. The teacher could also develop such an avenue in planning for the lesson. Note that the questions only are developed for two avenues and focus on a question which would provide a conclusion to the investigation.

For the sake of discussion, let us assume that your students, with guidance, generate the following topics: the growth of industry in the cities (technology); various ages of industry; inventions assisting the growth of industries and cities; the arrival of migrants and immigrants in the city. Many of these topics can be related to materials listed at the end of the lesson in the bibliography.

Students in teams select the topics and map out their questions using *Chart IV* (p. 165). Before they begin their investigation, they can judge each other's questions as to worth. Tell the students: In the "Ideal" column write the questions you wish to raise regarding your topic and indicate in parentheses the cognitive level of the question. Is the question centering on facts or your understanding, or requiring you to analyze or synthesize or evaluate data. As you are investigating the topic, jot down the questions you are really using or if you are asking these questions orally, record them on tape for later analysis. Record these "actual" questions you raise under the Actual column and see if they agree with the questions you originally planned. If they do put a plus under the agreement column; if they do not agree, place a minus. You should strive to have the questions you use in your investigations agree with the questions you plan to use. Here the students should also determine what types of information they wish to obtain from utilizing these questions. Once they determine they have questions that will assist their investigation they begin to process information relating to their particular topic.

The means of obtaining information in response to the questions raised can vary according to the materials available and student learning styles. Some students may wish to read support materials; others may combine the support materials with films and filmstrips; and others may analyze newspapers of the past century for information.

You must provide students sufficient time to process their information, to respond to their questions, relating to the topics selected. Perhaps two or three lesson periods can be scheduled for this lesson phase. Information gathered in response to the questions is recorded on data charts, and new questions indicated for further investigation and sharing with the total class are listed.

SAMPLE CHART

Name: _____

Lesson: _____

Your Objective/s: _____

Date: _____

First Question: *What were some reasons for the growth of the city in the 19th Century?*

(R) Arrival of people   (R) New inventions   (R) New values

(Q) When did some people begin arriving?

(Q) What were some of the inventions?

(Q) Where did the people come from?

(R) Steel, elevator

(Q) What were some reasons for these people arriving?

(Q) How did steel assist in the development of the city?

(R) Mid-1800s. Many came from central and southern Europe.

(R) Some people came for new opportunities, some came to escape famine, others came because of war situations.

(Q) Where did the people settle?

(R) In the eastern cities

(Q) What effect did these increased numbers have on the city's development?

(Q) What statement/s can we offer to explain why cities seemed to "take off" during the mid-1900s?

(R) = Response   (Q) = Question

According to our example, there are four major topics for investigation: growth of industry, various ages of industry, inventions helpful to the city's growth, and arrival of migrants and immigrants. While your students are investigating these topics, provide guidance where needed, suggest materials when necessary, and allow children the opportunity to visit the learning resource center as required, if you have one.

Here you may also wish to have some students use single concept film loops to view events that happened in the cities. Other students may wish to listen to tapes on appropriate topics.

The obvious outcome of this implementation stage of the lesson is that students will have obtained information about the American city in the nineteenth century. They will have gathered facts, understandings, and hopefully some conclusions relating to the various dimensions of the city's growth. But, the most important outcome is that your students will have had opportunities to work with several types of questions. They will have had time to plan questions to guide their investigations, and they will have had opportunities to utilize these questions in various investigatory sequences. They should have come to some conclusions about the power of questions and how one can utilize questions in the processing of information. They also should have gained some sense of appreciation of those peoples who contributed to the growth of American cities.

Predicted Outcomes

After several days of study, have your pupils share the results of their investigations. This sharing can take several variations: you can have pupils role-play historians at a conference on the American city to report their research findings. Other "historians" at the conference can challenge the conclusions of their "colleagues." This conference does not need to be a total class activity. Several groups of pupils can meet in separate sessions to consider conclusions relating to the growth of cities. Group conclusions can possibly be written as position papers to be presented to the total class convention.

Pupils also may wish to make special presentations to the class or to make video-reports for a television presentation to the school body via closed circuit video programming.

Assume that your lesson has the convention of historians as the selected activity. Pupils present their conclusions and address themselves to the challenges of their peers. The important aspect of this concluding activity is that pupils are encouraged and assisted to raise questions relating to the procedures of investigation, e.g., the questions raised and mapped out for the investigation. This they can do by completing the top half of *Chart V* (p. 166). Such analysis should increase pupils' consciousness of process and further emphasize the power of particular types of questions when inquiring into historical topics.

Concluding the Lesson

In this aspect of the convention, pupils can share their reaction avenues as recorded on *Chart III*, perhaps having them on transparencies for all to consider. Pupils would have to defend their questions. Pupils would also have to evaluate the effectiveness of their peers' questions and, by completing the bottom part of *Chart V*, especially the effectiveness of their own questions. Did my or others' questions raised really get me or them to focus on the types of materials and situations that would assist me or them in learning about the American city in the nineteenth century? Did my questions focus primarily on facts? Did my questions or those of others in the class assist me or them in gaining understanding of written materials, whether primary or secondary sources? Did the questions guide me in processing data such that basic assumptions relating to building cities were uncovered? Did my questions center on the central themes of some authors' statements? Did my questions enable me to analyze various hypotheses raised to determine if sufficient evidence existed to support them? Were my questions productive in guiding me in deriving certain generalizations? Finally, were my questions of any assistance in allowing me to judge whether tentative conclusions arrived at were warranted? Here some of the diagnostic schema might be used.

As part of their summation, have students list on a master data chart the major conclusions relating to the American city, as well as major conclusions relating to the question and its use in inquiring. An offshoot of this emphasis on questions could relate to having pupils at a later time begin to analyze specifically the questions used by historians and the ones they asked in their class investigations.

Predicted Outcomes

After experiencing this "convention," your pupils should have gained some understandings relating to the American city and should know the reasons for their conclusions. The focusing on the questions as well as the conclusions of the investigation also should make your pupils quite knowledgeable about the question and how it can be utilized in particular strategies to make investigations meaningful and productive. Certainly, with pupils continually focusing on their questions, they are becoming aware of the types of questions, and they are becoming analytical. Students throughout the lesson and certainly in the concluding section of the lesson have been active in dealing with the history of the city. At no time were pupils passive receivers of information presented by the teacher. For much of the time, they assumed prime responsibility for their inquiry; they had opportunities to make history exciting study.

Alternate Teaching Strategies

One alternate procedure has already been suggested, that of having pupils make special presentations for video-tape programs to the schools. Those who did this would, most likely, be individuals really interested in doing depth study of some aspect of the topic.

Another alternate strategy would be to have some pupils write "If. . .

then" stories in which they would focus on some "If" situation and then write a "scenario" of some possible development. For example, some pupils might have suggested that "if the masses of immigrants had entered the country on the west coast, then the development of cities in the last century would have been, etc." Or "if gold had been discovered in the Appalachian Mountains, then the migration of people would have been. . . ."

A similar avenue could have been to have pupils focus on cities not discussed in the lesson and to determine if similar factors were operating in their development during the last century. The findings could have been placed on audio-tapes for pupil use in interest centers set up in the classroom.

Of course, pupils also can generate alternative strategies for investigating this topic and we need to allow our pupils opportunities to demonstrate some creativity in how they will approach a topic.

Implications of This Lesson for Secondary-Level Students

Process objectives explicit in this lesson could readily be *applied* to other topics for consideration by secondary-level students. Inquiry into other topics might include questions those students could ask about current or possible future movements by ethnic or racial groups such as American Blacks, Chicanos, or Indians. Another topic for consideration could, in addition to the material which appears in Chapter 4, include a closer examination of the Women's Rights Movement in American history and its possible future. Each topic could begin with student examination of recent photographs depicting a selected movement and continue with application of the basic teaching strategies and accompanying data-questionnaires presented in this chapter. For that matter, the five data-questionnaires used in this lesson on the American city could be used in the suggested sequence by students as they begin to investigate any relevant topic of their own choosing which has origins in the American past and implications for the future.

Whatever the case, this chapter has presented a history lesson with an emphasis on particular content, but more importantly on the *process of questioning*. The lesson was designed to enable students to become knowledgeable of the types of questions, to become skilled in incorporating questions into strategies, and finally to achieve realization that questions are powerful tools in the processing of information.

The lesson presented in this chapter is to get the teacher thinking about ways to teach history that will involve students in the processes of the historian. The lesson was presented to demonstrate the centrality of the question to all phases of education, in this case the teaching of history.

As was stated at the beginning of this chapter, the quality of the question determines in large part the quality of the investigation. Students experiencing this lesson would hopefully have opportunities to generate and react to questions that will challenge them to arrive at meaningful conclusions. Without careful attention to the question, teaching history runs the danger of becoming mired in memorization and regurgitation of facts about events, places, names, and outcomes. But events, places, names, and outcomes do not comprise the study of history. The study of history in the schools is or should be involved in the analysis of events, places, persons and outcomes to determine the reasons why certain events occurred, to understand the roles persons played in these events, and to uncover the causes for particular outcomes and the consequences of certain outcomes for a particular era or even for the present and future. History is a quest for understanding the total fabric of people. Such understanding requires pupils to experience and to raise questions in meaningful strategies. This lesson offers some suggestions as to how to provide opportunities for working with the question and questioning strategies so that students will know what to ask, how to ask, and when to ask it in the study of history.

Additional References

The following references are not limited to the American city in the nineteenth century.* However, one may wish to utilize the basic ideas suggested in this lesson and apply them to the study of some other aspect of the city whether with a past or present focus. Also, some of these materials are appropriate for several grade levels. The grade level at which one is functioning would determine to some degree the depth of coverage and the types of questions to use with the materials. For example, some of the film loops on the city can be used at any level, the variations existing regarding time spent in generating questions relating to these loops, types of questions generated, and the degree of response sophistication accepted in the pupils' answers.

For those wishing to make comparisons of the cities of the last century with cities in the current century, see *Modern American Cities*, Quadrangle Press. This book, based on articles from the *New York Times Magazine*. *A Modern City: Its Geography* by Harold M. Mayer, published by the National Council for Geographic Education, provides information useful for a current geographical analysis of the city. Additional suggestions for study about the city can be found in Richard Wisniewski (ed.), *Teaching About Life in the City*, 42nd Yearbook, National Council for the Social Studies, 1972.

For expanding the topic of growth of American cities, the Urban Growth Transparencies produced by Hubbard Scientific are useful. There are eight transparencies: growth of urbanization, growth of a coastal city, growth of a river city, growth of an inland city, city shapes, city land use, standard metropolitan areas, and walled cities. These transparencies can be used to supplement some of the pupils' investigations when discussing why cities grew as they did in the last century.

In focusing on the many dimensions of the city, you may wish to use filmstrips stressing certain aspects of the city. Media Research Associates produces five

---

*The author expresses his appreciation to Ms. Judy Fichter of the Auburn, Washington, Public Schools for assisting in the materials search.

filmstrips under the collective title of *A City Is Many Things*. Many of these film-strips concentrate on the city as it currently exists, but they can be used to determine if the functions of today's city have changed from the functions of cities in the last century. The five filmstrips are "A City Is People at Work," "A City Is People at Leisure," "A City Is Services," "A City Is Transportation," "A City Is Buildings."

There are many kits available on the city. Most deal with the city today, but one can use these in a unit on urban development of which the lesson on cities in the nineteenth century could be a part. The *New York Times* produces a kit entitled *Embattled Metropolis* having filmstrips, LP records, and duplicating masters. The *Times* also produces a kit containing similar types of materials entitled *Problems of the City*.

For teachers wishing to stress the comparison of cities of the past century with those of the current century, there are several sources of filmloops. Earling Company produces nine color filmloops under the general title of *Today's Cities*. These filmloops deal with the size of the city, movement in the city, energy for the city, transactions within the city, renewing the city, problems in the city, taking care of the city, life styles in the city, and contacts between the city and country. Double-day Multimedia also produces nine filmloops under the title of *Life in a City*. The loops deal with modern industry in a city, modern transportation in the city, educational uses of land, cultural uses of land in the city, automation and its effects on modern industry, public recreation facilities in cities, obtaining water in a city, the supply of water for urban areas, and the motion picture and TV industry.

Urban Studies Filmloops produced by Hubbard Scientific provides pupils with opportunities to focus on specific dimensions of the city: aerial view, cross section, contrasts, population, occupation, recreation, culture, government, transportation, industry, commerce. These loops can be used to compare the current aspect of these dimensions with their beginnings in the last century.

**Student Materials for
"The American City in the Nineteenth Century—
Questions We Can Ask"
follow on pages 162–166**

CHART I

The City

Major statements about city	Major questions about city

Suggested ways to begin your research:

CHART II

Rationales for Considering the Topic of Cities

Rationale (need) for investigation of the topic	Information needed to satisfy the reason for the investigation	Specific example of a city

Key questions to trigger investigation:

CHART III

Name: _____

Lesson: _____

Your Objective/s: _____

Date: _____

- -

First Question:

CHART IV*

Name: _____

Lesson: _____

Date: _____

- -

Ideal and Actual Levels of Questions

Ideal   *Actual*   *Agreement*

1. _____   _____   _____

2. _____   _____   _____

- -

*Note: This form is an adaptation of a form for the teacher as found in Hunkins, *Questioning Strategies and Techniques*, Allyn and Bacon, 1972, p. 118. Used by permission.

CHART V*

Name: _____

Lesson: _____

My Objective/s: _____

Date: _____

- -

My Question	Whether knowledge, com-prehension, application, analysis, synthesis, or evaluation.	Purpose of Question
1. _____	_____	_____
2. _____	_____	_____

- -

My reactions to my questions and their use: _____

_____

_____

- -

*Note: This is an adaptation of a form for the teacher's use as found in Hunkins, *Questioning Strategies and Techniques*, p. 128. The pupils would have to have been introduced to the various cognitive levels of questions as defined by Bloom's Taxonomy. Used by permission.

"Use of historical data nonemotional in nature has become a vital part of having students analyze what opinions they possess about contemporary issues."

Marsha Hobin

8
Clarifying What Is Important

Use of historical data nonemotional in nature has become a vital part of having students analyze what opinions they possess about contemporary issues. Space limitations do not permit a listing of issues we now face or we might encounter in the future, but one, especially our recent preoccupation with what has become known generally as the Watergate Affair, vividly illustrates how a contemporary issue can initiate a series of questions both relevant and historical in nature.

Watergate in particular caused many Americans for the first time in their lives to begin to question seriously the extent to which the many aspects of a presidential campaign should be kept secret from the general public. Others wondered about what should be expected of an innermost White House staff in performance of its duties. More and more Americans even wondered about to what extent answers to such questions were in keeping with basic American traditions and values while others were compelled to recall what those traditions and values were in the first place.

Another sidelight of the Watergate Affair focused on what kind of person should occupy our highest elective office in the future. Consid-eration of this question seems especially appropriate for mention here as an example which can involve student clarification of an issue through use of historical data nonemotional in nature. The issue deals with what qualifications, both conventional and nonconventional, students might feel the President of the United States should possess. This was a concern which caused much discussion among delegates to the Constitutional Convention of 1787 and certainly is an issue which has continued to plague us to the present. More than likely, it will continue to be an issue as functions of the executive branch of the federal government have become increasingly complex since the administrations of George Washington.

One suggested means of having students seriously ponder what kind of person should occupy our highest elective office is to first have them consider what kinds of qualifications *any* President should possess. This they can do by beginning with an examination of biographical data about fifteen prominent Americans, past and present. Student use of those data as they relate directly to desired presidential qualifications will be the focal point of the lesson plan and student materials in this chapter.

Sample Lesson for Teaching:
Who Is Qualified for the Presidency?

LESSON PLAN

Intended Student Audience   Upper elementary and secondary levels.

Suggested Time for Classroom Use of Materials   1–2 class periods (50–100 minutes).

Materials for Classroom Use   15 data cards (pp. 178–186), each containing biographical information about a well-known American. Student question sheet (p. 187).

Major Objectives for the Lesson

Objectives Within the Cognitive Domain   Upon completion of this lesson the students will:

Knowledge goals

(a) Know what qualifications a person should have in order to serve as President of the United States.

Skill development

(a) *Interpret* data presented on a series of cards.
(b) *Recognize a problem* about what kind of person would be best qualified to serve as President of the United States.
(c) *Formulate a hypothesis* in answer to the problem.
(d) *Test the validity of the hypothesis* by examining evidence concerning the qualifications of fifteen prominent Americans, six of whom served as Presidents.
(e) *Form a generalization* or more definite conclusion about what kind of person is best qualified to be President.

Objectives Within the Affective Domain   Upon completion of this lesson the students will:

Social participation

(a) Be *willing* to work in groups while examining and discussing available evidence on possible or actual presidential candidates.
(b) *Publicly* state additional factors in deciding who is qualified to serve as President.

Value Clarification

(c) *Identify* their own *values* in deciding who is best qualified to serve as President.

Teaching Suggestions

As long as our present form of constitutional government exists, many citizens will continue to be concerned about what kind of person is best qualified to be President. This lesson focuses on that concern by having students (1) examine biographical data about fifteen individuals prominent in past or present American history, (2) determine if they feel that data reflects the background a person should possess before assuming the Presidency, and (3) consider what other information should also be examined when one tries to decide who would be the best Chief Executive.

Omitted from the available data are the name, sex, and time when each of the fifteen people was active in American life. This has been done in an effort to eliminate from consideration as many preconceived notions or prejudices as possible while the students begin to clarify their thoughts about what makes a person well qualified to serve as President.

Available biographical data on each of the fifteen cards are under six general headings: (1) colleges attended, (2) religion, (3) major occupations, (4) years married, (5) number of children, and (6) age. Actual identities and brief summaries about the fifteen Americans whose biographical data appear in the cards follows:

Card 1 Data about *Warren G. Harding*, as of 1920. Harding served as Republican President from 1921 until his death in 1923. During the third year of his administration, the public learned of the Teapot Dome oil scandal and other graft in some federal agencies. Although his administration was racked with scandal, no evidence to date has linked him with it. Scholars of the Presidency generally regard his term as one of the most ineffective in American history.

Card 2 Data about *Franklin D. Roosevelt*, as of 1932. The American people elected Roosevelt President four times. Because of his New Deal programs designed to combat the severe financial depression of the 1930's and his leadership during World War II, many historians have classified him as one of the most effective Chief Executives ever to hold that office. Some of Roosevelt's critics, however, felt that he misused the power of the Presidency by exerting extensive political pressure on Congress in order to secure passage of the New Deal legislation. He served as President from 1933 until his death in 1945. An attack of polio in the early 1920's left Roosevelt's legs partially paralyzed for the remainder of his life.

Card 3 Data about *Cesar Chavez*, as of 1974. Chavez, the son of poor migrant-worker parents, is the founder and leader of the National Farm Workers Organization. He has been especially active in unionizing the Mexican-American farm workers of southern California. His most notable success occurred with the NFWO's nationwide boycott of non-union-picked lettuce.

Card 4 Data about *Chester A. Arthur*, as of 1881. Arthur, who was nominated on the Republican ticket for Vice-President in 1880 through the efforts of Roscoe Conkling and his powerful and corrupt New York machine, became President after the assassination of James A. Garfield. Although associated with a corrupt political group, Arthur surprised most people upon becoming Chief Executive by actively lobbying for civil service reform to abolish the spoils system and by vigorously prosecuting members of his own party accused of defrauding the federal government. He served as President from 1881 to 1885.

Card 5 Data about *Eleanor Roosevelt*, as of 1949. Eleanor Roosevelt, wife of Franklin D. Roosevelt, became one of our country's most active champions of the poor, minority groups, women's labor unions, and civil rights. As Franklin Roosevelt's wife, she constantly served as an unofficial advisor for many of his New Deal domestic policies. After her husband's death in 1945, Mrs. Roosevelt was appointed a United States delegate to the United Nations.

Data Cards: Set II

Card 1 Data about *Benedict Arnold*, as of 1779. Before he joined the British in their attempt to defeat the rebels during the American Revolution, Arnold had served George Washington with distinction during military campaigns from 1776 to 1779. Distressed with financial worries and with a feeling of not receiving adequate recognition from the Continental Congress for his services, he abandoned the American cause and became one of the most well-known traitors in American history.

Card 2 Data about *Martin Luther King, Jr.*, as of 1968. Before he was assassinated in 1968, the Reverend Martin Luther King, Jr., had become one of the most active champions of the non-violent civil rights movement. Beginning with his successful boycott of segregated city buses in Birmingham, Alabama, King rose to become leader of the Southern Christian Leadership Conference—one of the most effective organizations to lobby for the federal civil rights legislation during the 1960's.

Card 3 Data about *Andrew Jackson* as of 1829. According to most historians of American life, Jackson was one of our most forceful Chief Executives. As President, Jackson asserted the supremacy of the federal government when South Carolina attempted to nullify federal tariff laws. His opposition to any form of monopoly was evident in his veto of legislation to recharter the powerful and half-public Bank of the United States.

Card 4 Data about *Ida M. Tarbell*, as of 1904. Ida Tarbell was among the more well-known muckrakers of the Progressive Era. Her articles exposing corruption appeared in popular magazines of the day, such as *McClure's*, and her detailed history of the economic activities of John D. Rockefeller and his Standard Oil Company helped to influence later Progressive legislation designed to curb the evils of monopolistic business practices.

Card 5 Data about *Alexander Hamilton*, as of 1804. Until his death in a duel with Aaron Burr, he had served his country as an advisor to George Washington. His arguments for adoption of the federal Constitution were instrumental in its final approval. His financial genius helped to establish the young U.S. on a firm financial footing during its early years.

Card 1 Data about *George Washington*, as of 1789. To George Washington fell the difficult task of organizing a national government that had to unite what had been thirteen separate states into one country. Historians of his two administrations are in general agreement that he not only succeeded in his domestic and foreign policy programs but managed to calm, as best as anyone could, the constant Thomas Jefferson-Alexander Hamilton disputes over what powers the federal government should have exercised during its early years.

Card 2 Data about *Henry B. Gonzales*, as of 1974. Henry B. Gonzales was the first Texan of Mexican ancestry ever to serve in the United States House of Representatives. Since his first term, which began in 1961, he has been an active spokesman opposed to any legislation upholding or facilitating the principles of segregation. He has also been active in slum clearance projects, in advocating stricter controls on lobby groups, and in attempts to provide and maintain conservation of our natural resources.

Card 3 Data about *George C. Wallace*, as of 1974. Until the attempted assassination on his life crippled him in 1972, George Wallace had been an active and outspoken proponent of the cause of states rights. This was especially evident when he began his first term as Governor of Alabama (a position he now holds), ran as a presidential candidate for the American Party in 1968, and campaigned as a Democratic candidate for the Presidency in 1972. Since the attempt on his life, Wallace has been paralyzed from the waist down.

Card 4 Data about *Shirley Anita St. Hill Chisholm*, as of 1974. Shirley Chisholm in 1969 became the first black woman ever to serve in the United States House of Representatives. A Democrat and native New Yorker, Representative Chisholm has been especially active in the cause of black America and equal rights for all women. In 1972 she was a candidate for the Democratic nomination for President of the U.S.

Card 5 Data about *Abraham Lincoln*, as of 1861. With the exception of George Washington and Franklin D. Roosevelt, probably no other President ever entered office facing such immense problems as did Abraham Lincoln. Historians of Lincoln's life generally agree that he did as much as any Chief Executive could have to lead the Union to victory in the Civil War, and attempt to heal the wounds of that conflict for both the North and the South. On numerous occasions before and during his Presidency, Lincoln suffered periods of severe mental depression. His untimely assassination occurred in 1865.

In the case of Harding, Roosevelt, Arthur, Jackson, Washington, and Lincoln the biographical data conclude just before they became President. Data on Arnold end when he deserted the rebel cause during the American Revolution. Information on Tarbell concludes after she had reached the height of her journalistic career. Data on Hamilton continue until his death at the hands of Aaron Burr. Material on King concludes with his death in 1968. Information about Chavez, Gonzales, Wallace, and Chisholm continues to 1974 since all four are still active in American life.

Introducing the Lesson

Before the students examine information about those fifteen Americans, ask the class for definitions of the terms (1) "qualifications" and (2) "qualified." Other than the requirements listed in Article II, Section I of the Constitution, what qualifications should one look for in a candidate for President of the United States? Record all student responses on the board. Here you may need to remind the class that according to Article II, Section I of the Constitution, any candidate for the Presidency must be a natural born citizen of the United States, must be at least thirty-five years old, and must have been a resident of this country at least fourteen years before the presidential election. Nearly all of those individuals whose biographical data appear on the cards possessed or now possess those qualifications.

Predicted Outcome

Whatever the students' responses to the central question, they will have *recognized a problem for inquiry* (What kind of person would be best qualified to serve as President of the United States?) and *offered some hypotheses* or tentative answers (We can begin to make a listing of qualifications we would like a President to possess.).

Implementing the Lesson

Then tell the students that they will now examine some qualifications possessed by a selected number of prominent Americans. For this part of the lesson you may wish to have your students work in six groups with five members each, duplicating two copies of each of the three sets of cards. This would allow Groups One and Two to examine the five cards in Set I; Groups Three and Four to examine the cards in Set II; and Groups Five and Six to examine the cards in Set III. For ease of handling and care, you may wish to dry-mount and laminate each of the cards. Depending on the make-up of your class, you may also want to have each group contain representative proportions of what you regard as slow, average, and bright students and allow each group, once formed, to select a leader to report its findings.

Once each group has selected a leader, have the class notice that no names or dates appear on the cards, only basic biographical data about each of the still unidentified individuals. Emphasize that the data on the cards are about actual people who have been or are still active in American life. Then tell the students that as they examine the data about those Americans, they are to decide how they would answer the following two questions, which you should write on the board:

1. Based on the data your group has available about these five people, which one of them do you think would be *best* qualified to serve as President of the United States?
2. Which do you think would be *least* qualified to serve as President?

Emphasize that while seeking answers to these questions, group members should feel free to express different opinions.

Once the students have made their decisions, each leader should then be prepared to report group conclusions. When those reports are made to the remainder of the class, each leader should tell *why* the group decided what it did. Here the important thing is not who was selected but *why* those individuals were chosen.

As each group leader reports, write on the board the card numbers of those individuals selected as best and as least qualified. Once all leaders have reported, beside each number write the name of the person they have selected for each choice. As you write the names of those individuals, ask the students what they can recall about each. To assist student responses, you may wish to rely on the summary-descriptions for each card which previously appeared in this lesson plan. Continue this identification until all fifteen people have been discussed, regardless of whether they were selected as the best or least qualified to be President.

During discussions which identify each of those fifteen prominent Americans, some students may be surprised that the person they selected as best qualified may be an individual they normally would not have endorsed in an election for the Presidency. The reverse could be true of those selected as least qualified.

To facilitate additional student discussion of data on the cards, ask, for example, why lack of a college education did not seem to thwart George Washington's, Andrew Jackson's, or Abraham Lincoln's chances to become President? Apparently many people in 1789, 1828, or 1860 did not feel Washington, Jackson, or Lincoln needed a college degree. Why do you suppose most people then felt that way? Do we think a President today should have a college education? Can this illustrate how we have changed in some of our attitudes about the Presidency since 1860?

Next point out that some of the people whose biographical data appeared on the cards came from poor economical backgrounds. This was especially true of Cesar Chavez, Henry B. Gonzales, and Abraham Lincoln. Should this keep Chavez or Gonzales or have kept Lincoln from holding our highest elective office? Abraham Lincoln also suffered from periods of acute mental depression. Should this have kept him from becoming our Chief Executive?

Concluding the Lesson

Before students consider the next part of this lesson, ask them if they used their earlier criteria (offered at the beginning of this lesson and recorded on the board) as the basis for why they selected whom they did as best and as least qualified to serve as President. Is an examination of limited data such as those which appear on the cards sufficient for a person to decide which candidate is best qualified to serve as President? Would you now add other factors to your original listing before deciding who would make a good President?

Someone in the class will probably maintain that more should be known about a prospective candidate for the Presidency. When this occurs, tell the students that they will now consider what other factors should be examined. Here you will need to duplicate and give each student a copy of "Who Is Qualified To Be President?". While students consider the fifteen questions on that sheet, you may prefer to have them work in groups again with group leaders reporting the groups' conclusions to the class. The questions ask if age, religion, marital status, children, education, and previous occupations should be factors in selection of a presidential candidate. The questions also ask if other factors should be considered (for example, a candidate's position on issues of the day). The last question asks the students to then form a more definite conclusion about when someone is qualified to be President. To facilitate student discussion of these questions, you may also need to ask: Do you think some voters would consider *only* data similar to those which appeared on the cards? Are those kinds of data important when considering a presidential candidate? Should other factors also be considered? If not, why not? If so, what other factors should be considered?

Once the students have discussed answers to all those questions, ask them what factors they can now add to their original listing. Why would they now add those factors?

Predicted Outcomes

In completing this part of the lesson the students will have *tested the validity of their earlier hypotheses* (by determining if any factors should be added to their original listing) and, finally, will have *formed a generalization* (by reaching a more definite conclusion about what kind of person would be best qualified to serve as President).

By beginning with objective historical data, the students will also have become more aware of the need to further *clarify* and *analyze* what opinions they have about a question which might concern them today and which should definitely concern them in the future.

Additional Teaching Suggestions

Some of your students might wish to use this kind of card format and compile a new set for classroom consideration of candidates prominent in upcoming city, county, or state-wide elections. Each of those new cards should also contain the candidate's stand on issues of the day.

Another suggestion especially for use by upper secondary-level students would be for them to use questions 1–15 from "Who Is Qualified To Be President?" as the basis for conducting a school-wide poll. Once they have made their compilation, your class could then decide what conclusions could be reached about school population attitudes toward desirable presidential qualifications.

Additional References

If your students wish to learn more about the individuals whose biographical data appeared on the cards in this lesson, they can consult the references listed at the bottom of each card. Sources with a more detailed examination of those individuals can be found under *biographical* card catalogue listings in most school and public libraries.

For more information about our Chief Executives, see the special issue by *American Heritage Magazine* entitled "The Presidency" (August, 1964). *Inaugural Addresses of the Presidents of the United States from George Washington to John F. Kennedy*, U. S. Government Printing Office, 1961, is available in paperback for classroom use. Another paperback which would benefit your more advanced secondary-level readers is *America's Eleven Greatest Presidents*, Morton Borden (ed.), Rand McNally, 1971. The Borden volume contains selected articles on how historians have rated Washington, John Adams, Thomas Jefferson, Andrew Jackson, James Polk, Abraham Lincoln, Grover Cleveland, Theodore Roosevelt, Woodrow Wilson, Franklin Roosevelt, and Harry Truman.

For additional studies concerning *value clarification of political issues* and about *political socialization*, see Part IV, "Political Science in the School Program," in *Political Science in the Social Studies*, edited by Donald Riddle and Robert S. Cleary, 36th Yearbook of the National Council for the Social Studies. Especially appropriate for teachers of elementary and secondary students are the articles by David Easton, Jack Dennis, John Jarolimek, Jack Allen, and H.H. Wilson. Additional references to value clarification can be found in footnote 20 of Chapter 1 in this yearbook.

For a recent study closely related to the question of who is qualified to be President, see James David Barber's *The Presidential Character: Predicting Performance in the White House*, Prentice-Hall, 1972. Barber examines in detail the personalities of Presidents from William Howard Taft to Richard Nixon and concludes that a study of their backgrounds could have led us to predict how successful their administrations would have been *before* they became President.

**Student Materials for
"Who Is Qualified for the Presidency?"
follow on pages 178–187**

SET I—CARD 1

College attended: Ohio Central College

Religion: Protestant

Career: *Major occupations*

　　Editor of a newspaper
　　Director of a bank, lumber company and telephone company
　　State Senator
　　Lieutenant Governor
　　U. S. Senator
　　Temporary chairman of a major party's national convention

Years married: 29

Number of children: None

Age at this date: 55

Source: *Dictionary of American Biography,* Charles Scribners's Sons, VIII, 1932, pp. 252–254.

SET I—CARD 2

Colleges attended: Harvard University, Columbia University

Religion: Protestant

Career: *Major occupations*

　　Farmer
　　Lawyer
　　State Senator
　　Assistant Secretary of Navy
　　Governor
　　Vice-Presidential candidate

Years married: 27

Number of children: 6

Age at this date: 50

Source: *The National Cyclopaedia of American Biography,* XXXVII, University Microfilms, A Xerox Company, 1967, pp. 1–3.

SET I—CARD 3

College attended: None

Religion: Roman Catholic

Career: *Major occupations*

Director for a community service organization
Founder and director of a farm worker's organization
Served in United States Navy
Honored for distinguished public service by the American Institute for Public Service
Second recipient of the Martin Luther King, Jr. Nonviolent Peace Prize.

Years married: 29

Number of children: 8

Age at this date: 47

Sources: *Who's Who in America*, Marquis Who's Who, Inc., 1972, p. 550; *Current Biography Yearbook 1969*, H.W. Wilson Co., 1970, pp. 86–89.

SET I—CARD 4

College attended: Union College

Religion: Protestant

Career: *Major occupations*

School teacher
Lawyer
Served in U.S. Army
Aid to a Senator
Collector for Port of New York
Chairman of major party's state committee
Vice-President of U.S.

Years married: 22

Number of children: 3

Age at this date: 51

Source: *Dictionary of American Biography*, I, Charles Scribner's Sons, 1928, pp. 373–375.

SET I—CARD 5

College attended: None (Private secondary schooling in England)

Religion: Protestant

Career: *Major occupations*

    Teacher
    Journalist
    Member of a labor union (trade union league)
    United States delegate to the United Nations
    Chairman of the United Nations Commission on Human Rights
    Endorsed by a President for the Nobel Peace Prize
    Noted public speaker

Years married: 27

Number of children: 6

Age at this date: 65

Source: *Current Biography: Who's News and Why, 1949,* The H. W. Wilson Co., 1950, pp. 528–532.

SET II—CARD 1

College attended: None

Religion: Protestant

Career: *Major occupations*

Investor
Druggist
Bookseller
Brigadier General in U. S. Army

Years married: 1st spouse: 5 years until spouse's death
2nd spouse: 1 year

Number of children: 3 by first marriage

Age at this date: 38

Source: *Dictionary of American Biography*, I, Charles Scribner's Sons, 1928, pp. 362–367.

SET II—CARD 2

Colleges attended:

Morehouse College, A.B. and L.H.D.   Harvard University L.L.D.
Crozer Theological Seminary, B.D.   Central State College
University of Pennsylvania   Morgan State College
Boston University, Ph.D., D.D.

Religion: Protestant

Career: *Major occupations*

Protestant minister
Teacher of Philosophy at Harvard
President of a civil rights organization
1 of 10 outstanding men for the year according to *Time Magazine*
Nobel Peace Prize winner
Noted public speaker

Years married: 15   **Number of children:** 4   **Age at this date:** 37

Sources: *Current Biography Yearbook 1965*, H. W. Wilson Co., 1966, pp. 220–223, *Current Biography Yearbook 1968*, H. W. Wilson Co., 1969, p. 457.

SET II—CARD 3

College attended: None

Religion: No specific denomination

Career: *Major occupations*

Land speculator and farmer
Lawyer
Member of U. S. House of Representatives
U. S. Senator
U. S. Judge
Commander of U. S. Armed Forces

Years married: 38

Number of children: none

Age at this date: 62

Source: *Dictionary of American Biography*, Charles Scribner's Sons, IX, 1932, pp. 526–531.

SET II—CARD 4

Colleges attended: Allegheny College
Study at the Sorbonne, University of Paris in France

Religion: Protestant

Career: *Major occupations*

Teacher
Magazine editor
Associate editor of *America Magazine*
Member of American Historical Association
Member of American Economic Association
Served on two Presidents' councils
Author

Years married: Unmarried   **Number of children:** None
Age at this date: 47

Source: *The National Cyclopaedia of American Biography*, Vol. 14, University Microfilms, A Xerox Company, 1967, pp. 111–112.

SET II—CARD 5

College attended: Columbia University

Religion: No specific denomination

Career: *Major occupations*

Writer
Served as Lieutenant Colonel in Army
Lawyer
Member of a congress
Member of a constitutional convention
Secretary of the Treasury

Years married: 24

Number of children: 8

Age at this date: 47

Source: *Dictionary of American Biography*, Charles Scribner's Sons, VIII, 1932, pp. 171–179.

SET III—CARD 1

College attended: None

Religion: No specific denomination

Career: *Major occupations*

> Surveyor
> Farmer
> Commander-in-chief of Armed Forces
> Chairman of a constitutional convention
> Member of Congress

Years married: 40

Number of children: none

Age at this date: 57

Source: *Dictionary of American Biography*, XIX, Charles Scribner's Sons, 1936, pp. 509–513.

SET III—CARD 2

Colleges attended: St. Mary's, University of Texas

Religion: Roman Catholic

Career: *Major occupations*

> Public relations
> Probation officer
> Member of city council
> State Senator
> Member of U. S. House of Representatives
> Served in U. S. Navy

Years married: 34

Number of children: 8

Age at this date: 58

Sources: *Who's Who in America*, I, Marquis Who's Who Inc., 1972, p. 1187; *Current Biography Yearbook, 1964*, H. W. Wilson Co., 1965, pp. 157–159.

SET III—CARD 3

College attended: University of Alabama

Religion: Protestant

Career: *Major occupations*

    Lawyer
    State Assistant Attorney General
    State legislator
    U. S. judge
    State Governor
    Party candidate for Presidency
    Served in United States Air Force
    Noted public speaker

Years married: 1st spouse: 26 years until spouse's death
                     2nd spouse: 3 years

Number of children: 4 by first marriage   **Age at this date:** 55

Sources: *Who's Who in America*, II, Marquis Who's Who Inc., 1972, p. 3300; *Current Biography Yearbook 1963*, H. W. Wilson Co., 1964, pp. 454–456.

SET III—CARD 4

Colleges attended: Brooklyn College, Columbia University

Religion: Methodist

Career: *Major occupations*

    Teacher
    Consultant on child welfare
    Member of state legislature
    Member of U. S. House of Representatives
    Candidate for nomination for the Presidency
    Named outstanding graduate of Brooklyn College
    Noted public speaker

Years married: 25   **Number of children:** none   **Age at this date:** 40

Sources: *Who's Who in America*, I, Marquis Who's Who Inc., 1972, p. 559; *Current Biography Yearbook 1969*, H. W. Wilson Co., 1970, pp. 92–95.

SET III—CARD 5

College attended: None

Religion: No specific denomination

Career: *Major occupations*

Postmaster
Lawyer
U. S. Representative
Store owner
State Congressman
Served as Captain in U. S. Army
Noted public speaker

Years married: 19

Number of children: 4

Age at this date: 51

Source: *Dictionary of American Biography,* XI, Charles Scribner's Sons, 1933, pp. 242–249.

Discussion Questions
Who Is Qualified To Be President?

1. Should age be a factor in choosing to vote for a presidential candidate?

2. Should religion be a factor in choosing to vote for a presidential candidate?

3. Should marital status be a factor in choosing to vote for a presidential candidate?

4. Should the number of children be a factor in choosing to vote for a presidential candidate?

5. Should educational background be a factor in choosing to vote for a presidential candidate?

6. Should a person's sex be a factor in choosing to vote for a presidential candidate?

7. Should previous occupations be a factor in choosing to vote for a presidential candidate?

8. Should personal appearance be a factor in choosing to vote for a presidential candidate?

9. Should personality be a factor in choosing to vote for a presidential candidate?

10. Should ethnic background be a factor in choosing to vote for a presidential candidate?

11. Should other factors be considered? If so, which ones?

12. Do you think most voters consider all those factors? Tell why or why not. How could you begin to determine how many factors voters consider about presidential candidates?

13. What qualifications are *most* important to you when considering who might make a good President?

14. What qualifications are *least* important to you?

15. When, then, do you think someone is best qualified to hold an office such as the Presidency?

*"When you do something, no matter how minor, you
set off an explosion of reactions whose often conflicting
effects scatter in all directions."*

Allen P. Lawrence

9
Am I Relevant to History?:
The Environment

What is environmental education? Is it important? Is it a fit subject for the social studies? The following is an excerpt from a government publication on outdoor environmental education; it sounds as though it were written expressly for this yearbook:

Stop and think a minute about the phrase, "side effect." Our use of that phrase says a lot about the kind of world we think we are living in—and about our need for environmental education. It is not what "side effect" means that is important, but what it presumes.

There is no such thing as a "side effect"! Every effect is a direct effect. When you do something, no matter how minor, you set off an explosion of reactions whose often conflicting effects scatter in all directions. Each effect emanates directly from the original act, but the great majority of effects are ignored or called side effects because *they weren't planned for*. The effects you planned for you call your purpose.

When we permit ourselves to plan and act with our thoughts only on the purpose we want to achieve, we do not see things as they actually exist. The world is simply not a well-oiled machine whose task it is to carry out our every desire. It is complex and dynamic, with perpetually interacting factors. *The world is a process which man, as a factor, affects in complex and contradictory ways. It is a process whose factors affect people in equally complex and contradictory ways. Within process, all these factors and their innumerable side effects create a highly interacting, constantly changing and evolving system.*

Viewing the world process only in terms of our immediate purposes is a distorted and dangerous practice. We miss the big picture and see unnaturally isolated factors in a frozen world. True or false, reality or myth, the way man perceives his world will largely determine the way he feels and acts toward his fellow man. If his perception is sufficiently distorted, man's actions may become a threat to his welfare and, ultimately, his survival.

As our understanding of process increases, we begin to see that the world constitutes a whole system. In this system we find that if we push in one direction, we affect the entire system. We find, for example, that if we depend on automobiles for transportation, we have affected our politics, our foreign policy, our life style, art, value systems, concepts of friendship, our national and personal economy, and on and on. No one can say that all these effects are good or all bad; man's finest works are inextricably related to world conditions we are ashamed of. *There are trade-offs in everything we do.* The unfortunate thing is that we never considered what kind of world we were building when we made our decisions. It is time to start considering the world we are building.

Our human institutions, value systems, practices, and procedures are having difficulty keeping up with rapid interaction and change in technology, communication, medicine, and science. As we become less able to cope, the troubling effects of our social conditions become increasingly apparent. Like it or not, all these conditions affect all of us in one way or another.

Two basic approaches to these conditions have emerged. The first assumes that man will not survive, or maintain a life of any quality, unless strong societal controls are instituted. This approach maintains that basic freedoms interfere with effective environmental policies and practices; that individual freedoms lead inevitably to worldwide excess and, possibly, suicide.

The other approach holds that man can act with environmental responsibility, without resorting to ideological, medical, or behavioral controls. In fact, this theory maintains that basic freedoms are indispensable. Without them, all of man's creativity and talents will not be tapped—and today every resource we possess is needed. So, systems and institutions must be devised which encourage the free circulation of new ideas and attitudes which develop within us a deeper perception of ourselves, and which give us the individual strength to avoid the seeming inevitability of living according to whatever seems fashionable during the time of our lives. . . .

To live real lives in a real world, change and interaction cannot be rejected—we must accept them. We must develop a new framework for seeing, knowing, and doing which lets us live lives of process in a world of process. We must create institutions—especially educational institutions—which are not rigid, but which are responsibly structured to evolve and adapt to the dynamic needs of our time.

Environmental education is the process of experiences and observations which makes a person aware of his relationship to the total environment, and his responsibility to it. It is a lifelong learning process which influences behavior patterns in a way that promotes a life of quality with survival potential. It is not a subject to be taught; it is a way of seeing the world which enables us to get a handle on where we are and where we are going.

Environmental education is man-centered, not because man is the center of the world, but because

he is an indivisible part of world dynamics (a fact he is only beginning to recognize), and because he alone has the conscious ability to alter the world's balances.

It is man-centered because it is designed to heighten man's awareness and widen his options in forming behavior and value patterns.

Environmental education is man-centered because it is *education for living*. It is not education for science or for philosophy, or for vocations, or for art, or for crisis. We do not use the environment to teach about history. We use history to teach about the environment. There is nothing shocking about this. . . .

Interrelation and interdependence and *continuity and change* are the dynamics of the world of process. Although dynamic, ours is also a cohesive world, because change and interrelation do not appear from nothingness—they exist alongside continuity and interdependence.

Only at our peril are change and interaction ignored or opposed; similarly, we can never act as if we, or the things we affect, are in isolation. Education must be designed to facilitate change; it cannot be purely didactic, but must be a base for a life of learning. At the same time, education cannot promote the idea that "progress" is good for its own sake, or that there are no lessons or values of the past, applicable to the present and future. Neither can our actions ignore interdependence; if our culture or way of life is not responsibly based on biophysical realities—the web of life—its survival is seriously threatened.

No content material is irrelevant in education. Irrelevance exists because things are seen out of context, in a vacuum. If a thing is "taught" in a way that ignores continuity and interdependence, if it is not student-centered, *if it does not reveal its relationships with the student's life, it is irrelevant*. A child would be better on his own. Nothing can be *honestly* described in isolation—or taught that way.[1]

A word about science as our savior: Perhaps because of the extent we live surrounded by the products of technology, we expect science to rescue us from possible "eco-disaster." Expecting this is much like looking to science to solve a host of other problems that are as much social as scientific; for example, the arms race, drug addiction, and unemployment.

Even looking at the matter scientifically, environmental problems are nowhere near so simple, because nature is so stupendously huge and complex. All that science has brought to bear on the study of nature has still yielded no more than a glimmering of that enormity. Responsible ecologists are the first to concede that whatever they might suggest as technical solutions would be no more than tinkering, and some say their function is only to help us become more aware of how we are wrecking what nature built up over billions of years.

Here is a classic example of how the social studies can really matter. Scientific tinkering is no long-range answer. Instead we must change our whole approach to life; from "bigger and better" to ways of living that are more responsible, more meaningful, more in keeping with the eternal fitness of things. Social studies do not have the "answers" either. They do offer students an opportunity to approach a critical problem by dealing with what life is all about. Some will say this is the job of religion, and indeed the social studies, meaningfully approached, deal with some of the same issues as religion.

* * * * *

About critics of the environmental movement: Some have complained that it distracts from the needs of the poor and those of minority groups. One trouble with this argument is that pollution affects everyone, whether black, white, brown, or green; in fact, there is more of it concentrated in central-city ghettoes than anywhere else.

Other critics say that just when the disadvantaged are taking hope that they may finally come into possession of the prizes middle-class people enjoy, they could be cut off from those goods by the anti-materialism of the environmental movement. But is the middle class happy with what it has won—the suburban home filled with gadgets beyond the wildest dreams of ancient potentates? It is not. Otherwise, how to explain in those same suburbs, dope, divorce, alcoholism, and boredom? A Chinese philosopher said centuries ago, "The greatest tragedy in life is, not to have your heart's desire; the second greatest tragedy is, to have it."

Such an argument may seem like pretty weak soup to the inmates of a ghetto—they are subjected to the same pitch about utopian suburbia as everyone else. But a turnaround in the nation's values (a return to older values?) may save them in the long run from the disillusionment of today's middle class. And the theme in the environmental movement of our common humanity should help dispel the prejudice that has contributed to second-class status. The message is ancient: Things don't make happiness.

Finally it needs to be said that saving the environment may be at once both the most difficult thing to accomplish, and the most difficult to teach about: "Those who are concerned about the quality of life will have to take risks and work hard to improve it. Do not think otherwise."[2]

FOOTNOTES

[1]National Park Service, *National Environmental Study Area: A Guide.* Superintendent of Documents, 1972, pp. 18, 21-23, 34.

[2]*Ibid.*, p. 5.

Sample Lesson for Teaching:
Am I Relevant to History?:
The Environment

LESSON PLAN

Intended Student Audience

Grades 5–12.

**Suggested Time for
Classroom Use of Materials**

2–5 weeks. Under certain scheduling arrangements could fill an entire year, if extensive environmental projects are undertaken, or if this study leads to one of the comprehensive programs listed in the bibliography.

Materials for Classroom Use

Seventeen handouts containing readings/discussion topics (pp. 198–214).

Major Objectives for the Lesson

**Objectives
Within the Cognitive Domain**

Upon completion of this lesson the students will:

Knowledge Goals

(a) Know the causes for several major kinds of environmental problems.
(b) Know a variety of solutions to environmental problems.

**Objectives
Within the Affective Domain**

Upon completion of this lesson the students will:

Social participation

(a) Be *willing* to share knowledge from library research with classmates.
(b) Be *willing* to participate in class discussions.

Value clarification

(c) Be *willing* to express personal opinions about approaches to solving environmental problems and to state personal values as they bear on environmental problems.
(d) Be *willing* to hear out and consider the viewpoints of others on those topics.
(e) Have developed a feeling of responsibility for the environment.

Teaching Suggestions

Lesson Overview

A set of lesson plans for a detailed study of the environment would take up far more than this short space. The unit is designed first to bring out what students already know about environmental problems, then to guide them in gathering more information about the problems. That is the usual emphasis of environment study but is only introductory here. This unit focuses on some of the larger implications of environmental problems, and especially on what people can do about them—young people, and the adults they will soon be.

Numerous open-ended questions point to the broad nature of the environmental issue. There are no pat answers to the questions, because there are none to the problems themselves. Instead, students must weigh options and values in the style of the "New" New Social Studies, as exemplified throughout this yearbook.

Because the environmental issue is so crucial to our survival, teachers are encouraged to consider working with students in taking some action toward environmental reform. If time, the law, or local convention make this impossible, there are plenty of ways this study can be broadened; for example, by undertaking some phases of outdoor environmental study suggested under "Additional Resources." Another approach would be to work toward the implementation of a comprehensive environmental study program, also suggested in "Additional Recources."

The handouts (pp. 198–214) are intended to be used in sequence, but this is not necessary if the teacher chooses to leave some out or change the order. The students' academic level would be the main determinant.

Additional References

1. **School sites:** This is the most easily overlooked resource for environmental study. A modern plant in a spacious, park-like setting would suggest itself for this purpose, but all too many a school is a dreary mausoleum left over from the nineteenth century, and jammed up against the street, "still standing beside the road, like a ragged beggar sunning."[*] Fortunately, no matter how old and run-down the building, how much the grounds are bare, any site can be used. For information on what other schools have done, get *Environmental Education/Facility Resources*. Price: $2.00. Educational Facilities Laboratories, 477 Madison Avenue, New York, N.Y. 10022.

For detailed plans on how to develop open grounds for environmental study, get *Planning Guide for School Sites*. Price: $1.25. Environmental Science Center, 5400 Glenwood Avenue, Minneapolis, Minnesota 55422.

2. **Outdoor study, away from school:** Environmental study is *not* just nature study or conservation study; it is about how people affect the total environment, and how the environment, in turn, affects people. One way to make education relevant is to get it out of the schools: "It is a very recent idea, and a crazy one,

---

[*]Educational Facilities Laboratories, *Environmental Education/Facility Resources*, 1972, p. 10.

that the way to teach our young people about the world they live in is to take them out of it and shut them up in brick boxes."[*]

The National Park Service has a program called National Environmental Study Areas. NESA's are natural and/or cultural locations with materials and ongoing procedures for studying the environment. A NESA usually serves many schools in a wide area. To find out if there is one near you, and how to get one established if there is not, write U.S. National Park Service, Department of the Interior, Washington, D.C. 20240.

The Park Service also has materials for outdoor use in its program NEED (National Environmental Education Development). NEED materials combine environmental studies with all other subjects (K–8), and are good for all kinds of schools, including those in the inner city.

There are permanent regional centers for environmental study scattered all over the country. Some are NESA's, some are not. At some the students spend a few hours, at others they stay overnight, and at certain ones they spend several days. The students they serve range from kindergarten through college. Some are in the inner city and some are in the wilderness. For more information get, *Environmental Education/Facility Resources.* Price: $2.00. Educational Facilities Laboratories, 477 Madison Ave., New York, N.Y. 10022.

3. **Teenage organizations:** The High School Project puts interested students in touch with local resource persons to help organize and work for the environment in the school and community. High School Project, 3130 M Street, N.W., Washington, D.C. 20007. Students who live in the following states can call toll-free: Connecticut, Delaware, Maryland, New Jersey, New York, North Carolina, Pennsylvania, Ohio, Virginia, West Virginia, District of Columbia. Call 800-424-9216.

The Ecology Council of America helps form local chapters of high school students (grades 9–12). Members carry out local environmental improvement projects. The organization provides a variety of helpful materials on how to get things done, publishes a newsletter, and awards prizes to local groups. ECO America, Room 2200, 99 Park Avenue, New York, N.Y. 10016.

The STEP (Students Toward Environmental Participation) program is sponsored by the U.S. National Park Service and the U.S. National Commission for UNESCO. STEP members are high school students who are trained by the organiation to establish local sites for environmental study, teach younger children environmental awareness, and evaluate local needs for special projects. Students Toward Environmental Participation, U.S. National Park Service, Department of the Interior, Washington, D.C. 20240.

4. **Other organizations:** The best source for international, national, and state organizations is the *Conservation Directory,* published annually by the National Wildlife Federation, 1412 16th Street, N.W., Washington, D.C. 20036. Price: $2.00.

A shorter directory is available for 15¢ from Public Inquiries, Office of Public Affairs, Environmental Protection Agency, Washington, D.C. 20460. Title: *Groups That Can Help.*

---

[*]National Education Association and National Park Service, *A Guide to Planning and Conducting Environmental Area Workshops.* Superintendent of Documents, 1972, p. 8.

5. **Study programs:** Educators wishing to develop comprehensive programs would do well to start with Stanley L. Helgeson, *et al., Environmental Education: Programs and Materials* (PREP Report #33). Superintendent of Documents, Washington, D.C. 20402. Price: $1.00.

Another guide is *Programs in Environmental Education.* National Science Teachers Association, 1201 16th Street, N.W., Washington, D.C. 20036.

NEED (National Environmental Education Development) is a program of the National Park Service that combines environmental studies with all other subjects (K–8). Both indoor and outdoor activities are included. Useful to all schools, including those in the inner city.

GEE! (Group for Environmental Education, Inc.) has a number of interesting materials for problem-solving and for using the ordinary facilities of school and community. Its series of workbooks intended for the 7th grade has been used by architecture students at the University of North Dakota, and *Time* magazine says that Book Seven is ". . . the best primer on architecture and urban planning yet published in the U.S."*

The Institute for Environmental Education draws upon experience with some of the first and most successful programs in the country. It specializes in helping schools start from scratch. Institute for Environmental Education, 8911 Euclid Avenue, Cleveland, Ohio 44106.

The Brevard County Schools, Cocoa, Florida, have developed a 296-page guide for environmental study: *Social Studies Resource Units.* Available as ERIC microfiche #ED 067 304. Order from Leasco Information Products, Inc., 4827 Rugby Avenue, Bethesda, Maryland 20014. Also from the Brevard County Schools is *The Curious Entanglement of Law, Politics, and the Environment* (369 pages). ERIC microfiche #ED 068 339.

For financial and other kinds of aid in organizing environmental studies, get *Environmental Education: Reference Sources for the Development of Programs and Sites* (free). Write U.S. National Park Service, Division of State and Private Assistance, Department of the Interior, Washington, D.C. 20240.

6. **Government publications:** Order from: Superintendent of Documents, Washington, D.C. 20402:

- *Environmental Education: Education That Cannot Wait.* Stock # 1780-0809. Price: 30¢. 1971.

- *National Environmental Study Area: A Guide.* Stock # 2405-0484. Price: 75¢. 1972.

- *Establishing Trails on Rights-of-Way.* Stock # 1 66.2:T 68/3 S/N 2416-00052.

- *Annual Report to the President and to the Council on Environmental Quality.* Stock #4000-0278. 1972.

- *Clean Air: It's Up to You.* 1973. (no other information shown)

- *Don't Leave It All to the Experts.* Stock #0-478-748. Price: 55¢. 1972.

- *Community Action for Environmental Quality.* Price: 60¢.

---

*Quoted in Eliot Levinson and Saul Yanofsky, "After the Water Is Clean (or Not), Then What? How? and Why?", *Social Education*, January, 1971, p. 71.

7. **Books:** So many are available that it is hardly proper to single any out. However, one is unusually commendable for its comprehensiveness, and also because it is especially useful to youth in career planning: Odom Fanning, *Opportunities in Environmental Careers.* New York: Universal Publishing Corp., 1971.

For a bibliography of paperbacks suitable for stocking a school bookstore, see the book cited above, pp. 230–35.

8. **Periodicals** (partial list): *Air Pollution Control Association Journal, American City Magazine, Atmospheric Environment, Audubon Magazine, Desalination, Ecological Monographs, Ecology, Environment, Environmental Education, Environmental Science and Technology, Journal of Environmental Health, Journal of Soil and Water Conservation, Journal of the Water Pollution Control Federation, National Wildlife, Mother Earth News, Natural History, Oceanology International, Pollution Abstracts, Public Works Magazine, Radiological Health Data and Reports, Sierra Club Bulletin, Water and Wastes Engineering, Water Research,* and *Water Resources Research.*

Not included: general science publications.

See also: *Social Education,* January, 1971 (entire issue). On environmental study in general. *Social Education,* April, 1972 (entire issue). On population.

9. **Audiovisual:** The National Park Service has over 30 films it will lend for the price of the return postage. An annotated catalogue is available. The National Park Service, Department of the Interior, Washington, D.C. 20240.

Numerous proprietary companies are producing multimedia kits and simulation games. See their catalogues.

10. **Simulation games:** A 26-page annotated list from the University of Michigan: *A Selected List of Urban and Environmental Gaming Simulations.* ERIC microfiche # ED 067 228. Order it from Leasco Information Products, Inc., 4827 Rugby Ave., Bethesda, Maryland 20014.

11. **Kits and instructions for testing the air and water:** Order, *How to Investigate the Environment in the City: Air and Water,* from the National Science Teachers Association, 1201 16th Street, N.W., Washington, D.C. 20036.

12. **Miscellaneous:**

Inexpensive materials on population control for older students: Optimum Population, Inc., Box 27, Charlotte, Vermont 05445.

Environmental Education/Facility Resources. Examples of sites and programs used in environmental study. Educational Facilities Laboratories, 477 Madison Avenue, New York, N.Y. 10022. Price: $2.00.

Law and Taxation—A Guide for Conservation and Other Nonprofit Organizations. Conservation Foundation, 1717 Massachusetts Avenue, N.W., Washington, D.C. 20036. Price: $1.00.

How to Plan an Environmental Conference. League of Women Voters Education Fund, 1730 M Street, N.W., Washington, D.C. 20036. Free.

Clean Water—It's Up to You. Izaak Walton League, 1800 North Kent Street, Arlington, Virginia. 22209. Free.

The National Wildlife Federation has a number of useful and attractive materials, including discovery units and reprints from its children's magazine, *Ranger Rick*. National Wildlife Federation, 1412 16th Street, N.W., Washington, D.C. 20036.

The Federation also has reprints of its *Environmental Quality Index*, published in its magazine, *National Wildlife*, in 1969, 1970, 1971, and 1973. Interestingly presented and highly adaptable for classroom use.

A complete bibliography of books and films, thoroughly annotated: *Education Product Report*, nos. 33/34, 1971, pp. 19-75.

To keep up with your students on little ways to help the environment get: *71 Things You Can Do to Stop Pollution:* Keep America Beautiful, Inc., 99 Park Avenue, New York, N.Y. 10016. Also, *Small Steps in the Right Direction: Some Things You Can Do to Improve the Environment*. Information sheets, Nos. 1 and 2: Johnny Horizon News Bureau, 1825 K Street, N.W., Washington, D.C. 20006.

For information about electric vehicles: Electric Vehicle Council, 90 Park Avenue, New York, N.Y. 10016. (General information.) Electric Auto Association, 815 Seamaster Drive, Houston, Texas 77058. (On conversion of internal combustion autos to electric, and general information.)

**Student Materials for
"Am I Relevant to History?: The Environment"
follow on pages 198-214**

Am / Relevant To History?

YOU ARE . . .

    If you understand how serious the environmental problem has become, and . . .

    If you learn how not to offend Mother Nature and how not to be thoughtless of other people, and . . .

    If you are willing to help bring about changes in society that will save the environment for everyone.

BUT IF YOU DO NOTHING . . .

    There may not be any future generations to have a history.

OR

    The world might not make it to even the next generation (YOUR children's generation).

OR

    Your own life may be cut short, and you wouldn't enjoy even that part very much.

Time is running out on the environmental problem. Some scientists
say that it is already too late, but most say the next few
years will tell the tale. That is why the 1970's
have been named "The Environmental
Decade." YOUR generation
may just be the most
important in the
history of
the
world.
EVER.

ARE _YOU_ RELEVANT TO HISTORY?

Our Abused Planet: Finding out more about the problems so you will know what you can do about them.

How much does your class already know about the conditions listed below? Get it together: While different ones tell what they know, someone can keep a running list on the board. Don't forget to include evidence about your own school and community.

- Air pollution
- Water pollution
- Solid waste disposal and litter
- Resource depletion
- Noise
- "Eye pollution" or "uglification"
- The "population explosion"

Next go to the school library and find out more. Magazine articles will be the best source. Find them by using the *Reader's Guide to Periodical Literature.*

Plan to tell the class later what you or your group found. The teacher will help decide who works on which topics.

Take notes in whatever form you want, but DO NOT COPY from the sources—use your own words.

Be on the lookout for ideas about WHY these problems exist: What do our habits, attitudes, and values have to do with all this?

Like little drops in a big bucket, the little acts of many people can add up to an environment ruined or an environment saved. Be looking also for little things people can do to improve the environment. The teacher may want to have a "brainstorming" session on these from time to time.

Here are some additional topics you could work on in the library. Your teacher will help decide who works on which topics.

1. Go through some recent editions of general-interest magazines and spot the ads for products or services, the making or using of which tends to damage the environment.

    Then try to reach some conclusions about connections between profits and the environment. Who stands to gain by using these goods and services? Who stands to lose?

2. Life in our cities today has a make-believe quality about it. Our gadgets and the services of other people protect us from every discomfort, every effort, every inconvenience. Meanwhile we are cut off from the majesty, beauty, and power of nature that is the real world. All this is dangerous in that it means we have grown so used to all this protection and support that we may not be able to function in the face of even the temporary failure of our crutches.

    To test the validity of this idea, check some news accounts of people caught in a power failure, or in a similar situation.

    Find some passages, in sources like the following, that show how independent we once were (and could be again):
    Thoreau's *Walden*
    Old Farmer's Almanacs
    A Boy Scout manual or any book on how to survive in the wilderness

3. In many countries people cannot afford our machines and products even if they wanted them. What of it? How do people survive in those countries?

    Use several issues of *National Geographic* (or other sources) to find out how people in poor countries satisfy their needs. What are likely to be the effects on the environment? On physical and emotional health?

4. How old is respect for nature? You may be surprised to learn that it is not just an "in" thing.

    Ask the librarian to help you find books of quotations or other works so you can assemble a collection of voices from the past. Examples:

    But ask the beasts and they will teach you; the birds
    of the air and they will tell you; or the plants of the
    earth, and they will teach you; and the fish of the sea
    will declare unto you.
    —*Job 12:7*

    Nature is not governed except by obeying her.
    —*Sir Francis Bacon*

These are discussion topics to help you understand some basics of the environmental problem. If you work in groups, make sure your group comes to some conclusions and can support them.

1. What do these situations have in common?
   - A community dumps raw sewage into a river, damaging the ecological balance of the water and sending pollutants downstream.
   - A car owner disconnects an emission control device to get better gas mileage.
   - A homeowner votes against a bond issue to overhaul the community's garbage disposal system because this would cause his taxes to go up.

   What is needed that would make incidents like these rare?

2. There never was a cause, no matter how good, that did not have its critics. Today some are saying that the environmental movement detracts from other needs, like those of the poor, the sick, the aged, and minorities. Where do most of the people in those groups live? Where is the environment the worst?

   By now you have probably realized that some changes in public attitudes will be necessary before the environment can be made right. What changes? Are they likely to help those groups at the same time? Can their needs and those of the environment be met at the same time? Why or why not?

3. See if you agree: We decided to reach the moon in ten years and did it in nine, so we should have no trouble solving our environmental problems. Exactly what is the "environmental problem"? Who is responsible for it? Which parts can science and technology do nothing about? The air and water belong to the whole world. How much responsibility for maintaining them belongs to the United States?

4. Would we all be better off today if modern science and technology had never come along? Exactly what is good about life today because of them? Make a list. Are those things worth keeping if they cost us damage to the environment? How much worth? How much cost?

5. People and pollution usually go together. What is good—really good—about living in a city? How do we get our ideas about where is the best place to live?

What If No One Gives In?

The individual's importance to society can be explained by an idea that environmentalists frequently refer to as "the tragedy of the commons." It comes from a pamphlet on population written in 1833, and goes something like this:

In the villages of both England and New England it was a general practice to set aside a piece of land called the "commons," where all the farmers could graze their cattle. Sooner or later the number of cattle would approach being more than the land could support. Each farmer would figure that if he added one more animal it would not affect very much the amount of food available for each animal, but the farmer stood to gain considerably by that addition. The trouble was that all—or many—of the farmers did the same, the commons was ruined, and no one benefited.

Can you see how the same principle applies, for example, to air pollution by automobiles today? To the reading that follows?

> There is an approved American way of doing things that has produced a high degree of freedom from material want and, at the same time, a rising number of crises that threaten not only this freedom but most of our other freedoms as well. Social custom teaches us to strive for a privately owned, single-family home in the suburbs, possessing a garage of at least two-car capacity, and filled with "conveniences" that assure us of more "leisure" time. Advertising urges us to consume and dispose. We spend much of our free time as spectators watching professional performers or in vigorous activity behind the wheel of some power-driven machine—a car, boat, or snowmobile. Life is frantic. Is this what you want? The decision is yours and you are free to say "no". [1]

If not enough farmers gave up grazing their cattle on the commons, it was destroyed, but the farmers could easily change to other agricultural activities and suffer little or no important consequences. But our situation with the environment today is literally a matter of life and death.

What will be the tragedy tomorrow if not enough people say no (or yes) to the right environmental questions? According to the reading above? What do your answers tell you about the needs of the environmental movement?

---

[1] Adapted from Paul Swatek, *User's Guide to the Protection of the Environment*, Ballantine Books, Inc./A Division of Random House, Inc., copyright © 1970, p. 9. Used by permission.

What Are Your Needs and Greeds?

Can you tell the difference?

Assume that you could not get to a store for the next year. Beginning now—before the year starts—you must buy supplies to last for 12 months. Assume that you already have a simple, empty shelter and the clothes you are wearing. You have only $120 to spend.

Then go to whichever stores you need to and make up a list of what you would buy, naming item, quantity and cost. It might be convenient to "shop" first at a large department store and then a supermarket, or at a large discount house that includes a grocery department.

Bring your list to class and be prepared to discuss these questions: How do you explain all those other items in the stores: in terms of the economy; the advertising industry; our dependence/independence; the environment?

OR

Live for a week in the simplest fashion possible. Report to the class your reactions to doing without the things you dropped.

OR

Imagine a typical family of four going through a day's activities. List in detail the goods and services they would use. Which ones would you say are necessary, and which unnecessary? Be prepared for some argument from the class about your choices.

For some people life in the city has become so artificial and so injurious to the environment that the only answer is a retreat to nature. If you were to abandon the city for a life away from civilization, what kind of person would you have to be to make a go of it? Many have tried it in recent years, but have given up and returned to the city.

Without going that far, what are some ways you could simplify your life style and live more in harmony with nature? For more ideas, see the magazine *Mother Earth News*, P.O. Box 38, Madison, Ohio 44057.

What Can *I* Do—Just Me Alone?
Attention: Word Mechanics

Are you good with the written word? What are some ways you could use that gift for the cause of the environment? Example: You could volunteer to write a regular column for a local newspaper on conditions in your community. If the paper already has a column, you could contribute to it or write occasional articles. You might even be hired eventually. If you don't get any money for your work, you would still be making a contribution. What could you do right in your school?

Here's another idea for someone especially creative: Much of what is written on the environment is filled with boring statistics. Could you take figures and turn them into interesting reading? Example:

> Every 7-1/2 seconds a new American is born. He is a disarming little thing, but he begins to scream loudly in a voice that can be heard for seventy years. He is screaming for 26,000,000 tons of water, 21,000 gallons of gasoline, 10,500 pounds of meat, 28,000 pounds of milk and cream, 9,000 pounds of wheat, and great storehouses of all other foods, drinks, and tobaccos. These are his lifetime demands on his country and its economy. . . .

> He is hailed as an enormous consumer in a nation that accounts for one-fifteenth of the earth's people but consumes half of its total product. In one year we use up enough big trees to build a ten-foot boardwalk thirty times around the world at the equator. . . .

> Up to the time he has requisitioned his last foot of lumber for his coffin and his three-by-six plot of land (probably arable), . . . an awe-inspiring amount of the soil's resources (for all things come from the soil) will have passed through him like earth through an earthworm and ended up in the watercourses and in the ever-mounting junk piles of the nation. [1]

Is radio or television your thing? In 1970 the Federal Communications Commission ruled that stations must spend a "reasonable amount of time" on environmental issues. See that your local stations do. If you have the talent you can volunteer to do environmental spots or to write for them. At least as a citizen you can demand that a station stick to the regulations, and if it does not, report the station to the FCC: Federal Communications Commission, 1919 M Street, N.W., Washington D.C. 20554.

A lot of people have talents but don't realize it. If you are not too certain about yours, how could you find out?

---

[1] From *Moment in the Sun* by Robert Rienow and Leona Train Rienow. Copyright © 1967 by Robert Rienow and Leona Train Rienow. Reprinted by permission of The Dial Press.

What Can *I* Do—Just Me Alone?
You Against "They": Business

Who Owns American Business?

What about the small businesses in your own community—the dress shops, the garages, the toy stores, and so on? How ordinary are the people who own them? For example, how do they spend their day? What part of town do they live in? If you don't know, how could you find out?

And big business? Who owns companies like General Motors, General Mills, and General Electric? You may be surprised to learn that there are over 1,250,000 shareholders in General Motors (think of writing that many dividend checks every three months!), and that anyone can buy stock in over 5,000 companies. What do the companies do with the profits they make? They give away billions, and often receive tax benefits by doing so. If you go to college on a scholarship, it is possible that the money will have come from business; if you don't have a scholarship, you still benefit from the donations business makes directly to the college.

Some stock sells for as little as $5 per share. What rights go with owning stock? Even if you have only one share, you are a stockholder and have the power to vote on motions other stockholders make, and to make motions yourself.

The communists often promise what might be called "people's capitalism" to countries they are trying to take over, that is, ownership and control of the economy by the people. If we gave up the system we now have for communism, what would be the loss or gain?

If you have some money saved, you are a "capitalist" already. When you go to work full-time you will have more, unless you are very careless with your money. How can you use your savings to help improve the environment?

The Power in Your Pocketbook

Today companies that pollute worry about what the public thinks. Can you see why? Some run costly ads that say they really aren't harming the environment. Find ads like these in magazines or newspapers, or take notes from some you see on television. Exactly what do they say and how do they say it? One way to find out if a company is misrepresenting is to check some of the many environmentalist magazines now in publication. *Environmental Education,* for example, has a regular feature called, "Debunking Madison Avenue."

You can affect what companies do about the environment by buying or not buying their goods. Or can you? Do you *have* to buy what a polluter manufactures? Why or why not?

What Can *I* Do—Just Me Alone?
What Price To Pay?

Make 'Em Squirm

Often someone who has just begun to think about the environmental problem pops up with something like, "Hey! If industries start installing pollution control equipment, they will have to charge higher prices!" But suppose pollutants could be turned into useful products—to reduce the cost of pollution control or even make a profit. They can. And suppose a company knew of that possibility, but did not try it. Why might that be? One reason could be that we are all creatures of habit, including companies' boards of directors. We often tend to do a thing today because we did it yesterday. "Business as usual" and, with it, pollution as usual just won't do anymore. What could be some other reasons? How could you go about getting a company to follow the lead of those that are doing something about pollution?

Who pays for all the goodies that industries produce—that flood of gadgets, chemicals, machines, junk foods, aerosol sprays, flashy cars, etc.? We do. Can we afford them? It all depends. Are there any other choices than these?

- Lots of goodies, lots of pollution
- Fewer goodies, less pollution
- Lots of goodies, less pollution, but with higher prices and taxes

Suppose you decide on higher prices and taxes. *Exactly* what are you willing to pay higher prices for? *Exactly* what products and activities would you tax (to limit their use)? *Exactly* what should be done with the tax money? Environmental decisions like these are called "trade-offs." They are necessary because you cannot have your environmental cake and eat it too.

What Can I Do—Just Me Alone?
You Against "They": Government

A Funny Kind of "People's Republic"

Neither business nor government need be thought of as an enemy, because fortunately in a democracy we control both. If we don't, whose fault is it? Consider an opposite kind of government such as a dictatorship. A communist dictatorship is much like any other kind, and the world has had dictatorships since the beginning of civilization. For example, in his novel about Russia, entitled *Dr. Zhivago*, Boris Pasternak has the central character fall in love with the communist government when it first starts, because of the way he thought it could get things done for the people (later he changes his mind): "What splendid surgery! You take a knife and with one masterful stroke you cut out all the old things that are wrong." [1] That should mean that Russia has no environmental problems—after all, who wants to be poisoned? But consider, for example, that the Soviet Union, organized around central planning, has created some of the most hideous cityscapes on earth, while ravaging the countryside with strip mining, industrial pollutants, and all the other environmental crimes that here in the United States are blamed on selfish capitalist interests. [2]

Communist governments are always calling themselves the "People's Republic" of this and the "People's Republic" of that. Why would the people in a "People's Republic" put up with the conditions like the ones described above? Review the reasons for pollution in this country. What could be some causes that are common to all countries that have pollution?

Where Is "The Government"?

In our country government can be made to do whatever is needed about pollution, but only if we the people make it happen. Unless you live in Washington, D.C., the environmental problems that concern you the most are the ones where you live. Look up "government" in the yellow pages of your telephone book (Washington, D.C. excluded) and count: How many entries are there under "city," "county," "state," and "United States?" What do your answers tell you about how far away "the government" is? What does this tell you about curing a sick environment?

---

[1] Boris Pasternak, *Doctor Zhivago*, Pantheon Books/A Division of Random House, Inc., copyright © 1950, p. 194. Used by permission.

[2] See Max Way, "How to Think About the Environment," in Sheridan D. Blau and John V. Rodenbeck eds.), *The House We Live In*, The Macmillan Co., 1971, 25.

What Can I Do—Just Me Alone?
A Tale of Two Cities

In Anmoore, West Virginia, one citizen, Dale Hagedorn, began a movement to stop a local factory from filling the air with black smoke and soot. Formerly the company treated complaints with, "Unfortunately, our product is black." Mr. Hagedorn reflects,

> I guess I thought all a citizen could do was write a letter of protest. It was somewhat demoralizing. The feeling was that the town was going down, but everybody else thought, "What's the use?" [1]

But he didn't give up. He began to distribute a newsletter to fellow citizens, and this led to the formation of an organization. The group filed a lawsuit against the company on the grounds that every citizen has the right to breathe clean air. Mr. Hagedorn:

> It's been a thrilling thing for us. Indeed, the citizen does matter—he matters very much. He has freedom of speech, and by golly he can use it—and use it with tremendous impact. I've learned that little people can count if they don't lie down or quit. [2]

This problem had been going on for years. Do you think it would have been solved without Mr. Hagedorn's efforts? Why or why not? Would it have been solved later without him? Why or why not?

Quite a different story came out of Steubenville, Ohio, in 1970. In the summer of that year the government ranked Steubenville as having the dirtiest air in the country. The town was shocked, but did nothing: the local steel companies provided most of the smoke, but also most of the jobs. Months went by. When primaries for city council came up, 11 candidates ran, but none took a stand on air pollution.

In one town there was an individual who spoke out. In the other there was none. Could this be the whole explanation for action in one, and inaction in the other? What other kinds of information would you want before deciding?

What risks does an individual take in speaking out against powerful institutions? Where are the risks greater—in a small town or a big city? Why? If the risks are great, why might a person take them?

How could the decision to take such a step be influenced by personal factors, like married/single, man/woman, parent/childless, rich/poor, old/young?

---

[1] National Geographic Society, *As We Live and Breathe*. National Geographic Society, 1971, p. 215. Used by permission.

[2] *Ibid.*, p. 217.

Getting Organized

How do you accomplish something that you can't do alone? The name of the game is ORGANIZE.

(Isn't it enough to "throw the rascals out" and put in better people?)

Here is an idea of what goes on at the centers of power, while you are trusting your vote to do everything:

> In the day-to-day practice of American politics, . . . the voices most heard will be those of organized groups with officers responsible for knowing what is going on. The potential interest groups have influence only because those who make decisions know they are out there and must not be offended—too much.
>
> If a group does not organize and post a guard, decisions will be made without the knowledge of the members of the potential group. They wake to the news that they may be dying of pollution; a slice is torn from a park for a wider freeway; the estimated time of arrival of doom has been advanced again. The lesson for those who want to save the environment is plain. They should organize and hire a guard, a staff to keep watch against offenders, an information center to keep members informed, and a quarterback to call plays for the offense in legislatures, stockholders' meetings, local governments, state governments, national government, executive, legislative, and judicial branches, factories, retail stores, banks, insurance companies. Decisions about the use of the environment are made in all these places and more, and decisions can be influenced best while they are being made. [1]

If you are ready to do something besides vote, you can start tomorrow. Organizations are already at work in every state. You can join one. If one is needed in your community you can help form it. You don't have to be any particular age to make a contribution. What are the government and business institutions in your own community that need watching?

---

[1] James L. McCamy, *The Quality of the Environment*, The Free Press, Div. of The Macmillan Co., 1972, pp. 198–199. Used with permission of the publisher.

Take Action

- Suppose a candidate is running on an environmental platform, but not enough people are responding. How could you help—either as an individual or with others in an organization?
- Suppose no candidate takes a position on the environment. What could you do?
- Suppose someone is elected on a platform to work for the environment, and then doesn't deliver. What is your duty?
- Suppose the persons who make environmental decisions are appointed, not elected, or suppose they are in business, not in government at all. Then what?

Citizens' groups do make a difference.
- Voters in New York state approved $1.2 billion in bonds to clean up the air and water, and to create parks.
- Congress voted down the SST (Supersonic Transport).
- The Cross-Florida Barge Canal was abandoned after $50 million had already been spent on its construction.
- Californians voted to protect the coastline from further development, and to make loans to private companies for pollution control.
- In New Jersey the voters defeated a bond issue of $650 million, most of which was to be for highway construction.
- Freeway construction was stopped in San Antonio, Texas.
- Pollution of Lake Erie began to be reversed.
- Environmental protection was made a proper function of the state of North Carolina.
- The Los Angeles–Long Beach harbor was cleaned up.

Citizens' organizations do complicated things in a big way, but they depend on the efforts of ordinary people for what they accomplish. Can you see how a citizens' group can use these resources?

Scientists	Environmental control agencies
The courts	The news media
Legislatures	Other environmental groups
Libraries	

Who is the opposition likely to be? Why? Would they use any of the same resources? If so, which ones, and why?

Youth Power!

Events of the 60's and early 70's proved that young people *do* have power. But just what is the nature of that power? Exactly what do you have to offer the environmental movement—any movement—that older people cannot or do not provide?

What Others Are Doing

Here are six examples of what your generation is doing—only six out of thousands:

- In Houston, Texas, teenagers converted a ghetto garbage dump into a park.
- In Albuquerque, New Mexico, teenagers established a low-cost spaying and neutering clinic to reduce animal overpopulation.
- In Roanoke, Virginia, a youth group obtained the passage of laws to protect endangered species of wildlife.
- In Iowa City, Iowa, teenagers exposed pollution by local industries.
- In Fort Worth, Texas, teenagers started a newspaper recycling campaign that led to the city's collecting enough paper to save 34,000 trees a month.
- In Denver, Colorado, a group of *6th graders* has written and brought about the passage of environmental bills for both Denver and the state of Colorado.

Start Thinking: *What environmental jobs need doing in your community?*

Teenage Organizations

- The High School Project, 3130 M St., N.W., Washington, D.C. 20007.
- The Ecology Council of America, Room 2200, 99 Park Ave., New York, N.Y. 10016.
- The STEP Program: U.S. National Park Service, Department of the Interior, Washington, D.C. 20240.

If you organize a group at school, naturally you will need the school's permission. Get at least one social studies teacher and one science teacher to sponsor you, and present your idea to whomever has the say-so on clubs. Think ahead: What are some questions the administration is likely to ask?

Study Programs

Environmental study is *not* just nature study or conservation study; it is about how people's activities affect the total environment, and how the environment, in turn, affects people. There are programs of many different kinds, but all emphasize studying the environment directly. A list is in the teacher's bibliography for this unit.

Environmental studies are definitely "in". In Haverton, Pennsylvania, 120 seniors have spent their entire year studying the environment; some school districts have amazingly complete programs, run by environmental specialists. If you do not feel your school is doing an adequate job on the environment, how would you go about getting some changes made? Exactly what would you do first, and then next, then next?

Youth Power
Example of How To Get Things Done

A Library Is a Friend
Facts are one of the environmentalist's most important weapons, and an "information explosion" on the environment continues. But detailed information takes a bit of looking.

Whenever you want to find out something—anything—the best place to start is the library. Librarians have sources of information and knowledge of how to find things you never dreamed of, unless you are a librarian.

Example: Starting in 1971 the Environmental Information Center began publishing *The Environmental Index.* It's a huge volume you will probably find in the reference department. It lists magazine articles, books, conferences, and patents (hundreds of new ones on environmental protection every year). The organization can supply copies of the materials.

Example: New environmental publications are coming along all the time. Some of them concern only the technology of environmental protection. Libraries are taking more and more of them. Older magazines are adding or expanding their coverage of the environment. *American City*, for example, carries numerous articles on how different communities are solving their environmental problems.

Spreading the Word
Over 30 environmental information centers have been established around the country, some doubling as action centers. Take the one in Berkeley, California. It operates an environmental bookstore, answers telephone questions, receives thousands of visitors a year, and maintains communication with other groups. Within six months of opening it had some 60 projects going on.

If there is a center where you live, you can volunteer to work in it. If not, you can help organize one. What is to prevent making your school the headquarters for environmental information and action in your community?

Even on a "one-shot" basis, your class could:

- Identify a local environmental problem.
- Assemble a collection of articles on various ways to solve it. Start with the information on this page.
- Turn over a complete set to the city council or other governing body, and if the law permits, make an oral presentation. In other words, teach them what you have learned. Chances are it will be far more than they knew before, and your work could be the first step in turning your community around. Think of it.

You and the Future

Your Career

When you leave this school, what will you do with the rest of your life? When your working days are over forty or fifty years from now, what kind of career will you look back upon? Many high school students—even graduating seniors—have no idea what they want to do, because they haven't thought very much about what they want out of life.

Be honest with yourself: What do *you* want? If your wish is to leave the world better than you found it, an environmental career is one to consider. What are some questions you should ask yourself in deciding about this? Maybe the first one should be, "How selfish am I?" Then go on from there.

How much education does it take to improve the environment? If you quit school today and never returned the rest of your life, could you still help the environment? How? What do you think the author of the following reading saw as the most important requirement for a person to be useful to the environment?

> Let no man jump to the conclusion that he must take his Ph.D. in ecology before he can "see" his country. . . . The weeds in a city lot convey the same message as the redwoods; the farmer may see in his cowpasture what may not be revealed to the scientist adventuring in the South Seas. Perception, in short, cannot be purchased with either learned degrees or dollars; it grows at home as well as abroad, and he who has a little may use it to as good advantage as he who has much. [1]

There are careers in environmental work to match any level of education. Check in the library; especially see Odom Fanning, *Opportunities in Environmental Education.* Universal Publishing Corp., 1971.

Your Generation, Your World
Which is better?

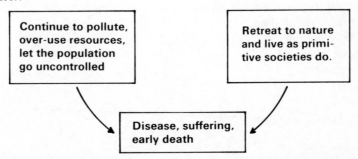

Will either extreme actually lead to the same result? Do we have to choose one or the other? In order to have an ideal physical environment, is it necessary to have also an ideal social world? Why or why not?

---

[1]Adapted from Citizens' Advisory Committee on Environmental Quality, *Annual Report to the President and to the Council on Environmental Quality.* Superintendent of Documents, 1972, p. 31.

Am I Relevant to History?

A movement typically starts with one person who sees a need *and* does something about it. The movement succeeds only if other individuals catch the sincerity of the first one, *and* take action. What kinds of people do you think these would be?

Why do you think some people, when they realize what they *can* do about a problem, do nothing? What are likely to be some excuses for not trying great things? Little things?

Where the environment is concerned, what could be some causes for a person to stop making excuses and start doing something?

Suppose a few years from now you begin to notice improvements in the environment, like the air and water getting cleaner, litter disappearing, here and there a place beautified with greenery, a landscape restored. When you see them, how will you know if you have helped—whether you have been relevant to history? And if you work hard now, but see no results then, how much will be the loss, how much the gain?

> I am only one,
> But still I am one.
> I cannot do everything,
> But still I can do something.
> And because I cannot do everything,
> I will not refuse to do the something that I can do.
>
> *Edward Everett Hale* (1822–1909) [1]

> Our natural environment is dying.
> If it dies, we all die.
> What will save it?
> Hope? Wisdom?
> The Law?
> "They?"
> You?

---

[1] John Bartlett, *Familiar Quotations*. Little, Brown, and Co., 1955, p. 624.

"If our goal is to effectively teach American history as a quest for relevancy, students never need ask: 'What good's all this gonna do me?' They'll already know."

Allan O. Kownslar

10
What Materials Are Relevant for the Future?

As teachers, one of our biggest problems is finding instructional materials which best meet the needs of our students. Publishing-house salesmen bring forth an unending supply of textbooks and audio-visual aids in such profusion that frequently it is almost impossible to adequately cull through and locate materials most appropriate for our classes.

During a workshop conducted at Trinity University in 1972, sixty Bexar County (Texas) social studies teachers and supervisors pondered this problem and compiled the following curriculum analysis questionnaire as an evaluation tool for judging new social studies programs. This questionnaire is an adaptation of the *Curriculum Materials Analysis System: Long Form* as devised by the Social Science Education Consortium at Boulder, Colorado.[1] The workshop participants preferred using the *CMAS Long Form* when there was enough time. However, many of the participants of the workshop were required to serve on local textbook selection committees without a subsequent reduction in class loads. In those cases, they preferred to use the following shorter version in evaluating programs under consideration for adoption.

A primary purpose of this quesionnaire is to serve as a system by which teachers can begin to determine how relevant history and other social studies programs are for intended student audiences. Many teachers recommended that students also be allowed to use this questionnaire and thus participate in the evaluation of available programs. The questionnaire is included in this chapter with the thought that other teachers might also find it useful. During the past two years it has been used by social studies personnel on textbook committees in approximately one hundred school districts throughout the San Antonio and South Texas areas.

---

[1] This social studies curriculum analysis short form is an adaptation from Irving Morrissett, *et al., Curriculum Materials Analysis System: Long Form*, SSEC Publication #143, 1971, by the Social Science Education Consortium, Boulder, Colorado. For more information about how curriculum analysis might benefit your school district, see the November, 1972 issue of *Social Education:* "New In-Depth Evaluations of Social Studies Curricular Projects, Programs, and Materials." Workshop participants who devised the CMAS abbreviated form included in this chapter were: Henri Ella Wix, Opal Maxey, Nora Forester, Tommy Ford, Norma Roberts, Charles E. Neff, Heston R. Gumm, Arthur Smith, and Jerry Pennington—Northside (Texas) ISD; William Guardia, James Sutton, Katherine Perry, Elizabeth Kefauver, Shirley Villarreal, Elmer F. Brandenberger, and Don McAskill—San Antonio ISD; E. Albert Sauter, Carolina Pena, Violet Lahourade, Lillian Kelly, Juan R. Lira, Tony McAdoo, Aurelia Navarro, Naomi Brown, Sidney Hilton, and Carrie Harris—Edgewood ISD; Deurene Morgan, Virgil R. Wadsack, Diane Crowe, Marguerite Medlock, Barbara Wagner, and June S. McSwain—Northeast ISD; Tessye Wheeler and Marion Chandler—Ft. Sam Houston ISD; Sister Jan Maria Wozniak and Paul Matula—Providence, San Antonio Archdiocese; Sally Andrade, and Federico Viduarri—Crystal City ISD; Nancy Hagen, Roland Gusman, and Bruce Bell—East Central ISD; Karen Pena, Frances M. Rhodes—Our Lady of the Lake College; Jan Stebbins, Vernon Adams, Linda Wilson—Alamo Heights ISD; Virginia Folger, Jeanette John, Nita Cox, and Catherine Beseda—Kerrville ISD.; and Sarah Cannon, Hardy D. Cannon, H. Charles Dulling, Nancy B. Thompson, Pearline Miller, Beverly Westbrook, LaRue C. Diviak, Penny Taylor, Florene Allen, Helen L. Kershaw—Harlandale ISD.

217

Social Studies Curriculum Analysis Short Form

Name of analyst _____

Social studies position _____

Total years of teaching experience _____

Subject areas taught and total number of years taught for each _____

_____

Grade levels taught and total number of years taught for each _____

_____

Name of program to be analyzed _____

Author(s) of program to be analyzed _____

Publisher of program to be analyzed _____

Grade level(s) for which the program is primarily intended _____

_____

Product Characteristics

1. What does the author consider the most appropriate length of time in weeks or years for use of the whole set of materials?

    _____Weeks

    _____Years

2. Check which of the following items are covered in this analysis. If any listed in a.–f. are unavailable, list as such and why they are unavailable.

    a. Student _____   e. Workbook _____

    b. Teacher's guide _____   f. Rationale _____

    c. Audio-visual materials _____   g. Other _____

    d. Testing program _____   (explain)

Content

3. What is your general overall judgment of the physical and technical (not substantive) durability of *all* materials in the program?

0	1	2	3	4	5	6
Inadequate			Adequate			More than adequate

Explanation:

4. To what extent are pictorial sources, maps, graphs, charts, tables, and other illustrative material integrated and utilized with textual narrative and questions?

0	1	2	3	4	5	6
Not at all			To a moderate extent		To a great extent	

Explanation:

5. To what extent are key terms and concepts defined for the student in student materials?

0	1	2	3	4	5	6
Not at all			To a moderate extent		To a great extent	

Explanation:

6. To what extent are adequate data readily available in the student materials to questions asked of students?

0	1	2	3	4	5	6
Not at all			To a moderate extent		To a great extent	

Explanation:

7. In general, how accurate do the factual data and interpretations of the data seem to be in all parts of the program?

0	1	2	3	4	5	6
Very unsound			Moderately sound		Very sound	

Explanation:

8. To what extent is a multi-ethnic approach integrated in the student materials?

0	1	2	3	4	5	6
Not at all			To a moderate extent		To a great extent	

Explanation:

9. List the ethnic groups included in the materials _____

_____

_____

Explanation:

Is the multi-ethnic approach presented in the materials sensitive or suitable to the needs of ethnic groups within your school population? Answer "yes" or "no."____

Explanation:

10. How is the role of women portrayed in the student materials?

_____

_____

_____

Is that portrayal sensitive or suitable to the needs of females within your school population? Answer "yes" or "no."____

Explanation:

11. Indicate the disciplines most prominent in the program. Mark them "1", "2", or "3" in order of prominence. If they cannot be distinguished, mark them all "1". If more than three disciplines are prominent, mark them "interdisciplinary".

Anthropology	____	Psychology	____
Economics		Sociology	____
Geography	____	Social Psychology	____
History	____	Other (explain)	____
Political Science	____	Interdisciplinary	____

Explanation:

12. The acquisition of knowledge which includes concept formation (the many meanings which can apply to one word such as "horse", "war", or "revolution") and the development of basic study skills (such as those listed in a.–l. in question 13) and critical or analytical thinking skills (such as those listed in m.–q. in question 13) are generally referred to as cognitive processes. In general, how clearly does the author state and define his cognitive objectives in behavioral terms (expected student performances) in the teacher's manual?

0	1	2	3	4	5	6
Not at all			Fairly Clearly		Very Clearly	

Explanation:

13. To what extent do the student materials and suggestions in the teacher's guide include cognitive learning processes which focus development on the following:

a. Observing or perceiving (If it occurs, list in which item(s) of the program where it is suggested or asked of the students) _____
_____
_____

0	1	2	3	4	5	6
No emphasis			Moderate emphasis		Much emphasis	

Explanation:

b. Listening (list where) _____

0	1	2	3	4	5	6
No emphasis			Moderate emphasis		Much emphasis	

Explanation:

c. Discussing (list where) _____

0	1	2	3	4	5	6
No emphasis			Moderate emphasis		Much emphasis	

Explanation:

d. Defining and expanding the meanings of key terms or concepts (list where) _____

0	1	2	3	4	5	6
No emphasis			Moderate emphasis		Much emphasis	

Explanation:

e. Reading (list where) _____

0	1	2	3	4	5	6
No emphasis			Moderate emphasis		Much emphasis	

Explanation:

f. Writing (list where) _____

0	1	2	3	4	5	6
No emphasis			Moderate emphasis		Much emphasis	

Explanation:

g. Contrasting and comparing for the purpose of noting similarities and differences (list where) _____

0	1	2	3	4	5	6
No emphasis			Moderate emphasis		Much emphasis	

Explanation:

h. Locating, gathering, and classifying information relative to a particular study in progress (list where) _____

0	1	2	3	4	5	6
No emphasis			Moderate emphasis		Much emphasis	

Explanation:

i. Interpreting globes, maps, or other types of map projections (list where) _____

0	1	2	3	4	5	6
No emphasis			Moderate emphasis		Much emphasis	

Explanation:

j. Making maps (list where) _____

0	1	2	3	4	5	6
No emphasis			Moderate emphasis		Much emphasis	

Explanation:

k. Interpreting tables, graphs, or charts (list where) _____

0	1	2	3	4	5	6
No emphasis			Moderate emphasis		Much emphasis	

Explanation:

l. Making tables, graphs, or charts (list where) _____

0	1	2	3	4	5	6
No emphasis			Moderate emphasis		Much emphasis	

Explanation:

m. Recognizing a problem for further inquiry (list where) _____

0	1	2	3	4	5	6
No emphasis			Moderate emphasis		Much emphasis	

Explanation:

n. Drawing inferences or making tentative conclusions (stating hypotheses) (list where) _____

0	1	2	3	4	5	6
No emphasis			Moderate emphasis		Much emphasis	

Explanation:

o. Testing the validity of hypotheses (list where) _____

0	1	2	3	4	5	6
No emphasis			Moderate emphasis		Much emphasis	

Explanation:

p. Forming generalizations (list where) _____

0	1	2	3	4	5	6
No emphasis			Moderate emphasis		Much emphasis	

Explanation:

q. Synthesizing information from a variety of sources and experiences (list where) _____

0	1	2	3	4	5	6
No emphasis			Moderate emphasis		Much emphasis	

Explanation:

14. In all the materials, then, what is the author's emphasis on memorization of data as opposed to critical or analytical thinking such as the steps noted in m.–q. in question 13? _____

0	1	2	3	4	5	6
Much memory work (recall)			Some of each			Much critical or analytical thinking

Explanation:

15. To what extent does the teacher's manual include specific teaching strategies and additional lessons within the cognitive domain for use of the materials with the following kinds of students:

a. Slow students

0	1	2	3	4	5	6
Not at all			To a moderate extent			To a great extent

Explanation:

b. Average students

0	1	2	3	4	5	6
Not at all			To a moderate extent			To a great extent

Explanation:

c. Gifted students

0	1	2	3	4	5	6
Not at all			To a moderate extent			To a great extent

Explanation:

The Affective Domain

16. Learning concerned with a closer look at one's attitudes, value clarification, empathizing, and any behavior which causes a student to be *willing* to perform as a responsible person both inside and outside the classroom (social participation) is part of the affective domain. In general, how clearly does the author state and define his affective objectives in behavioral terms (expected student performances) in the teacher's manual?

0	1	2	3	4	5	6
Not at all			Fairly clearly		Very clearly	

Explanation:

17. To what extent do the student materials or suggestions in the teacher's guide encourage students to explore, clarify, and act:

a. On their own values?

0	1	2	3	4	5	6
Not at all			Moderate emphasis		Much emphasis	

Explanation:

b. On values held by others?

0	1	2	3	4	5	6
Not at all			Moderate emphasis		Much emphasis	

Explanation:

c. On the presentation of alternative and conflicting points of view.

0	1	2	3	4	5	6
Not at all			Moderate emphasis		Much emphasis	

Explanation:

18. How are values and attitudes presented in the student materials by the author?

0	1	2	3	4	5	6
Imposed values by the author			Balanced		Free of imposed values by the author	

Explanation:

19. To what extent does the teacher's manual include specific teaching strategies and additional lessons within the affective domain for use of the materials with the following kinds of students:

a. Slow students

0	1	2	3	4	5	6
Not at all			To a moderate extent		To a great extent	

Explanation:

b. Average students

0	1	2	3	4	5	6
Not at all			To a moderate extent		To a great extent	

Explanation:

c. Gifted students

0	1	2	3	4	5	6
Not at all			To a moderate extent		To a great extent	

Explanation:

20. To what extent does the testing program or other evaluation processes provided with the program test the students for factual recall?

0	1	2	3	4	5	6
Not at all			To a moderate extent		To a great extent	

Explanation:

21. To what extent does the testing program test for basic skill development such as that listed in a.–1. in question 13?

0	1	2	3	4	5	6
Not at all			To a moderate extent		To a great extent	

Explanation:

22. To what extent does the testing program test for critical or analytical-thinking skill development such as that listed in m.–q. in question 13?

0	1	2	3	4	5	6
Not at all			To a moderate extent		To a great extent	

Explanation:

23. To what extent does the testing program test for continued development of concept formation?

0	1	2	3	4	5	6
Not at all			To a moderate extent		To a great extent	

Explanation:

24. To what extent does the testing program test for value clarification such as that noted in question 17?

0	1	2	3	4	5	6
Not at all			To a moderate extent		To a great extent	

Explanation:

25. To what extent does the testing program take into account the learning abilities and capacity for learning of the slow students?

0	1	2	3	4	5	6
Not at all			To a moderate extent		To a great extent	

Explanation:

26. To what extent does the testing program take into account the learning abilities and capacity for learning of the average student?

0	1	2	3	4	5	6
Not at all			To a moderate extent		To a great extent	

Explanation:

27. To what extent does the testing program take into account the learning abilities and capacity for learning of the gifted student?

0	1	2	3	4	5	6
Not at all			To a moderate extent		To a great extent	

Explanation:

The Author's Rationale

28. How much evidence is there that the development of the program was guided by a clear rationale? In essence, can the author's rationale be found explicitly in all materials of the program?

0	1	2	3	4	5	6
No evidence			Moderate amount		To a great extent	

Explanation:

29. To what extent do you, the analyst, agree with the author's rationale?

0	1	2	3	4	5	6
Not at all			To a moderate extent		To a great extent	

Explanation:

Summary

30. Suppose the following types of students were to be in the grade level for which this program is intended. Imagine, too, that these students asked: "What good's spending a year on this program gonna do me?" What do you think would be her/his answer?

a. A slow learner or a student with reading probelms.

0	1	2	3	4	5	6
It would be little if any benefit to me.			It would be of some benefit.		It would greatly benefit my needs.	

Explanation:

b. An average student who reads at the grade level for which the program is intended.

0	1	2	3	4	5	6

It would
be little
if any benefit
to me.

It would
be of
some
benefit.

It would
greatly
benefit
my needs.

Explanation:

c. A gifted student who reads above the grade level for which the program is intended.

0	1	2	3	4	5	6

It would
be little
if any benefit
to me.

It would
be of
some
benefit.

It would
greatly
benefit
my needs.

Explanation:

31. Considering the grade level for which this program is primarily intended, how *relevant* do *you* think this program would be in meeting the needs of the following kinds of students in your schools?
    a. Slow students

0	1	2	3	4	5	6

Unsuit-
able

Suitable to
a moderate
extent

Very
suitable

Explanation:

b. Average students

0	1	2	3	4	5	6

Unsuit-
able

Suitable to
a moderate
extent

Very
suitable

Explanation:

c. Gifted students

0	1	2	3	4	5	6
Unsuit-able			Suitable to a moderate extent		Very suitable	

Explanation:

d. Other types of students (explain) _____

_____

_____

_____

_____

32. Considering the entire program, what type of teacher do you think would be most effective in using these materials?_____

_____

_____

_____

33. In general, to what degree would you recommend that these materials be used for the designated level(s)?

0	1	2	3	4	5	6
Not recommended			Recommended with quali-fications		Highly recommended	

Explanation:

34. How adequately does the analyst think her/his analysis represents the materials analyzed?

0	1	2	3	4	5	6
Very inadequately			Somewhat adequately		Very adequately	

Explanation:

Epilogue

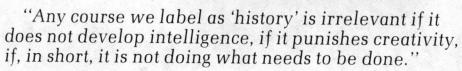

*"Any course we label as 'history' is irrelevant if it
does not develop intelligence, if it punishes creativity,
if, in short, it is not doing what needs to be done."*

Vernon O. Adams

11
What Could Happen If . . .

If the medium is indeed the message, then it is not only content we try to convey to students but instead the *way* we go about having them use it to perceive better the total environment which affects what they do and how they feel about themselves both as individuals and as members of that mini-society we call the classroom. In contrast, acquisition of content only for content's sake more often than not creates an environment which teaches students that passive acceptance is a more desirable response to ideas than active criticism; that discovering knowledge is beyond the power of students, and is, in any case, none of their business; that recall is the highest form of intellectual achievement, and the collection of unrelated facts is the goal of education; that the voice of authority is to be trusted and valued more than independent judgement; that feelings are irrelevant in education; that there is always a single, unambiguous, *right* answer to a question; that English is not history and history is not science and science is not art and art is not music and art and music are minor subjects and English, history, and science are major subjects, and a subject is something you take, and when you have taken it, you have had it, and once you have had it, you are immune, and need not take it again.[1]

If one accepts the assumption that some of these criticisms have merit, and if, after reading through this yearbook one has the feeling that it only contains a few lessons that can be extracted to fill gaps in a particular history course, then one should read it again. There is much more than mere lessons here. There are strategies, techniques, methodologies—true—but there is a transcending theme which gets at the very core of what schools are all about—a theme which takes into account the needs of all learners. Each lesson presented has students as the focal point, not as peripheral objects that are incidentally present. Students are put into context in such a manner that they can see themselves in perspective with this ever increasingly complex world in which they must live their future lives. The lessons look forward, not backward. The lessons are a vehicle by which students can further attempt to find harmony with the world around them, can learn to search in a meaningful, systematic way for a life style with which they can identify and can function within. And this gets at the very heart of what our educational system is all about, that is, to help students equip themselves so that they can function, and function well in a democratic society.

In his opening chapter, Allan Kownslar set the

235

theme and the tone of what the "New" New Social Studies is all about. The emphasis is clearly in the affective domain. In other words, we are allowing people to not only have feelings about themselves, their friends, their society, but we are encouraging them to express these feelings. What a simple, straightforward idea, yet how complex! This requires much more of teachers. It means they can no longer be just dispensers of knowledge. They must use that knowledge to get involved with students as real human beings who live in a real world that has real problems. Seen in this light, one statement made by Kownslar sticks most vividly in mind: "Our responsibility is not one of training students but in educating them, not in indoctrinating them, but in developing classroom strategies which produce a knowledgeable sense of values that will endure for a lifetime."[2] Again, the emphasis is on the needs of the learner. Each lesson presented gets at this point from a different perspective, but the goal is ever present, ever important.

It is downright presumptuous to assume that social studies teachers who disagree with major points made in this yearbook will completely change any of their classroom strategies after reading it. It is even more undesirable that any teacher blindly accept the rationale of this yearbook without asking the question "Why should I change?" After all, we are again in the affective area, and, as educators, we are all aware that it can be very difficult to change attitudes, even of young people who are still theoretically open-minded enough to at least entertain a new idea.

On the other hand, if the premise of this yearbook is not valid, it will not withstand the test of usage. On this ground, the people who developed and class-tested these lessons have an advantage. They *know* they work because they have tried them. They also know that as time passes, all of us develop our own style within the general framework of inquiry. As O. L. Davis stated: "Teachers . . . must consider how it 'fits' them, not as a new fashion but life style."[3]

But what if some teachers decide to try some of the lessons, and what if they work well with their students? An educated guess would be that if at least two people in each school building try this approach, they, in turn, will be the catalyst to bring about changes in others. Even so, will this solve our problems of pollution, crime, corruption, wars, or racism? Of course not! But it will be another small step in a long journey that will help equip our students to start asking the right kinds of questions, to take highly controversial, emotional issues and deal with them in a systematic, rational manner. If that step is *not* taken, the trip into the future will happen anyway.

That future is now. Today. The past is now. Today. A play on words? Not really. The point is that the journey into the future can be much more meaningful, much more productive for many more people, if the use of history can help them discover the ways and means to cope with what presently seem to be insurmountable problems. Who could have predicted with certainty fifty years ago that man would walk on the moon? Who can predict with certainty that man will not reach the outermost limits of the universe by a method of transmitting human beings via high frequency waves? No fantasy is too far out. No dream is impossible.

Perhaps our students can say it best, as illustrated in the following entry by a student in a Humanities class. Her topic for discussion was "The Ideal School—A Personal View."

Education is the battleground of society. For this reason, the average child and school are unsure of what they are, where they are going, and what they will be when they reach their goal.

From a personal point of view, education is merely to help a person live life as fully as possible. Going to school is to help a person learn about himself, to give him the materials and opportunities to discover the world and new worlds. A school is only a building which houses the facilities and equipment which help education, in one convenient location. The educational system should help children learn about themselves, their lives, and the world they live in.

The first thing a child should be taught is the process of inquiry and questioning. Children should be taught with materials which abound in their environment. This doesn't mean they shouldn't be taught history or read the classics. It does mean that current events [should be] taught in history. Schools have to keep in step with the times. . . .[4]

For this student there seems to be little uncertainty about what she expects the school to be. Her feelings are not uncommon ones, and the fact that a student raises such pertinent questions should give all of us who teach history a feeling of optimism about the future.

Perhaps what I am saying is that any course we label "history" is what it is because we have made it that way. If it is irrelevant, if it educates for obsolescence, if it does not develop intelligence, if it is based on fear, if it avoids the promotion of significant learning, if it induces alienation, if it punishes creativity and independence, if, in short, it is not doing what needs to be done, it *can* be changed, it *must* be changed.[5] That, in essence, is what each of these yearbook authors are saying directly or indirectly in their chapters.

FOOTNOTES

[1]See, for example, Marshall McLuhan, *The Medium Is the Massage*, Bantam, 1967; and Neil Postman and Charles Weingartner, *Teaching As a Subversive Activity*, Dell, 1969.

[2]See page 8, Chapter 1 of this yearbook.

[3]See page 41, Chapter 3 of this yearbook.

[4]Nancy Carnes, "The Ideal School—A Personal View," 1973. This is a theme by a student written at the end of a unit of study on Education Systems in a special Humanities class at Alamo Heights High School, Texas.

[5]For additional information on the points in this last paragraph, see Norbert Wiener, *Ex-Prodigy: My Childhood and Youth*, M.I.T. Press, 1966; John W. Gardner, *Excellence: Can We Be Equal and Excellent Too?* Harper and Row, 1961; Jerome Bruner, *Relevance of Education*, Norton, 1971; John Holt, *How Children Learn*, Dell, 1972 and *Freedom and Beyond*, Dutton, 1972; Carl Rogers, *Freedom to Learn: A View of What Education Might Become*, Merrill, 1969; Paul Goodman, *Like a Conquered Province: The Moral Ambiguity of America*, Random House, 1967; and Edgar Z. Friedenberg, ed., *The Anti-American Generation*, 2nd ed., Society Books, 1972. I am particularly indebted to Mrs. Helen Bernal for allowing me to use some of her ideas in the introductory and concluding paragraphs of this chapter. Mrs. Bernal is presently a doctoral student in the Department of Sociology, the University of Texas at Austin, and a consultant with McDonnell Douglas Automation Company, Educational Services, St. Louis, Missouri.

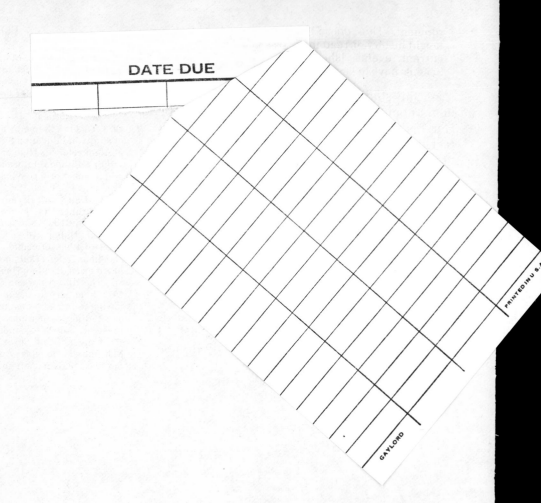

DATE DUE

GAYLORD

PRINTED IN U.S.A.

Book design and production
by Willadene Price